D0328546

De-Coca-Colonization

De-Coca-Colonization
Making the Globe from the Inside Out

by Steven Flusty

ROUTLEDGE
NEW YORK AND LONDON

Published in 2004 by
Routledge
29 West 35th Street
New York, NY 10001
www.routledge-ny.com

Published in Great Britain by
Routledge
11 New Fetter Lane
London EC4P 4EE
www.routledge.co.uk

Copyright © 2004 by Steven Flusty

Routledge is an imprint of the Taylor and Francis Group.

Printed in the United States of America on acid-free paper.

10   9   8   7   6   5   4   3   2   1

All rights reserved. No part of this book may be printed or utilized in any form or by any electronic, mechanical or other means, now known or hereafter invented, including photocopying and recording, or any other information storage or retrieval system, without permission in writing from the publisher.

Library of Congress Cataloging-in-Publication Data

Flusty, Steven, 1963–
    De-Coca-colonization : making the globe from the inside out / by Steven Flusty.
        p.   cm.
    Includes bibliographical references and index.
    ISBN 0-415-94537-2 (alk. paper)—ISBN 0-415-94538-0 (pbk. : alk. paper)
    1. Globalization—Social aspects.   2. Globalization—Economic aspects.
3. Anti-globalization movement.   4. Social change.
I. Title.
HN17.5.F58   2003
303.4—dc21
                                                                    2003010247

This work was produced with the generous support of the Southern California Studies Center, University of Southern California.

Further support was provided by the Department of Geography at the University of Southern California, and by Haynes Foundation and USC University Fellowships.

Portions of this book draw from, reformulate and elaborate upon earlier work that has appeared elsewhere under the following titles: "Y la Revolución se Combirtio en Mercancia." In ed., *Los Nuevos Actores en América del Norte,* edited by Edit Antal (México City: CISAN-UNAM, 2003). *The Spaces of Postmodernity: Readings in Human Geography* Michael Dear and Steven Flusty (Oxford: Blackwell, 2001). "The Banality of Interdiction: Surveillance, Control, and the Displacement of Diversity," *International Journal of Urban and Regional Research* 25, no. 3 (2001): 658–64. "Adventures of a Barong: A Worm's-Eye View of Global Formation." In ed., *Postmodern Geography: Theory and Praxis,* edited by Claudio Minca (Oxford: Blackwell, 2001). "Thrashing Downtown: Play as Resistance to the Spatial and Representational Regulation of Downtown Los Angeles," *Cities* 17, no. 2 (2000): 149–58. "Postmodern Urbanism," *Annals of the Association of American Geographers* 88, no. 1 (1998): 50–72. "Icons in the Stream." In *Icons: Magnets of Meaning,* edited by Aaron Betsky (San Francisco: San Francisco Museum of Modern Art/Chronicle Books, 1997). *Building Paranoia: The Proliferation of Interdictory Space and the Erosion of Spatial Justice.* West Hollywood: Los Angeles Forum for Architecture and Urban Design. 1994.

Contents

Introduction

> The beetle took off his glasses, looked me up and down, and said very angrily: "Please, captain, I beg you not to interrupt me . . . I'm studying about neoliberalism and its strategy for dominating Latin America." "And what good does that do a beetle?" I asked him. And he answered angrily: "I have to know how long your struggle is going to last and whether you are going to win . . . so as to know how long we beetles have to be careful not to be squashed by your huge old boots." . . . "And what have you concluded from your studies?" I asked. . . . "You can't tell exactly. You have to take into account many things: the objective conditions, the maturity of the subjective conditions, the correlation of forces, the crises of imperialism, the crises of socialism, etc. etc."
> —Subcomandante Marcos, *Shadows of Tender Fury*

Subcomandante Insurgente Marcos, in this story written for a ten-year-old in Mexico City, employs his alter ego Durrito the Beetle to parodically sum up two commonplace propositions about globalization. First, it is analytically opaque. Second, and more important, it is embedded in neoliberal economic policies that cause the immiserization of vast populations. It was this sense of globalization as a boot pressing down upon the less powerful that impelled, within minutes of the inauguration of the North American Free Trade Agreement (NAFTA) on midnight of January 1, 1994, the sudden appearance of the Zapatista uprising in Mexico's Chiapas State. The uprising has since spread, for example, to Seattle where, from November 29 to December 2, 1999, highly visible protests from without and within monkeywrenched the third ministerial meeting of the World Trade Organization (WTO). Activists

1

claimed that, in the words of one graffito, "We Are Winning," and indeed a formalized international legitimation of 'corporate globalization' was, for the time being, squelched. There was, however a glaring lacuna in the week's dissident proceedings, casting protesters in a reactionary light while suggesting future victory was anything but assured. There was no well-articulated alternative to 'corporate globalization,' no "agenda for 'globalization from below'" (Wainwright, Prudham, and Glassman 2000, 9).

Perhaps, were the beetle only to elaborate upon the specifics of the many things to be taken into account, he could resolve this lacuna. Perhaps he fails to do so owing to the difficulty of explaining such things to those as young as the recipient of Marcos's communiqué. But then again, it may be due to some uncertainty on Marcos's part himself. If so, then Marcos is not alone. Such uncertainty is something we all share when attempting to wrap our heads around such behemothic symptoms of globalization as the North American Free Trade Area.

We understand implicitly that globalization is big, and complex. It is, after all, a *global* thing. But beyond this, what exactly *is* globalization? Is it a mechanistically economic phenomenon, as seems to underlie its construction in the business press? If so, then globalization is about raising the living standards of all by removing political obstacles to fluid investment and flexibly utilizable factors of production.

Is globalization a strategic maneuver in an internationalizing class war? If so, then it is intended to displace peasants, discipline labor, and generally subjugate much of the planet's population (not to mention "nature") to enrich an investor class and its financial institutions.

Or is globalization perhaps a psychosociological phenomenon? If so, then it may be a manifestation of an emergent worldwide community of civilizations. Such a community could engender a more broadly shared culture across the continents. Simultaneously, it could drive a counteracting retrenchment of nationalism as we are all circumstantially compelled to define ourselves against growing perceptions of the "other."

These differing conceptions of globalization make use of a verdant lexicon: free trade, transnationalization, neocolonialism, tribalism, Americanization, coca-colonization, liberalization, ethnic cleansing, structural adjustment, relativization. Many of these terms are arranged in diametric opposition by those advocating competing versions of a shared discourse, one observer's structural adjustment program being another's neocolonialism. Other terms are predicated upon such divergent assumptions as to be impossible to deploy in the same analysis: the utility-optimizing "rational man" of much free-trade theory and the polysemic self implicit to sociological models of relativization inhabit incommensurable discourses that are, for all intents and purposes, alternate realities. Some of these terms refer to broad or even universal structures, others to specific institutions. All rest upon assumptions of what globalization *is*.

What can be said with some certainty is that the meaning and effect of globalization is currently a contested arena in which how one sees determines what one champions. Those who embrace entrepreneurial opportunities within an evolving world economy will know globalization differently from those who oppose the expansion of a global web of exploitation, or from those who concern themselves with an emerging order of global civilizations. Such diverse conceptions of globalization in turn rest upon very different intellectual foundations, very different readings of how an imperialist past has manifested as either a post- or neocolonial present and, most important, very different (and more often than not unstated) assumptions about the roles of space and everyday life.

Yet these alternative visions of globalization do have one thing in common. All proceed from presumptions of globalization's bigness, tacitly adopting approaches and underlying assumptions focusing upon globalization as a structural phenomenon. As a result, dominant conceptions of globalization persist in explaining the phenomenon from a panoptic perspective, attempting to model it as a whole from imagined overhead vantage points. While this perspective does not necessarily ignore more earthbound locales, they are commonly limited to serving as the sites in which particularistic responses constitute obstacles to, and defenses against, globalization as a higher-order imposition. And despite attempts to the contrary, this tendency has not much abated with the increased acceptance of globalization as an object of study. As late as 2000, for example, I attended a lecture in which Anthony Giddens made clear his intention to address how local kinship relations play a role in constituting the global but, faced with the challenge of finding the global in the household, emerged instead with generalized remarks upon how globalization transforms localized familial relations (see also Giddens 2000).

The sheer scale of global processes, it would seem, boggles our capacity to imagine them as both embedded in and dependent upon the immediate and the intimate. As a result, there may well be no formally articulated alternative to globalization from above, whether corporate or otherwise. There already exists, however, a counterpart. While less ostentatiously visible than its from-above equivalent, this alternative globalization constitutes a potent globalization from below. It is less a globalization from below, however, than it is a globalization that reaches ever outward from within particular places, social collectives and even single persons. Thus, it is less a counterpoised grassroots globalization than it is a concomitant and even a prerequisite to any globalization from above. It is even, in a vital sense, not a globalization at all. Rather, it is a combination of distinct spatial and temporal practices that, in their execution and their accretion, exercise globally formative effects. These practices are brought about through the quotidian business of conducting daily life within and across ever widening distances and by means of ever more distended social relations. It thus entails a redefinition of globalization not as an extrinsic quasi-opaque imposition from above, an irresistible structural imperative, or a commandment unifying capital markets. Rather, it is globalization as both immanent in, and increasingly intrinsic to, our everyday practices.

At its broadest my claim is that globalization *is* only because it is woven through the planet's social fabric from the ground up (or, much more correctly, from particular grounds outward) by everyday life's hyperextension—the increasing spatial reach of emplaced social relations. Further, I will argue that the sites in and through which this quotidian weaving occurs are predominantly the "world cities." Thus, this is an investigation into the mutually productive relationship of the world city's everyday life to the global. It is not the first such investigation. Present thinking on globalization is neither wholly negligent toward nor indifferent to localized everyday life, especially not in its urban manifestations. As will be apparent in the coming chapters, the contrary is the case: there has been, and continues to be, much discussion of how globalization is received, and its impacts felt and modulated, in urban locales. There have even been some forays into how relatively more localized practices and relationships inflect globalizing economic processes regionally—for example, research into the operations of diasporic Chinese business and social networks across the Pacific Basin (Ong, Bonacich, and Cheng 1994; Tao and Ho 1997). But overwhelmingly, investigations into the global/urban nexus have been concerned with how globalization, commonly taken as a structural given, turns cities into world cities with distinctly opportunistic entrepreneurial polities. This top-down bias has persisted even in treatises claiming to reveal precisely the opposite (e.g. Short and Kim 1999).

In these pages, I too attend to globalization's transformative impacts upon the city. But my primary focus is to invert deterministic assumptions of the global-to-urban relationship by exploring the social construction of globalization within, between, and through world cities. Further, I will identify specific ways in which the work of so constructing globalities, *in the plural,* is accomplished. This work, I claim, is done by the stuff of everyday life—its persons, spaces, artifacts, and, most important, the practices that constitute their relationships. Such quotidian minutiae, I will show, have simultaneously concentrated within cities and splayed out across the planet in highly specific ways so as to inform both globalization and the world city. Finally, in that everyday actors, artifacts, and the spatial performance of their relations differ from one another, so too do the urbanities and globalities they construct. Such differences give rise to divergent globalizations and world cities that coexist, cross-pollinate, and contend with one another. This book will concretely describe examples of these diverse globalizations and world cities, while teasing out the peculiarities of their interaction. And in so doing, it will recast globalization as immanent within, and an intimate creation of, our everyday undertakings.

This *re-placement* of globalization into the everyday, however, does not contradict its manifestation at "upper-circuit," "structural," or (more simply) larger scales. Nor does it entail a voluntaristic perspective blind to the clear presence of proliferating social and spatial injustices. To the contrary, some globally formative everyday practices are inextricably intertwined with what I term *plutocratic corporatism*—hegemony through superior pocket depth. And the more-or-less autocratic imposition of such globally formative practices can indeed impart the distinct sense that a particular globality, one of cash and commodities in transit, has descended crushingly from on high. As Bauman (following Karl Marx) makes clear, there was a time when the state endeavored to impose panoptic order "down" upon daily life. But now, capital organized as corporations (and masquerading beneath the rubric of a "free market") seeks to make similar impositions upon the state and, through the state, upon daily life (Bauman 1998). This is what Marcos himself refers to as "neoliberalism as a global system . . . a new war of conquest for territories" (Marcos 1997). Although phrased here as high theory, this is not an abstract assertion. Returning this discussion to January 1, 1994's happenings in southern Mexico, those events did not remain southern Mexican for long: by January of the following year, a memo from Chase Manhattan Bank counseled, "While Chiapas, in our opinion, does not pose a fundamental threat to Mexican political stability, it is perceived to be so by many in the investment community. The government will need to eliminate the Zapatistas to demonstrate their effective control of the national territory and of security policy. . . ." (Roett 1995). And, within three weeks of the memo's issuance, then president Ernesto Zedillo did order soldiers into Chiapas on a hunt for Zapatista leadership. This is a clear empirical indication that capital does indeed secure itself globally by instructing states how and where to put the boot in. But what do we mean by "capital" here? An identifiable person, Riordan Roett, occupying an identifiable position, consultant to a major financial institution's emerging markets group, generated this memo in a particular place, New York City. It was generated to assuage the perceptions of other emplaced people, and for the perusal and instruction of still others.

This is not to reduce plutocratic globality's formation to some shadowy cabal of elite conspirators, skulking about with state bureaucracies and a phalanx of black helicopters in tow. Of course, it is not to deny this possibility either. The power of such theories lies in the logical impossibility of proving the nonexistence of a thing, and indeed a column of matte black Humvees could be issuing forth from the bowels of the United Nations building as you read this. (There is, oddly enough, a black helicopter hovering directly over my apartment as I type this.) But black helicopters are hardly key to an explanation of "corporate globalization," that supposedly ineluctable upper-circuit process of globalization with a capital G. The key, instead, lies in identifying how particular everyday practices are brought together so as to embody the effect of a globalization from above. By considering globalization as immanent, "corporate globalization" is revealed as the reification of an elite plutocratic subset of globally formative practices, institutional practices managing global formation that are undertaken in real places in the everyday. Such practices, grouped under the rubric *globalism* (Nederveen Pieterse 1995), thus become vulnerable to the intervention of other commonplace practices that hyperextend to great lengths across global space.

In the case of the aforementioned Chase Manhattan memo, these practices consisted of electronic mass forwardings of the memo to Zapatista sympathizers throughout the United States. The resultant popular outcry (see, e.g., Silverstein and Cockburn 1995) in turn impelled Chase Manhattan to distance itself from the memo and its recommendations, with bank spokespersons asserting that Roett was an independent consultant who had been promptly terminated (Rothberg 1995). And while Mexican troops were not withdrawn from Chiapas, their direct assault was terminated in lieu of a war of attrition coupled with protracted rounds of negotiation that continue to the present in fits and starts.

The goal of this book is to begin the work of explicating how everyday practices assemble far-reaching constellations of urban places and, through those constellations, construct the global in its many versions. In the process, this work will also demonstrate globalization's immanence; what I term *nonsovereign globalization* or, more correctly, *everyday globalities*. And as a result, this book will simultaneously foreground globalization's quiddity, its everydayness: how globalities are "coordered and concerted" in "actual activities by actual individuals" (Smith 1987, 123), their ongoing creation, dissemination, reception, and adaptive reutilization by real people in the real world. Thus, this book will be a step toward answering questions others have implied and left open, and will begin to explicate how all sorts of globally formative practices intersect, interact, and interfere at various scales.

In the process, this work takes on a critical agenda of immediate political significance: to undermine the widely propagated idea that globalization in its current form is preordained by some unassailable macroeconomic logic underlying the very nature of contemporary society. This pseudolocalization of global formation in the nonspace of transnationally "freed" markets and flowing capital has for too long now legitimized the imposition of globally determinant initiatives like NAFTA and the WTO, facilitating their institutionalization by relatively unaccountable national-cum-supranational elites. Simultaneously, this discourse of naturalized global neoliberalism has functioned to marginalize dissent as anachronistic, isolationist, and even as a manifestation of paternalistic racism toward the excolonial world (Krugman 1999). By indicating that global formation is first and foremost the product of identifiable human actions in identifiable locales, this book affords new possibilities for more informed and effective responses to any allegedly inevitable globalization imposed from on high.

But first, some groundwork is necessary. What, precisely, has been said about globalization? How many visions of global formation are presently at play, and what is the historical trajectory of their development? What are their respective strengths and weaknesses, from what perspective? To what extent are these visions of the global embedded in place and in daily life, and thus how might this embeddedness be enhanced? And how do we go about answering these questions to begin with?

Framing an Analysis of Global Quiddity: From Sovereign to Nonsovereign Globalization

The persistent focus on globalization, extrinsic and overhead, must be redressed by conceptions of global formation that look to specific *in situ* everyday activities. Such activities must be treated not just as informed by the global, but as formative of globalities and, through their interoperation, the global. Cribbing from Michel Foucault's critiques of the nature of power (1982b), we must shift our focus away from an external "sovereign" globalization-as-object to be grasped and wielded. Rather, we must imagine a "nonsovereign" production of the global that is as increasingly immanent in, and emergent through, our day-to-day thoughts and actions as it is in the mass movement of capital, information, and populations. In short, the formation of the world must be seen as embedded both in space and in the lives of emplaced persons. To this end, I look to the inhabitants of the world as globally formative actors. In the process I seek to enter the terrains and interstices of their worlds, a task to be undertaken by engaging the mundanities of the everyday in lieu of transcending them (Fiske 1992). This will efface the scalar distance between the global and the local, and also the theoretical distance between structural abstractions and the viscerally commonplace. In so doing, I will also demystify the supposed juggernaut that is globalization, opening it to analysis and intervention.

Accomplishing this task entails an imperative to tell the stories of the everyday practices of global formation in ways that are more than just illustrative and impressionistic, something that can not be done so long as everyday life is regarded as self-evident. Thus, I will constitute the everyday world as problematic, as "various and differentiated matrices of experience." Such matrices are "the place from which the consciousness of the knower begins, the location of her null point." (Smith 1987, 88). And therefore, concretely, my approach will be to adopt the standpoint of the insider, that of "knowers who are members of the society . . . and who know the society from within their experience of it as an everyday world." This "experience locates for us the beginning of an inquiry" (Smith 1987, 88). To this end, my analytical focus will privilege "agency; [or] more correctly . . . the *habitat* in which agency operates and which it produces in the course of its operation" (Bauman 1992, 190–91). In the case of this particular inquiry, however, the experiential matrices in question are global in scope. In accordance with this, I will proceed from a conception of habitat that can be simultaneously localized and globally distended.

Pulling all this together, my assumption at its simplest is that globality is the product of specific persons in specific locales. These emplaced persons do specific things that more or less formally engender globally "extended social relations" (Smith 1987, 133), hyperextended relationships that may support, parallel or interfere with one another. Part and parcel of this is the conventional assumption that global relations are necessarily inflected by how they are received in different locales. But such locales are as much sites for the inception and transmission of globally extended relations as for their reception. Thus, hyperextended relations are necessarily multiply inflected from their very start, and the ever-shifting place-bound peculiarities of those inflections necessarily constitutive of global formation. Considering the bias of the literature to date, this last may seem an outlandish claim. Thinking beyond the presumptive gap between the global and the local, however, indicates otherwise. As Roy Bhaskar points out, "society" is an expression of the sum of each person's distinct relations with one another (1998, 207). And even the most economistically structural depiction of globalization must acknowledge that the physical, historical and cultural peculiarities of resource distribution entail irregularities that render the global a highly eccentric production. Nor can this be reduced to a matter of local difference converging toward a larger process that is in some way a unidirectional constant. Contra classic Newtonian mechanics, small deviations do not necessarily average out at larger scales, and it is not only big things that have big effects. As James Gleick notes, "Just as turbulence transmits energy from large scales downward through chains of vortices to the dissipating small scales of viscosity, so information is transmitted back from the small scales to the large" (1987, 261). Thus scale is jumped all the time, small uncertainties are magnified into large-scale patterns and the idiosyncrasies of local deviations need remain neither local nor idiosyncratic.

Dorothy Smith imparts a methodological implication to this scale-jumping of the particular in her observation that "[i]f you've located an individual experience in the social relations which determine [or inform] it, then although the individual experience might be idiosyncratic, the social relations are not idiosyncratic" (Smith, quoted in Nast and Pulido 2000, 724). This methodological prescription also entails the surprising rehabilitation of a much-maligned data form: the anecdote. According to Smith, the anecdote becomes "a means of pointing to the socio-spatial conditions out of which individual experiences emerge or in which they are situated." I further add that when we fully incorporate the implications of particularities' capacity to percolate into the macroscale, we are no longer merely considering how social relations inform people's experience but also how each person's experience constitutes the social. Thus, to demonstrate this at a global scale and explicate its workings, I will make extensive use of empirical examples. These examples constitute instances of the discursive and material production, dissemination and utilization of particular objects, persons, and places. While I refer to these as examples, or even as "cases" at times in this book, I do not intend them as exemplary case studies in any classical sense: they are neither average nor ideal microcosmic representations of larger processes. This does not, however, render these examples merely individualistic anecdotes. I am deploying them to build outward from an everyday world that is problematic. Further, I am building outwards from a problematized world of contemporary (or, per Bauman, *postmodern*) habitats. Bauman makes clear that such habitats are complex systems possessed of two crucial attributes: "they are unpredictable" and "they are not controlled by statistically significant factors (the circumstances demonstrated by the mathematical proof of the famous 'butterfly effect')." Thus, "[s]ignificance and numbers have parted ways" (1992, 191–92). And therefore, the extent to which any one of my cases authoritatively typifies generalized social conditions is not at issue. Rather, each one constitutes both a "point of entry, the locus of an experiencing subject or subjects, into a larger social and economic process" (Smith 1987, 157), and a vital component of those larger processes.

Explications of particular globally formative practices are necessary points of departure, but in and of themselves they do not reveal how social action assembles globalities and brings the global into being. Globally formative practices do not just float freely and happily bump into one another as fellow travelers, amicably retaining their frequently incommensurable worldviews along the way. In hyperextending across space, everyday practices make the globe through the specific ways they are socially coordinated and concerted, and through the attenuation of their forms as they stretch between particular places. The global is thus much like any other material reality, an articulation of multiple everyday life worlds and worldviews. But the problematics of coordinating and concerting are particularly complex when the historical processes in question are not just local but translocal, transnational or, as I generally prefer, *nonlocal*.

All of these terms refer to concerted practices that manifest in, and bind together as one place, locales that are ever more extreme in their spatial discontiguity. Such a discontiguous place may be called a *translocality* (see Appadurai 1996), or as an alternative may be seen as a *transnational field* or a *transnational geography* (see Bailey et al. 2002). Each of these terms has its own utility and I deploy many of them at various points across this book, particularly in instances where the term has become an institutionalized descriptor, as has *transnational corporation*. But these terms also have their own pitfalls, most of them scalar. Strictly speaking, *translocal* can imply anything from across the world to across town. *Transnational* implicitly assumes the nation as the base unit of reference (while leaving the notion of nation unproblematized) and, in the process, can result in the mischaracterization of hyperextended social relationships whose most salient characteristic may be not how they transit between nations but perhaps their intercontinentality, the irregularity of their dispersion, or simply their prodigious span between widely distant points.

Thus, I have cribbed the term *nonlocal* from quantum physics, a term that describes the simultaneous, causative occurrence of a particular event at two or more locations that are distant from one another in space-time. In so doing, I do not in any way subscribe to suppositions of ageographicality or some technological conquest of space. All the practices of global formation entail located practitioners, and even their most seemingly dematerialized practices rest upon located transmission (whether in the form of satellite uplink stations, buried copper cables, airflight itineraries, or the like). Nonetheless, the fact that localities remote from one another may now experience an event as if they were one and the same locale is often a far more salient factor of a globally formative relationship than is that relationship's breaching of national boundaries. Where this is so, I will employ the term *nonlocal* to mark fields of human activity constituted by social relationships in which more-or-less simultaneous cause and effect relationships are radically discontiguous in space. Further, this linkage of widely disparate causative and effected places forges what are functionally and experientially single locales, but spatially dislocated ones with specific addresses that are "out of joint" with one another. Such discontiguous addresses of nonlocal fields I term, simply, *dislocalities,* and I use the term *dislocalization* to refer to the process by which presences in a particular dislocality of a given nonlocal field manifest in other dislocalities within that same field.

To apprehend the presence and coordination of nonlocal material realities and the dislocalities in which they are embodied, we require a framework that moves us beyond the innumerable subjective representations of divergent life worlds. In the absence of such a framing device, we are left with "this is how it looks to me" as an endpoint (Smith 1987, 121–22). Further, we are deprived of the capacity to assess relationally constituted social injustices implicit to global formation, and are thus blinded to globalization's "asymmetrical power-geometries" (Massey 1993). For her part, Smith sees such a result as the inescapable end product, and fundamental failure, of postmodernist polyperspectivity. Against this she prescribes Karl Marx and Friedrick Engels's materialist method to accomplish this work. I, however, see things the other way around. The materialist framework, when applied to the practices of global formation, is indeed sensitive to the problematics of asymmetrical power geometries on a global scale. And materialism offers a great deal more as well, from the antiessentializing relationalism with which Marx defines objects of analysis to his keen cognizance of how ideas and materiality are mutually produced and reconstituted through social relations. Conversely, though, Marx's lens provides little space for multiple worlds or for plural knowledges of those worlds, but instead simplifies the practitioners of everyday life to first and foremost either workers or owners emergent from an ontologically privileged base of production. Thus, the materialist frame imposes overarching a priori structural propositions that preclude the specificities of everyday life as the analytical prime mover.

Conversely, I will deploy a postmodern ontology and poststructural epistemologies as my framework for explicating everyday life. This approach is consistent with my analysis of the global as the contingent articulation of multiple voices (Dear 2000, 34–37; see also Dear and Flusty 2001). It is also in keeping with Bauman's assertion that "postmodernity renders accurately the defining traits of the . . . present social condition . . . marked by the overt institutionalization of the characteristics which modernity—in its designs and managerial practices—set about to eliminate and, failing that, tried to conceal" (1992, 187–88).

While this book is not a treatise on postmodernism or poststructural thought, it is such thinking that tacitly underpins the articulation of my case studies. I am, however, cognizant of the critique of postmodernism as encapsulated by Smith's aforementioned dissent. Postmodernism has a tendency to disarticulate the social into so many equally valid divergent versions and viewpoints. Such disarticulation can act to undermine the apprehension of any material reality and its embedded injustices. Recent writings in poststructural geography, however, have countered this danger with such prophylaxes as "discursive materialism" (Yapa 1996) or "materialist poststructuralism" (Peet 1996). By way of example, Lakshman Yapa reveals how 'poverty' is simultaneously such material experiences as hunger and malnutrition, and a discourse that "conceals the social origins of scarcity" (1993, 707). Further, he demonstrates how the latter (re)produces the former, and in so doing identifies poverty as a "discursive materialist formation." Thus, discursive materialism is not simply a synthesis of resolutely material and irremediably semiotic perspectives. It is a powerful analytical framework that investigates space as the medium in which the way things are informs how we think and, simultaneously, the ways in which we remake how things are. Thus, the image and the concrete reciprocate in giving form to one another and, over successive iterations, produce complex discursive/material formations (see Entrikin 1991 for a humanist presaging of this theme). Such a "postmodernism of method" elegantly bridges the material/discourse divide, recognizing that the concrete literally has no meaning without the cognitive but also that the cognitive assembles meanings from the kit of parts the concrete describes.

Thus, I will deploy my cases in conjunction with a framework that is discursively materialist, attentive of the interaction of the represented and the real, and in so doing will also indicate how the postmodern is no less (re)produced in the practice of everyday life than the global.

In short, I am making claims about the global impacts of the stuff of everyday life, and it is this same stuff that will build and test my claims—particular people and artifacts, and the locales they inhabit. I will narrate stories about the material *and* symbolic interrelations of these spatially situated people and artifacts. And I will show how these interrelations hyperextend to intersect and inflect others, at ever greater distances, so as to become present and efficacious on a global scale. Thus, the stuff of everyday life becomes arterial pathways through the emergent social body of the planet—pathways that are material, meaningful, and transformative, that can be shown to simultaneously enact globalities and, in so doing, bring the global into being. In a very deep sense, then, the everyday interrelations of people and artifacts are, in and of themselves, the processes of global formation. They are the stuff from which the world is made, a rich panoply of stuff that more often than not yields a world of contradictory dynamics and polyvalent outcomes.

The Sources of Globalities

At its most literal, this project is an investigation and locations-outward theorization of the everyday practices of global formation, an explication of the specific, commonplace, lived geographies of globalization. But in spirit, in the telling, and as an overarching methodological theme, this project is a planetary *dérive*. The dérive is the favorite practice of situationist psychogeography, a practice of wandering between multiple points of psychic attraction (Debord 1958).

Such wandering will include each chapter's shuttling back and forth between the theoretical and the quotidian. But it also includes the production of the work itself, a task that has led me by the nose on dérives across numerous world cities and the places in between. My own personal dérives to and through the spaces of these places were, in turn, attempts to follow other passages of particular persons and peoples through these points of psychic attraction. I have not, however, set out upon these wanderings unequipped. I have gone as a bricoleur, carrying a sack full of methods. These methods include ethnographic participant observation, material culture studies, and the network, fluidic, and folded spaces of actor-network theory and its successors. As with any good bricoleur, I have applied these methods singly and in combination, depending upon the peculiarities of each case as I have run across it.

My reliance upon bricolage has enabled me to engage in another situationist strategy, that of *detournement*. Detournement is the practice of adapting found objects to new purposes in, and constitutive of, new settings. And I have indeed seized upon the stories of persons, places and things to turn them to the purpose of explicating global formation. I believe this is entirely appropriate as it is from out of, and by means of, persons, places and things that globality itself is kluged.

Of course, in the pages of this story I am the one doing the kluging. And in narrating others' everyday practices, I will necessarily be translating them into discourse. It is regrettably but unavoidably the case that discourse about a practice is not, by definition, the practice itself (Bourdieu 1977, 110). In fact, the two can be quite divorced, with the worldview of the narrator doing the divorcing. I know of no prophylaxis against this. But as a hedge, I will in the course of these wanderings follow feminist prescriptions to explicitly situate my knowledge (Haraway 1991). I will make myself visible wherever possible, and repeatedly touch back to my own lived and practiced experiences.

The substantive focus of this work, however, is not my own relation to the global but the densifying skeins of practiced relationships that constitute globalities. Documenting these relationships has necessitated both literally following them across space, and gaining entré into these attenuating hyperextended interrelations by building my own interpersonal relationships with their participants. To accomplish this I have traveled both extensively and intensively, through hard cities and across the hard planet. The rationale for these travels, however, has been to explore the articulation of others' soft cities and soft planets, and their impacts upon the hard. To accomplish this I have engaged in forms of participant observation that range from formal interviews, through journalistic inquiry and conversational encounters, to extended socializing of the most informal sort. Throughout my approach has been, in keeping with Donna Haraway's strategy of 'mobile positioning,' to experience as best I could others' local knowledges and, through this, establish dialogues between those knowledges and my own.

A portion of this work was accomplished in Los Angeles, where I have lived and worked for much of my life. My narrative of L.A.'s hardening into a world city is drawn largely from my own professional experience as a perpetrator of that hardening, having worked as an architectural consultant, urban designer, and employee of the city's Community Redevelopment Agency. These experiences had the additional benefit of providing me access to many other Angelenos who as designers, sales agents, administrators, legislators, researchers, dissidents, and simple residents have witnessed L.A.'s world citification for decades longer than I have. I augmented these sources with my own legwork. This entailed months-long street-by-street surveys of the city for surveillantly controlled sites like privately administered "public" plazas and gated "communities." It has also included the collection of crime data at the national, metropolitan and neighborhood level drawn, with the invaluable assistance of Rachel Kuzma, from such sources as the FBI Uniform Crime Reports, the crimes-per-reporting-district enumerations of the Los Angeles Police Department, and mappings of individual crime incidences available through neighborhood watch organizations. Finally, I have dragged others along on many of these research expeditions to gauge their responses to the same phenomena. Some of these expeditions have entailed as few as two or three other people. Others, however, have involved tour groups of as many as thirty persons, including members of nationwide architectural organizations, a cohort of young Baltic geographers and, upon two occasions, approximately two dozen urban administrators assembled from a wide selection of nonaligned and post-Soviet countries.

Similarly, my redactions of L.A.'s life worlds emerge from their intersections with my own. Through these intersections, I have interfaced with innumerable facets of L.A.'s diverse community landscapes. Some of these engagements have been relatively brief and superficial, as with my encounters with the city's variegated Thai, Armenian, and South Asian communities. Others have become active engagements that continue to the present— particularly my ongoing interactions with predominantly Ishan/Edo segments of the city's Nigerian community and a self-identified "dyke" subset of the city's lesbians. Most commonly, members of these collectives collaborated in my research by means of open-ended conversations in which I asked a lot of questions. Often, the questions predicated upon the most mistaken assumptions proved the most valuable, eliciting enthusiastically elaborated corrections. To ensure I have not subsequently abused my collaborators in this work, I have whenever possible submitted my write-ups back to them for review and, at their discretion, rejection. This has as often as not elicited clarifications and corrections, which I have invariably included. In addition to conversations, however, there was much watching, and much acting on my part. Through these practices I have attempted to engage the varied sensory and sensual modes through which the realities of the world city are experienced, imagined, represented, contested, and (re)generated.

Given that the purpose of my work has been to pursue connections among world cities as well as within them, I have been attentive to how my engagement with the diverse populations of the city has pointed to linkages beyond Los Angeles. In some instances, such linkages provided secondary source material. My discussions of Japanese supranational politics, for example, benefited immeasurably from Angelenos who vouched for me to otherwise recalcitrant United Nations personnel stationed in Central Asia and at UN headquarters in Manhattan. But in other instances, I have traveled internationally to pursue these linkages actively. This has included repeat journeys along the length of Japan's Tokaido urban corridor, extended stays in Fennoscandia bracketed by Joensu on the east and Stockholm on the west, and numerous travels to Mexico centered on three locales: Oaxaca to the south, Tijuana at the *frontera,* and the Federal District of Mexico City in the center. Throughout this fieldwork my methods have been the same as those I used in Los Angeles, although in some instances necessarily deployed via translators. And as in L.A., this has entailed some rather unconventional acts, including taste testing prototype curry formulations in the laboratory of a Nagoya confectionary factory and falling in with a mass march against plutocratic globality through Mexico City's central axis. Further, these excursions were not, strictly speaking, mine alone. Were it not for the intercession of people like Khadija Mohammed, Odion Okojie, Sheri Ozeki and Tara Thierry in their respective communities in Los Angeles; Alejandro Mercado at Mexico's core and Tito Alegria at its northern periphery; Makoto Araki and Shusaku Morinaga along Japan's megalopolitan spine, and Marko Tiirinen in the deepest exurbs of Stockholm, many of the milieus in this book would have proved impenetrable.

Thus, this work utilizes widely varied categories of data. Such data ranges from built landscapes to corporate histories (and counterhistories), criminal incident statistics to the showings and tellings of persons' specific life-experiences. And in so far as different data require different techniques for their interpretation, this work likewise deploys a wide range of methods including participant-observation, landscape semiotics, historiography, and a raft of material culture methodologies melded with actor-network theory and commodity chain delineations. This multimethod approach has enabled me to engage in the critical realist practice of triangulation, whereby I narratively conjoin numerous and diverse partial perspectives, each a constituent social facet of the phenomenon that is the global. But referring to the sources of this work as "data" is neither respectful nor strictly honest. More often than not, this data has shown and told me what it is I should be studying. It has continually set and reset the direction of my research, as opposed to docilely following my own agenda. Therefore, in most instances such sources have not been data at all, neither object nor subject, but collaborators. Certainly this is true of the people and social collectives involved in the narration of this text. Their participation in my own open-ended methods of participant observation, applied both at home and abroad, have provided the lion's share of source material for my work. And it is no less true of those who have contributed behind the narrative and as such safeguarded its completion and its quality. In fact, there have been four teams of such collaborators: a principle committee headed unflaggingly by Michael Dear and comprised of Todd Boyd, Laura Pulido and Jennifer Wolch; a protocommittee including David Sloane and Greg Hise, a shadow committee more or less unwittingly comprised of Eve Oishi, Pauliina Raento, Ralph Saunders, and David McBride—my tireless editor; and a cadre of key facilitators including Angela Chnapko at Routledge, Billie Shotlow at the University of Southern California's Department of Geography, and Chris Conley and Carey Embry at the Casbah Café, the latter two having kept this text well fueled with a constant torrent of yerba mate.

But many of the collaborators in this work are not human at all. Rather, they are inanimate objects, artifacts, particular pieces of material culture. The logics of these artifacts have determined the axes along which I have organize my source material, and provided the prism through which I view the concerting of globally formative practices. Thus, such objects have become for me both subjects and collaborators in their own right. It is the multiple fluid faces, both material and symbolic, of these artifact-collaborators that concretely explicate the twisting paths of global formation in its broadest dimension. And simultaneously, they have kept my explorations grounded in the emplaced everyday, despite the fact that the progression of my work has floated (and the book's narrative floats) increasingly free from Los Angeles to journey through globalities and across the globe at large.

Working with the "Stuff" of Life: Biographical Mappings of People and Things Together

Of course, artifacts are not so adept at speaking for themselves as are my more animate collaborators. Thus, extra effort is necessary to coax artifacts into explicating the specific hyperextended relations in which they participate. We interact with thousands of artifacts every day from the moment we take our head off the *pillow,* sit up in *bed* and put our feet on the *rug.* Yet the overwhelming majority of such artifacts are so commonplace, so deeply embedded in our surroundings and routine activities, that we scarcely notice this "daily conspiracy of inanimate objects" (Hotz 1998, 8). As with any conspiracy, this relative anonymity hides power and complexity. Artifacts are a unique form of material evidence, possessed of a twofold nature (Miller 1987, chapter 7). On the one hand, a given artifact exhibits a recognizable form regardless of place or mode of employ. On the other hand, the same artifact is attached to differing functions and meanings that depend upon the social context of its use. Thus, the artifact is simultaneously thing and image. But it is more than a thing to be utilized and filled with meaning. According to Carl Sauer and Franz Boas (in Agnew et al. 1996), it is the product of unique human/environment relationships, and it is an indicator of the geographical extents of particular cultural influences.

The artifact is also an active mediator of people's relations to one another and their environment (Schlereth 1990; see also Kingery 1998, chapter 1). Material culture is not the passive embodiment of human intentions, but "a cause, medium and a consequence of social relationships" (Riggins 1994, 1). It is a synecdoche for a larger society, an active component of social reproduction that exhibits its own agency, and even the physical environment within and upon which societies sustain themselves (Jackson 1984).

Thus, artifacts may be read as mediators, translators, and participants in everyday global formation. This task includes mapping the artifact's migratory itinerary. But such a mapping must be joined to the stories behind the generation, transportation, and use of that artifact. The artifact thus becomes a constituent component of multiple material and social contexts, and "we have to follow the things themselves, for their meanings are inscribed in their forms, their uses, their trajectories. It is only through the analysis of these trajectories that we can interpret the human transactions and calculations that enliven things" (Appadurai 1986). Seeing objects as not just denoting social relationships but also as participants in them generates a narrative material culture that erodes firm divisions between the user and the thing used.

This will be my approach as I make use of artifacts throughout the following chapters, and it will enable me to simultaneously generate social histories and cultural biographies of people and things together (see Kopytoff 1986). I will use narrative material culture to reveal two things: how artifacts are embedded in diverse and disparate (sub)cultural narratives and locales, and how artifacts collaborate with people to inscribe those narratives and condition their interoperation. In so doing, my artifacts will show how those narratives and locales are indeed diverse but are not really all that disparate. Rather, it will become apparent they are intimately conjoined by the increasingly hyperextended activities of daily life.

Throughout this book, the artifact's multifold makings, meanings, and mutations through adaptive reutilization will be critical tools for the exploration and explication of the specificities of global formation across multiple scales. But under these mobile circumstances, the artifact also tends to deco-here as a discursive/material formation. It takes on a commodity form that drifts from its underlying production processes while, simultaneously, the artifact's image and branding become a "sign" that floats ever more freely from the artifact itself. Yet despite this drifting and floating, the artifact itself remains of a piece.

This polyvalence of the solitary artifact is complicated by how it is ag-gregated with others into "commodity landscapes." Such landscapes are the "world of goods" each of us consumes and displays, the materialization of a "subjective fantasy" in the form of a specific represented identity we use to distinguish ourselves from others (J. Friedman 1994b, 11). Commodity landscapes, unsurprisingly enough, are underpinned by a particular type of artifact: the commodity. From a Marxist perspective the commodity is a thing produced not for its use value, but as exchange value (see Marx 1978). In the process, the labor of workers producing the artifact becomes alienated from the total production process, and symbolically invisible in the artifact's eventual consumption. In this devalorization and disappearance of its underlying material production processes, the artifact's symbolic content is evacuated. Seemingly extracted from the social relations of production, the artifact becomes a commodity fetish bereft of any meaning except that which is arbitrarily ascribed to it as a means of enhancing exchange value (this being the function of advertising, in conjunction with the systemic production of chronic dissatisfaction; see Helm 2000). Thus, in addition to its materiality, the artifact becomes a readily reconfigurable sign, ren-dering the artifact cum commodity complicit in ongoing crises of meaning (Baudrillard 1994; after Debord, 1994) wherein ever more fluid symbolic systems embed human society in an unmoored hyperreality of mediated representations and simulacra, simulations of an imagined reality that need never have existed.

By turning to Michel de Certeau's (1984) idea that meaningfulness inheres as much in ultimate utilization as in production, however, a more ambiva-lent (and less damning) perspective on the commodity and the commodity landscape emerges. From this standpoint, the status of an artifact depends upon its deployment at any given moment. Thus the commodity gives way to a state of "commoditiness," a potential phase in an artifact's life. As an artifact is deployed in various contexts of use, its potential for employment in exchange relations will differ. When the artifact undergoes exchange, it becomes a commodity, with its candidacy for "commoditihood" depending upon "the standards and criteria (symbolic, classificatory and moral) that define the exchangeability of things in any particular social and historical context" (Appadurai 1986, 13–14). Thus an artifact may move in and out of a commodity state numerous times over the course of its existence and, as it transits globally between the symbolic networks of divergent culture complexes (Gurnah 1997, 130–31), slippage of meaning occurs as the artifact (and any associated symbolic value claims) is recontextualized by its receiver.

In the process, the artifact enters into relationships with others to describe larger systems of cultural meaning (Eco 1976). In so grounding our conception of the commodity landscape upon the everyday assimilation and deployment of its constituent artifacts, the commodity becomes more than a vessel of meanings manipulatively inscribed and prescribed by external authorities. Of course, it remains that too. But there is no guarantee that how we choose to mundanely use the commodity, how we enact it, will subscribe to such prescriptions and inscriptions. By enacting commodities in ways that adapt them to the exigencies of our daily lives, we transform artifacts in unauthorized and often unpredictable ways (see Latour 1995; Pfaffenberger 1992). In the process, global products and images are locally appropriated to create particular lifespaces. And subsequently, those novel appropriations and lifespaces may be dislocalized for reappropriation elsewhere. Thus, the "crisis of meaning" is also an efflorescence of opportunities. It may well be that we are all now subject to a condition of global dependency, but its local orchestration (J. Friedman 1994b, 17) entails that global formation depends in turn upon the diffusion of all sorts of particularities along very irregular paths. This will become clear as, in the progression of this book, I increasingly highlight the polyvalency of the "things" in my biographical mappings of people and things together. But at the same time it must not be forgotten that such abstractions as "the global," "the city," and "particularity," in all their differing and contending versions, exist only insofar as they are brought into being through embodied practices. Bodies, then, are the matter that matters most, and in keeping with this there is a common theme guiding my selection of artifacts for narration: all are things that are put on, taken into, representative of, or employed to exert control over, the body.

In following the ever-metamorphosizing artifact as it traces circuits that link lives lived at particular addresses and in varied contexts, my approach dovetails with actor-network theory (ANT), which is predicated upon the supposition of "rhizomatics"—that humans and nonhumans enter into networks of relationships, and that such relationships change each component member through processes of mutual translation. The resulting networks, hybridized of coadapted humans and nonhumans, may be considered complex agents in their own rights (Latour 1998). ANT's network entities are thus very similar to the human/artifact hybrid objects constituted in a narrative material culture.

I will make tacit use of rhizomatic conceptualizations as I pursue interpenetrating human/artifact relations about the planet. This will not, however, be an exercise in ANT-ic rhizomatics, for two reasons. First, I will not be focused exclusively, or even largely, on ANT's principle object of analysis: tightly coordinated networks of hard and clear relational lines, constituted and maintained by means of authorial delegation. Rather, the relations I will be chiefly concerned with are the product not of intentional and directed delegation, but of happenstance connections. These are relations of elements that have drifted into one another's paths over the course of more or less random walks, to subsequently miscegenate and propagate. Second, the relations I am here interested in are not constituted exclusively by and within the network. They are looser, more contingent in their coming together and staying together. And they are reliant upon fluidic spaces and processes (de Laet and Mol 2000) outside the network as a location in which to drift and interpenetrate. Therefore, I implicitly reject ANT's explicit ageographicality, the assertion that there is nothing and no space outside the lines and points of the network (Latour 1997). To the contrary, I will be equally focused on the artifact's locales of appearance, and on its influences in the production and experience of space and place. This serves to emphasize that human/nonhuman interactions comprise not just networks, but also "social practices [that] are inherently spatial, at every scale and all sites of human behavior" (Dear and Wolch 1989, 9). Such social practices constitute hybrid entities of particular people, places, activities, and artifacts that hyperextend spatially and so form the global from emplaced persons outward.

The (Dis)Order of the Work

Throughout the remaining pages I will bring together numerous located biographies of interwoven people and things to assemble what I hope will be a new and useful lens with which to view what the global is and how it comes into being. This process of assembly will proceed in three steps, each with a chapter of its own. First, I explore the different ways global formation has been grappled with in theory, and how these theories have been fused with understandings of the world city. Second, I adopt a perspective from within a particular world city to describe the global implications of how its everyday relations are ordered in space, and how the growing reach of those relations dis- and reorder the global. And finally, I explicate how the practices of such hyperextended everyday relations enact a wide variety of intersecting global realities or, more simply, globalities.

The vision of global formation I assemble here is neither comprehensive nor definitive, it does not pretend to be a panoptic encyclopedia of globalization. I believe this is appropriate. Panopticity is an impossibility, and pyrrhic attempts to attain it inevitably inflict disappearances and injustice. In response, and as a hedge against claims to panopticity, I will leave many threads loose at every end. Corollary to tracing these threads, I will also digress a lot, frequently going off on tangents. In fact, I will predominantly follow tangents. Within the frame of this project, digressions are not digressive and tangentiality is not synonymous with irrelevance. To the contrary, digressions and tangents are the meat of the matter. Globalities, after all, are woven of tangents that intersect to form dense skeins of social relations hyperextending outward through space. Thus, this project is an exercise in abductive reasoning. What I present here is an entirely partial exploration and explication of "the global" from within, following the skeins of networks and the meandering paths of diffusing influences. It is an excursion into heterotopia, Foucault's 'impossible space' of coexistent 'fragmentary possible worlds' (Hetherington 1997). It is a driftwork, a quasi-random walk across varied material and discursive terrains, following their lead and recording the journey, equipped with an array of devices for interpreting the world in relation to my own position.

This journey comes replete with all the attendant dangers of being hopelessly lost at sea or swallowed by monsters at the edge of the world. It may even seem a mess, a tangled knotty hotbed of disorder. At least I hope so. According to John Fiske, "the organization of bodily behavior in space and time forms the basis of the social order" (1992, 161). Conversely, the messiness of the everyday disorders, both theoretically and experientially. And when the order in question is a would-be panoptic one, imposed as though from on high for the purpose of instrumental control and even gross exploitation, is such disordering a bad thing? It is my hope, then, that this quotidian deregulation of daily life can dis-order a world presently subjected to some very draconian new orderings.

PART I

From the World to the City to the Street, and Back Again

Kublai Khan remains silent, reflecting. Then he adds: "Why do you speak to me of stones? It is only the arch that matters to me."
[Marco] Polo answers: "Without stones there is no arch."
—Italo Calvino, (*Invisible Cites*)

As I begin writing this, a compact disc plays in the background. My chosen soundtrack for the afternoon is martial brass of the Ottoman Empire, a civilization long predating that of Enlightenment Europe. Despite this, European powers of the period regarded the Ottoman Empire as the barbarously decadent "sick man of Europe," at least until its 1923 reconstruction as a properly modern nation-state, the republic of Turkey.

The compact disc, one of a series from the "World Music Library," was purchased from a local outlet of Tower Records. Twenty years ago such recordings would have been considered arcana, confined to Smithsonian ethnographic recordings and a handful of titles under such small, independent labels as Nonesuch. Now, hundreds of titles ranging from those of the U.S./Mexico border Norteño music to Tuvan throat singing are available from most major recording labels. These products are sold in every entertainment media outlet from an ever-growing linear footage of display bins identified by the problematic heading "world music."

My changing listening habits are mirrored by the change in neighborhood composition just out the window to my right. As a child, my playmates on this street may have had great-grandparents from various parts of Europe and parents from other U.S. cities, but they were with few exceptions native English speakers and pale of skin. Over the past few years, however, I began to encounter woman in hijabs on my walks around the block and, peering across the front lawn into the window of a new resident's home, I noticed enameled samovars. But it was not until the day following the earthquake of 1994 that the full extent of what had been occurring came, quite literally, out in the open. The residents of roughly every fourth house had relocated onto their front lawns with tea and flat bread. Discussions with these forced picnickers revealed Armenians, Iranis, and West-Central Asians fearing their homes might collapse like those caught in the Near Eastern seismic disturbances of the 1980s.

This normalization of formerly "exotic" influences in my home, and in the neighborhood in which it is embedded, is both symptomatic and generative of a larger condition. In New York City, I have watched Filipina care-givers tending to dowagers in Greenacre Park. In Frankfurt, I have watched from Dönner-Kebab stands as municipal workmen stencil black and yellow cautionary text in Serbian, Tamil, and Greek beneath the existing German and Turkish on high-voltage junction boxes. And my disc of Turkic militaria is produced by a subsidiary of Sony, the Japanese multinational also responsible for the stereo playing that CD. The disc is available at Tower outlets in the larger cities of thirteen nation-states spread across North America, the British Isles, East Asia and the Middle East (hence one of Tower's more recent mottos, "It's a global thing").

This widening dispersion of diverse goods, ideas and people(s) is the face of globalization, the process of the rendering of the world as a single place (Robertson 1992). But what flows, in which configurations, produce this face, and how has this face manifested over time? Further, what kind of single place is being rendered, and is it a single, unitary place at all, or a place of places? And what, or who, is making it so?

1
The World Defined

When we refer only to one form of globalization or, worse, to globalization in the singular, we beggar the question of just how many forms there may be. In so doing, we neglect their corollary implications. Thus, we find ourselves at a loss for theoretical tools with which to get a handle on the spectrum of occurrences giving recent rise to what may (or may not) be an entirely new world order (Smith and Borocz 1995).

Yet, a wide selection of tools for coming to grips with the global is already at hand. The most common, of course, is the analysis of globalization as a neoliberal ("free market") macroeconomic process. But there are more critical and academic perspectives, most notably three alternative models that highlight three distinctly different prime movers of global formation: a metastasizing capitalist ecumene, a planetary compression of cultures, and an erratically densifying net of eclectic worldwide "flows." Each of these models has its own utilities and its own implicit (but often unstated) spatial underpinnings and ramifications. But at the same time, certain problematic assumptions are common to these models of global formation, specifically:

- the counterposition of the global with the local
- their corollary identification with homogenizing upper-circuit economic imperatives and locally sticky heterogenizing cultural necessities, respectively

Such assumptions, and the overarching categorizations they reify, require dissolution.

The Conventional Wisdom: A World Market

The first use of the words *globalize* and *globalization* dates to the mid-1950s, where the terms emerged in a business context with reference to the growing significance of international trade (Weiner and Simpson 1991). The timing is no surprise. Following World War II, war-weakened European, Japanese, and affiliated colonial markets suddenly became readily accessible to the victorious United States. This relatively unipolar expansion of world trade interacted with capital surpluses in the mature markets of the United States to create a push and complementary pull into transnational trade for both U.S. capital and firms. These investments were soon to be followed by non-U.S. capital and firms as economic recovery took hold in Europe, Japan and, finally, numerous newly industrializing countries. While geographically widespread trading systems are hardly unique to the twentieth Century (Abu-Lughod 1989; Braudel 1984), these postwar developments were to result in two significant economic phenomena. First, intensifying flows of transborder investment, abetted by the hegemony of the U.S. dollar and the advent of "quicksilver capital" following the collapse of the Bretton Woods Agreement in the early 1970s. And second, the resultant generation of the transnational corporation (TNC, or MNC for multinational corporation; see Pitelis in Pitelis and Sugden, 1991). In time, these quicksilver capitalized TNCs would take on such forms as contingent alliances between TNCs of differing nationalities, and geographically "distributed multinational enterprises" that, considered as total entities, have no single de facto nationality whatsoever (such as Nike, Incorporated; see also OTA 1993, 28).

These massive institutions, and their even more extensive subcontracting networks, are at the heart of globalization as envisioned from the perspective of the business and newsweekly press. Such institutions dominate the production and dissemination of commodities, capital, and information worldwide, and so cast globalization as a planet-wide process of standardization in all spheres of human endeavor (Barnet and Cavanagh 1994). In response, popular debate has polarized between two opposing factions. The first is comprised of those who champion macroeconomic models of globalization, extolling an allegedly generalizable standard of affluence permitted by commodity capitalism. The second consists of those who seek to bolster local particularity, decrying the same affluent standards of living as available only to elites and, thus, not generalizable at all. For this latter faction, macroeconomic globalization is necessarily destructive of local cultural variation informing alternative ways of life, and offers the majority little in return (e.g., Mattelart 1983; see also the debate between Eisner and Lang 1991).

From this debate has emerged a model wherein globalization is homogenization imposed from on high, pitted against localization as a fragmented and fragmenting reaction from below (Barber 1996). This scenario has been further complicated by management theories acknowledging that TNCs have failed to provide for local taste, and to make use of unique local talent. Such failures hobble large firms' competitiveness in local markets relative to both local competitors and to more locally accommodating transnational firms (Dunning, 1993; *Economist,* 1994). From this latter position has emerged the notion of "glocalization," an imperative to adapt transnational business and marketing practices to local exigencies. Some have gone so far as to assert that in the absence of glocalization's increased sensitivity to local culture, the macroeconomic globalization of the TNCs will sabotage itself. In this scenario, localizing response will tend toward resistance, giving rise to such phenomena as protectionism and even terrorism. In turn, these will impel the collapse of both national and world markets (Friedman 1999).

Beneath this contemporary debate over the pleasures and perils of transnational homogenization, however, is a subtext of colonialist practice in general, and Eurocentric diffusionism (Blaut 1993) in particular. Broadly, Eurocentric diffusionism proceeds from the idea of a "European miracle" accounting for an endogenous dynamism in certain European peoples. This supposedly inherent quality propels the European to a "higher" stage of development constituting true civilization. It is this path that allegedly "backward" societies (sometimes equated with racial inferiority) must follow if they are to attain the material rewards of "becoming civilized." In this formulation, privileged sectors of Europe bear the "white man's burden" of assisting in a civilizing process commonly depicted as lubricating the transition from gemeinschaft to gesellschaft. In its most self-congratulatory polemical form, this process of predeterminate sociopolitical evolution will arrive (or, some argue, has now arrived) at an "end of history," wherein a best of all possible worlds with a neoliberal economy and a politics of liberal democracy reigns supreme (Fukuyama 1992).

Of course, this juxtaposition of "civilization" against "barbarism" and "backwardness" is no colonialist European invention. Peoples as diverse as the Attic Greeks and Shang Dynasty Chinese have seen their city states and imperial capitals as the cardinal point of civilization, with barbarism increasing as a function of distance from that center (Marshall 1991, 168). What is perhaps unique about the civilization/barbarism dichotomy's expression in Eurocentric diffusionism is the potential for all persons and peoples to undergo conversion to civilization. This missionary position was complemented by emerging technologies in transportation, communication and warfare to engender a *civilizade. Civilizade* is a term coined circa 1870 characterizing proposals to forcibly eradicate such "civilizationally regressive" practices as polygamy in the Middle East (Weiner and Simpson 1991), but it is in no way a defunct conception. The civilizade finds recent expression in the rhetorical justification for the seemingly never-ending aerial bombardments of Iraq as a restoration of the rule of law, or in arguments for the 1990s military intervention in ex-Yugoslavia as an assertion of civilization against the alleged tactical barbarism of *Chetniki* combatants.

But the notion of a civilizade persists most dramatically in modernization theories that recommend the emulation of Europe's socioeconomic evolutionary trajectory as the remedy to "underdevelopment." Such theories prescribe a preset sequence of modernization phases (e.g., the takeoff stage at which development commences), performance standards derived from late- and post-industrial societies (Gereffi 1989), and the absorption of Western European modes of thought, techniques of environmental transformation, and material standards of living. These "modernizing" Euro-American constructs are thus deployed as the benchmark against which other societies are evaluated, and often evaluate themselves (Arruda 1996; Weisband 1989).

These benchmarks do indeed have much to offer, and have not infrequently made good upon such offers to confer benefits like the eradication of numerous life-threatening diseases, radical decreases in infant mortality and illiteracy, and even such too-frequently underappreciated creature comforts as indoor plumbing. From a broader perspective, however, critics contend that the pursuit of such benchmarks under the auspices of Western financial and technical authority has resulted in development that is grotesquely uneven at every geographical scale. According to this line of reasoning, developmentalist modernization concentrates influence, discretion and capital ever more asymmetrically into the economies of the "developed world" and their principal investors (King 1991; Gorostiaga 1984) to the point of undermining and even eradicating local autonomy. In the process, the imposition of both broader development regimes and specific restructuring programs produces a host of dysfunctions. Most viscerally, they spatially displace and, in the process, economically undermine broad populations (Weisband 1989). They extirpate diverse local lifeways by imposing unitary product and production regimes upon varied peoples (Shiva 1993). They restrict those who are othered in the world marketplace to the roles of raw input and commodifiable exotica. Finally, and perhaps most ominously, they advance ecologically unsustainable overdevelopment worldwide (Anton 1995). Further, it has been asserted that these are not accidental side effects, but part and parcel of harmonized initiatives by de facto alliances of state and corporate high functionaries. Such initiatives institute a debt-leveraged imperialism that secures the privileges of global hegemony (Chomsky 1991). Nor is this dynamic necessarily seen as limited to the "developing world." Rather, the growing prevalence of "backwardness" in the "developed world" indicates that the concentration of overdevelopment's perquisites may rely upon a very thorough global diffusion of underdevelopment's privations.

A critical analysis of all these claims is well beyond the scope of this book. The broader argument about the developmentalist production of unevenness, however, is borne out by World Bank and United Nations Development Program statistics on planetary resource disposition. Between the 1960s and the 1990s the income of the world population's most affluent 20 percent increased from 70.2 percent to 84.7 percent of the planet's liquid assets, up from thirty to over sixty times that of the world's poorest 20 percent. And while this is a relative measure, the poverty of the latter cohort, disproportionately concentrated in the excolonial world, will likely increase throughout the coming years in the absolute sense as well, with foreign direct investment ever more prone to flow between "developed" economies and bypass "developing" regions entirely. Meanwhile, the lion's share of concentrated wealth wasn't in the hands of persons at all (except in the legally fictive sense). As of the mid-1990s, 60 percent of the world's twenty trillion dollars worth of productive capital was in the 'hands' of the world's fifty largest financial companies, and the three hundred largest nonfinancial companies (employing roughly .3 percent of the world's population) owned 25 percent of the world's productive assets (Korten 1996).

Advocates of globally deregulated trade disparage these arguments as just one of the many flavors of "globaloney" (Krugman 1996), asserting instead the market certainty that a rising tide of globally distending sweatshops will eventually float all boats (no matter, it would seem, how small or leaky). With even more such globalization, inequities will be overcome (*Economist* 2001a). This prescription, however, has failed to prevent the statistical symptoms of inequality from growing ever more marked, turning "the gap between rich and poor...into an economic chasm" (*New York Times* 1999; see also Wade 2001).

Thus, theories of globalization as a process of macroeconomic integration readily become discourses for legitimizing the continuation of precisely the colonial praxis that rendered "less developed countries" less developed to begin with, accomplished concretely by rendering the societies of the excolonial world penetrable to large financial and international aid institutions (McMichael, 1996; also see Krugman and Venables, 1995). And under these circumstances, glocalization becomes merely an admonition to "oppress global, recruit local."

Model 1: A World System

Immanuel Wallerstein's world-systems model of globalization expands upon critiques of global developmentalism's dark side, mobilizing Marxism in combination with dependency theory and decolonialist economic criticism. The world-systems model provides a counternarrative to the valorization of European success as a by product of superior efficiency or innovativeness. As redacted by James Blaut (1993), this counternarrative commences with resurgent Islam conquering Constantinople and so severing Europe from East Asian trade. While seeking a way around this closure, the Iberians bump into the Americas. Next, pillaged American animal, vegetal, and mineral wealth pour into Europe, throwing the continent into hyperdevelopment. This in turn facilitates technological advance, generating a well-armed European capitalist political economy and abetting the materially motivated subjugation of peoples previously at a level of development similar to (or in advance of) that of Europe.

Colonialism and contemporary neocolonialism thus constitute a different type of globalization, the worldwide diffusion of a capitalist division of labor to engender an international division of labor. The internationalization of the division of labor opens new markets and creates new proletariats for the expanded extraction of surplus value, and for the avoidance of downcycles generated by the contradictions inherent in capitalist accumulation itself (Wallerstein 1984). Global alienation is a necessary corollary of this attenuative hyperextension of capitalism. As workers are separated a world away from the product of their work, commodity fetishism is reinforced and rendered omnipresent. This globalizes a commodity culture rife for penetration by such institutions as commercial mass entertainment media, where meanings are manipulatively assigned for marketing purposes. Cultural components of globalization are thus exploitatively ideological, generated epiphenomenally and strategically deployed by the internationalized mode of material-economic production and its controllers (Wallerstein 1990).

The immediate end product of this historically materialist process is planet length, readily relocatable commodity chains, linked place nodes in which a given product's production occurs. The relative ease with which such chains can be moved from place to place for the purpose of reorganizing production and extracting capital in turn gives rise to flexible accumulation (Harvey 1989), and to disorganized capitalism (Lash and Urry 1987). And the long-term end product, some maintain, is the global spread of class conflict and the synchronization of capitalist crises, possibly leading to the eventual establishment of world socialism.

Globalization defined by world-systems theory is thus a process of continuing incorporation into a single, ever more adaptable economic regime. This incorporation is accomplished by means of an explicit spatial strategy. Constantly shifting commodity chains anchor the division of labor in each geographical periphery, yoking that periphery into endemically unequal exchange relations with core regions either directly, or via the mediation of an ever-changing cast of semiperipheral locales (Weisband 1989). The dichotomy of homogenizing universality and the heterogeneity of the particular is thus removed from the realm of culture and recast as neoimperium versus resistance. Within this formulation a global, class-based movement is best suited to overcoming the imperium and its ideological manipulations. While cultural particularity is not stripped entirely from the picture, its value is limited to the creation of collective identities that can serve as a crutch "to combat the falling away from liberty and equality" (Wallerstein 1997, 105).

World-systems theory is a powerful tool for explicating a critical lynchpin of global formation, the restructuration of (post)industrial production and its corollary spatial consequences both intended and otherwise (e.g. Davis 1992b; Knox and Taylor 1995). Such restructuration is driven by the global imposition of an integrated capitalist political economy, shifting industrial production from a Fordist mode of vertically integrated mass-production complexes to a post-Fordist mode distributed across multiple spatial clusters of small-size, small-batch subcontract producers (Scott 1988a, 1988b; Storper and Walker 1989; Castells and Hall 1994; for the high-technology and labor-intensive craft technopoles of Southern California see Scott 1993).

This shift in production entails that corollary shift in how capital accumulates, David Harvey's flexible accumulation or, per my own neologistical penchant, simply *flexism*. Flexism is a pattern of production and consumption characterized by rapid delivery and redirectability of resource flows, predicated upon cheaper and faster systems of standardized transportation and communication, capital market interoperability, and concomitant flexibly specialized "just-in-time" production processes enabling short production runs and product cycles. These result in highly mobile capital flows able to outmaneuver geographically fixed labor markets, located communities, and to a more limited extent bounded nation states. Global scope and rapidity thus permit capital to evade long-term commitment to place and the emplaced, enabling the acquisition of far-flung labormarkets and consumersheds at a discount and their subsequent abandonment at the drop of a profit.

These exchange asymmetries produce and perpetuate the core/periphery divide, and do so at multiple geographical scales to embody a *new world bipolar disorder*. Within the new world bipolar disorder, tremendous decision-making discretion is concentrated in the hands of those contracted to oversee the management of globally formative processes, whether chief executive officers or celebrities. Conversely, those lacking such authority find themselves in progressively weaker positions, pitted against each other globally, and forced to accept shrinking compensation for their efforts. Thus, world-systems theory not only accounts for flexism in general, but it also accounts for everyday life under flexist accumulative regimes: the global emergence of elite command-and-control entrepreneurs, and the corollary creation of hordes of precariously employed expendable labor called upon just in time to perform as-of-yet-unautomated McDonaldized tasks when flexist production processes require servicing.

Conversely, world-systems theory's predilection for envisioning global formation as the outcome of capitalism's long-term hyperextension confers upon globalization the status of a force as irrepressible and irremediable as the weather. And like upper-atmospheric windstorms, globalization thus becomes something that emerges from the high-pressure zones of affluent regions to buffet the low-pressure zones of poorer locales with gale force. Further, world-systems theory's privileging of capital flows renders global cultural flows junior traveling companions that, entrained behind capital, blow from such high-pressure zones as the U.S. and descend upon low-pressure zones in the homogenizing forms of Americanization or, less parochially, coca-colonization. While this propensity for clothing global formation in meteorological metaphors does not necessarily depeople global formation, it explicates people's globally formative roles in highly problematic ways. By way of example, Zygmunt Bauman (1998, 99–102), after Jonathan Friedman, has analyzed global formation as the product of a cosmopolitan class possessed of high degrees of fast geographical mobility. Such cosmopolitans, or "globals," are globetrotting jet-set inheritors of the bourgeoisie: affluent, continuously in transit, emancipated from space, and subject to experiences of disjuncture, in-betweenness, and deessentialization. According to both Bauman and Friedman, these latter caste-bound experiences form the basis of the privileged perspective informing what the authors claim to be globals' ideology, postmodernism. Subject to these cosmopolitans and their postmodern doxa are the 'locals.' Inheritors of the proletariat, locals constitute a class denied the privileges of mobility and imprisoned in place. In response, locals are retrenchantly particularistic, prone to (self-) essentialization as a survival strategy and *jihad* (cf: Barber 1996) as a corollary means of reclaiming power.

These are compelling characterizations. But do they obtain, or are they caricatures? As Saskia Sassen (1996) has pointed out, so-called cosmopolitans can be quite homogenized in their experiences, and so-called locals can be quite cosmopolitan in their diasporic scattering and simultaneous international connectivity (also see Featherstone in Bird et al. 1993). Where does the Ghanaian taxi driver negotiating the streets of Tokyo fit into Bauman and Friedman's model? Where do the Filipino contract construction worker in Bahrain or the Michoacaña hotel maid walking the picket line in Toronto fit in? Are not such people, clearly on the short end of globally formative processes, liable to experience disjuncture, in-betweenness, and very visceral deessentialization? Further, how are such people less cosmopolitan, less in-between, and more parochially particularistic than the "cosmopolitan" who travels first-class from airport lounge to airport lounge, from Hilton to Hilton, able to pay for the privilege of never having to speak an alien tongue or negotiate a foreign street? Certainly, the refugee compelled by circumstances to cross a border is situated very differently within the asymmetries of global power relations than the tourist who chooses to cross borders. But greater degrees of control over the material exigencies of one's everyday life do not necessarily correlate with cosmopolitanization. In fact, the opposite can clearly be the case.

World-systems theory is indeed useful for explicating the economic components of global formation and for apprehending their asymmetries. But faced with the challenge of situating such explications in everyday life, the theory is too rife with a priori structural positions, meteorological tropes, and procrustean assertions that juxtapose parochially shattered localities against the homogenizing global.

Model 2: A Compressed World

Roland Robertson's theory of globalization through "relativization" takes an alternative approach. It undermines narratives of European cultural superiority by denaturalizing the European as the benchmark against which other cultures are to be assessed. In the process, the singular civilization becomes plural civilizations. Simultaneously, the question of deviation from a single standard of civilization is rephrased as questions of differences among civilizations. This undermines normative standards by which civilization is to be determined, and generates uncertainty over how such standards can be legitimized. Thus, analytical focus shifts to how societies and their particular members construct one another, and how this construction process is influenced by intersocietal contact.

In relativization theory, *compression* puts the problematic of how societies construct themselves relative to one another at the center of globalization. For Robertson, compression is the growing interdependencies between peoples and places, structuring the world as a whole and bringing societies into increasingly interpenetrative contact. Through compression, previously separated societies are brought (or forced) into enduring contact and so create globalization. Thus Robertson's compression resembles world-systems-related depictions of how new transport and communication technologies shorten time and shrink space to cause time-space compression (e.g. Harvey 1989), or Anthony Gidden's (1991) idea that similar developments "stretch" societies across time and space to produce time-space distanciation.

Relativization theory, however, advances no unitary historical or technological dynamic that generates compression. Nor is compression a relatively recent phenomenon. Rather, relativization theory postulates numerous globalizations, deglobalizations and reglobalizations of various scales throughout history, caused by agents as diverse as military hegemony (e.g., imperial Rome), religious activism (e.g., the first Islamic Caliphate), or monopolistic trade (e.g., the Dutch East India Company). Each of these globalizations in turn may be seen as having facilitated the scope of the next, resulting in the current globalization of globalizations. The current globalization is attributed to a complex cascade of factors. These factors include, but are not limited to (per Robertson 1992):

- the extended reach of the Catholic Church
- the dissemination of the idea of the nation-state following the Treaty of Westphalia
- the three-way competition in the mid-twentieth century between liberalist, fascist, and communist modernisms
- the representation of both long-standing and postcolonial nations in such internationalist forums as the United Nations

At the level of concrete effects, such compressions bring people and peoples into closer day-to-day contact, heightening perceptions of the differences and similarities among them. Thus, global relativization may be seen as predicated upon conceptions of the spatial separation of more or less distinct culture areas, and the widespread local impacts of bridging these separations with increasing frequency and pervasiveness. This dynamic generates (or, more precisely, intensifies the potentials within) the global field.

The global field consists of four elements; the self, the national society, the world system of societies (e.g. international relations), and humankind. With compression, the interelationships of these elements attain a new prominence. Most significant is that compression heightens the visibility of humankind and a world system of societies relative to the self as person and social monad. This fourfold problematic destabilizes, and forces the continual redefinition of, such social attributes as (per Robertson 1992):

- citizenship (the relationship of nation to humanity)
- one's own cultural identity (the relationship of self to society and to humanity)
- the unique value of a nation in comparison to others (the relationship of national society to the system of societies)
- And of greatest import, the very existence of a given national society as its solitary citizens undergo redefinition by relativization

Thus, the world is currently undergoing an unprecedented reformation in the differential relations within, and produced by, the global field.

As in world-systems theory, globalization in relativization theory is very much a product of exchange. In relativization theory, however, what is most crucial is the exchange of self and collective representation (or the refusal of such exchange; see Perrin 1979) across the boundaries that separate societies. These exchanges define each society, and its members, relative to one another and thus establish worldwide a field of negotiated difference. Within these clusterings of relationally constructed identities, the dichotomy of homogenization versus heterogeneity is converted into a synthesis—the universalization of the particular, and the particularization of the universal. "The universalization of the particular" refers to how a need to identify what makes one's self and society unique becomes a compulsion shared by peoples worldwide. Simultaneously, "the particularization of the universal" refers to how every society will develop its own particular notions of what should constitute global first principles and will embody these putative first principles in a plethora of movements advocating their own universally applicable truths to the world (Robertson 1992, 177–78). This reciprocating dialectic will play out differently depending upon a wide variety of potential responses in local settings (Morley 1991). In some postindustrial settings, it has spawned the planetary spread of flexibly specialized and internationalized post-Fordist people (Barns 1991). In Japan, it has engendered an occidentalism that retrenches social identity by valorizing Japanese technological prowess and denigrating the West (Morley and Robins 1992). It can even entail the impending demise of societies with mind-sets ill-adapted to a global context, as with the U.S. tendency toward centrifugal atomization or the People's Republic of China's toward centripetal insularity (Tuan 1996).

Relativization theory's world matrix provides a schema for analyzing the cultural operations that inform the global from the intersocietal macroscale to the fine-grained particularities of the person. The formulation of universalizing particularism and particularizing universalism, however, tends to presume these dynamics' omnipresence and operational consistency, and as such pays less attention to the geographical unevenness and power asymmetries of the global field.

This weakness is located in relativization's depiction of global space as singular (a problem shared with formulations of both time-space compression and distantiation), and of nations as the mediators of that space's compression. Do national societies, a problematic enough construct to begin with, have so common a configuration as to comprise consistent and standardized functional-analytical units that constitute the same space? Even a cursory comparison of the "national" social identities of, say, Kuwait, North Korea, and Euzkadi would suggest otherwise. Further, this diversification of functional social typologies and the spaces they produce runs rampant when other types of social collectives predicated upon other dimensional axes of identity formation (e.g., the religious, sexual, or techno-professional) are regarded as societies as well. Thus, there are more kinds of societies with far more diverse operating parameters than just the national sort. And if we grant that such societies are also compressors and similarly compressible (something to which Robertson [1997] himself alludes), then they articulate their own distinct world systems of spatialized societies predicated upon criteria that can be quite different from (inter)nationality. Relativization's fourfold problematic thus becomes an N-dimensional one, wherein many different ways of bounding and playing the global field are simultaneously at play. More recent work in the relativization vein, especially work on the spatially disjointed communities established through diasporization, have accounted for this by pluralizing the global field into transnational fields or, per my preference, *nonlocal* fields. Such fields are geographically discontiguous but socially integrated terrains in which the dialogics of the universal and the particular, the "us" and the "other," play out according to distinct internal logics. Further, the logics of different nonlocal fields can be deeply incommensurable and at the same time influence one another profoundly (e.g., Portes 1996; Smith and Guarnizo 1998).

Less readily elided, however, are the tendencies toward cultural reification and essentialization implicit in the reliance upon unitary notions of national societies. While Robertson's work is too nuanced to fall into this trap, others have been less attentive. Perhaps the most famous instance of this to date is Samuel Huntington's geopolitical scenario that combines relativization's heightening of people's senses of cultural difference with a social Darwinist conception of the global field as a boxing ring. In Huntington's global arena, societies battle one another to preserve and enrich their own cultural values. According to Huntington, this combination must produce a bellicose assertion of philosophical and territorial boundaries between major cultural formations. As a result, "the world will be shaped in large measure by the interactions among seven or eight major civilizations...." Huntington identifies these civilizations as Western, Confucian, Japanese, Islamic, Hindu, Slavic-Orthodox, Latin American, and "possibly African...." These civilizations, it is proposed, are ready to rumble and already resurgent from beneath the rubble of the "modern" West's hegemony, a resurgence that will ultimately manifest as alliances and open conflict between civilizational blocs (Huntington 1993, 1996).

Critiquing the cultural essentializing and panoptic boundary-drawing implicit in Huntington's perspective has become something of an industry of its own (see, e.g., Rashid 1997), and an industry that has subsequently led Huntington to pull back from many of his own propositions. Among the best critics is Faoud Ajami, who responds that Huntington has chosen the wrong unit of analysis. Clearly cognizant of how nonlocal fields and local conditions mutually interoperate, Ajami dismantles Hutington's civilizational actors with examples of intracultural rifts made evident by the early 1990s Persian Gulf War, and by the failure of solid civilizational support to form around the respective parties in the Bosnian and Karabakh

Wars. Faced with the countercivilizational conundrum of Iran's support for Armenia in the 1990–94 Karabakh conflict, for instance, Ajami foregrounds two alternative and overlapping players: the nation-state, a globalized Western Enlightenment construct (albeit often shallowly indigenized) whose boundaries rarely coincide with those of civilizations, and intracivilizational formations, such as the fractions of Shiites, Sunnites, Persians, and Turks that could theoretically be lumped together as an Islamic bloc. Ajami thus constructs a model of relativized geopolitical formation based upon a fusion of cultural allegiance and the realpolitik of nation-states, in which people cast into new and tightened relations with one another make recourse to civilizational discourses while simultaneously pursuing goals of national identity and economic growth (Ajami 1993).

Model 3: A World of Landscapes

World-systems and relativization theory advance different prime movers for globalization, and then proceed to the business of identifying secondary globally formative factors and the tightness of their coupling to the prime mover. In world-systems theory globality's generator is the internationalized mode of economic production, to which culture has a tightly epiphenomenal relation (if it is acknowledged to exist at all). In relativization theory the prime mover is the emergent sociopsychology of a global field, relative to which economies are afforded a greater degree of "wiggle room." Neither model agrees on an axis for global enactment, as one advances class and the other cultural formations. Further, they offer two distinct and contradictory spatial metaphors with highly divergent ways of depicting relations across space. Wallerstein presents us a world machine generating a daisy chain of master, slave, and overseer territories, whereas Robertson presents a tightening mosaic of relatively autonomous hearths jointly and somewhat awkwardly negotiating their interdependence.

Arjun Appadurai's reconceptualization of globalization within the rubric of chaos theory dissolves these oppositions by asserting that either unit is correct for the sphere of analysis in question. But both the economic and the cultural realm, along with others, are themselves the outcome of turbulent flows of matter and mentation. And in turn, these flows are the product of human action, especially actions (and related technologies) that have overcome time and distance to command resources and sustain long-distance communication. Such undertakings result in cultural transactions among social groups previously separated by such circumstance as geographical barriers or collective intent.

Cross-cultural contact prior to the present phase of globalization was commonly a product of warfare, religious conversion, or a combination of both. Similar to relativization theory, Appadurai sees this contact as productive of miniglobalizations in recent centuries by such "aggressive social formations" as the Aztecs and Incas in the Americas, the Mongols and their descendent Mughals and Ottomans in Eurasia, the Buginese in islandic Southeast Asia, and the Dahomey kingdom in Africa. The maritime, print and electronic broadcasting powers of Europe and the United States are now in turn swallowing these miniglobalizations (Appadurai 1990, 1996) to yield a penultimate globalization of globalizations.

The resultant consolidation of planetary contact has produced sustained flows of commodities, data and ideas (most importantly ideas of peoplehood and selfdom). These flows may be metaphorically categorized as five landscapes or 'scapes for short—fluid and irregularly shaped perspectival constructs inhabited to varying degrees by actors as diverse as persons, families, neighborhoods, diasporic communities, even nations and multinational institutions:

- ethnoscapes, the interconnections of social affinity groups.
- mediascapes, the distribution of the capacity to disseminate information and the mediated images of the world so produced.
- technoscapes, the global configuration and flow of technologies and related know-how.
- finanscapes, the shifting global disposition of capital.
- Ideoscapes, the global dispersion of politicoideological constructs, generally statist or antistate and couched in Enlightenment discourses of "freedom," "welfare," "democracy," and so on.

These flows are present with differing degrees of intensity at different locations. And different actors will occupy and move (or not move) through these different locations in different sequences and at different levels. Thus, the subset of 'scapes experienced, the perspectives from which they are apprehended, and the relationships between them will differ radically. The personally and collectively held aggregate orderings of experienced 'scapes comprise imagined worlds. In chaos theory, it is these imagined worlds and their varied relations that are central to the process of contemporary globalization. Globality takes form in the propagation of imagined worlds, their differences and overlaps, their negotiation of disjunctive global 'scapes, and the capacity of these diverse and often contradictory visions to subvert the orderings of "the official mind" (Appadurai 1990, 7).

Globalization in chaos theory is thus not a continuously expanding imperium of peripheries and semiperipheries yoked to cores, and cores to one another, by lines of capital flow. Neither is it the coming together of an overarching field of differences shared back and forth between the permeable, reflexively determined boundaries of adjacent societies. Rather, chaotic globalization is distinct types of highly irregular material and immaterial flows that coagulate unevenly in specific places. This chaotic landscape generates a multiplicity of disjunctive domains that are fractal in shape and "polythetically overlapping in their coverage of terrestrial space" (Appadurai 1990, 20). As persons and social collectives negotiate these geographies daily over the course of their lives, the unique sequences with which actors encounter and contingently inhabit these disjunctive domains determine how actors structure their worlds.

While the components of these worlds may be a "variety of instruments of homogenization (armaments, advertising techniques, language hegemonies, and clothing styles)," these instruments are invariably "absorbed into local political and cultural economies" (Appadurai 1990, 16). Further, those local economies are themselves concatenations of globally distributed 'scapes, meaning that no matter how purportedly homogenizing the instruments and how locally they are absorbed, those instruments will inevitably end up transformed and reexported "as heterogeneous dialogues of national sovereignty, free enterprise and fundamentalism." The "idea of the triumphantly universal and the resiliently particular" so becomes a chimerical misperception of "the infinitely varied mutual contest of sameness and difference" that plays out in the "radical disjunctures between different sorts of global flows and the uncertain landscapes" those disjunctures create (Appadurai 1990, 17).

Thus, chaos theory forgoes attempts to divine *the* global order and instead shifts focus to the explication of "the order of global disorder." Rather than an aerial reconnaissance over globality, this exploration is one of spelunking through the chasms that riddle the settings in which different globalities are generated. Such chasms are so convoluted as to disrupt the consistency of relativization theory's twinned mechanisms of particularized universalism and universalized particularism. Similarly, the explanatory power of world-systems theory's cores and peripheries yoked together by investment flows is challenged by the demotion of these chains to just one of a number of discontiguous global landscapes. Conversely, chaos offers little to replace these conceptual tools for organizing the global. Chaos theory does present a new and rich conception of landscape lending itself well to generating thicker descriptions (Geertz 1973) of wide relevance. Further, it accommodates both economic and cultural dimensions within the multiplicity of its unevenly presenced global landscapes. Nor need Appadurai's catalog of landscapes be either exclusive or exhaustive. After all, the ethnoscapes of diasporic populations would fall apart without the technoscapes providing inexpensive telephony and jet travel; by the same token, were it not for the ethnoscape generated by the dispersal of European colonizers it is likely that contemporary technoscapes would have some very different configurations indeed. And what of commodityscapes, or laborscapes generated by the diffusion of professional specializations, or erotoscapes born of dislocalized sexual orientations, preferences and practices? And don't laborscapes and ethnoscapes fuse with one another in such phenomena as the diaspora of Filipino construction workers, or erotoscapes with mediascapes and financescapes in the globalization of the sex industry? The creative and recombinant possibilities are rich indeed. But conversely, these richly evocative non-Euclidean landscapes remain unmapped, are perhaps unmappable, and to date constitute not apprehendable territories but suggestive topological metaphors.

Bringing Theory to Ground

Each of the models of globalization I've presented herein constitutes a prominent but partial perspective, illuminating diverse aspects of global formation in their broadest impacts. They demonstrate that when viewed in the aggregate, globalization entails radical shifts in modes of production, identity formation, and cultural assertion. If such diverse notions of globalization could be applied concurrently, there would emerge potentials for polyperspectival global analyses. Yet these varied takes on globalization are also so divergent as to leave them talking across one another. Each assumes the ontological primacy of a different field of inquiry, and each is driven by very different sociostructural mechanisms.

This presence of sociostructural mechanisms in all three theories points to a broader problematic, their shared conceptualization of globalization as an object. Each aforementioned approach to the global entails a predisposition toward conceptualizing globalization as first and foremost a complex system of higher-order aggregate processes. These processes, in turn, account for the increasingly hyperextended and interculturalized experiences, responses, and resistances occurring at the level of the local. Each approach thus locates globalization "out there," a result of the inevitable dynamics of the planet imploding under its own socio-, politico-, or cultural-economic weight. In the process, localities become merely illustrative of globalization, its impacts and its discontents, confining space and those who abide in it to the role of something upon and against which globalization acts. As a result, albeit with a partial exception for Appadurai's 'scapes, all these perspectives on the global represent processes of globalization in which real places, their inhabitants, and their particularities are recipients and respondents at best, residual by-products at worst.

Such a dilemma, however, is neither necessary nor irremediable. We all know through firsthand experience that modes of production, identity formation, and cultural assertion are not disparate realms, nor are they phenomena that can be meaningfully ranked in order of primacy. Translate these abstractions into real experiences: being precariously employed at a McDonalds, checking more than one racial classification on a census form, playing Persian pop music loudly in public without authorization. Suddenly it becomes apparent that the diverse aspects of global formation come together where we are. They are not merely copresent, but intermeshed to form the settings of our daily lives. And although it may seem a truism, it is worth repeating that without such settings and their experiential correlates there would be nothing from which we could derive "higher order" theoretical abstractions to explain global formation. This suggests adopting a very different standpoint in discussing globalization, one that puts us on the ground and in situ.

A setting-up (or setting-out) view of globalization situates the dialogical engagement of otherwise incommensurable theories on globalization. Seen in this new context, such theories may be recast as interwoven perspectives on the same emplaced processes of global formation. The particularities we share with others (and may even strive to universalize) across ever greater distances concatenate into nonlocal fields. Such nonlocal fields are the globe as we experience it most directly, and thus define the parameters of our imagined worlds. Of course, we also act in keeping with our imagined worlds, and so enact them across assorted landscapes. In so doing, our imagined worlds contend with one another to materialize as alternate global realities or, more simply, globalities—imagined worlds made real. And of course, contention implies highly variable outcomes: neither globalities nor their respective fields of origin are all equal in scope, scale, gravity, and acumen. The result of this asymmetry is currently manifested as the hegemony of financescapes, and their conditioning of global space into gradated hierarchies of cores and peripheries. In total, this grounding of globalization theories yields what might be called a chaotically relativized world system, one consisting of multiple, ever-shifting, alternate globalities with highly differentiated spheres and degrees of dominance.

One critical implication to be drawn from seeing global formation in this manner is that globalities do not occur in isolation. They are reliant upon how nonlocal fields overlap, interpenetrate, and exchange particularities in specific places, and upon the ways and degrees to which such overlaps and interpenetrations are regulated or even prohibited. Thus, globalities are generated where nonlocal fields are most inclined to congeal and dislocalities most prone to cluster—in the large city linked to others of its kind. It is in such places that the everyday praxis of global formation is at its most intense.

2
The World in the City

Theories of globalization imply space in their operation. They are, however, commonly remiss in proposing a specific geography of globalization that links "the rendering of the world as a single place" to the many places where this rendering must occur on a quotidian basis. World-systems theory does point toward a system of world cities, and both Roland Robertson and Arjun Appadurai do invoke the names of particular cities in the course of illustrating the workings of their larger global problematics. But neither urbanism nor its significance appears in these theories, and it is indicative the words *city* and *urbanization* do not appear in Immanuel Wallerstein's or Robertson's indices.

Yet the world-system's commodity chains must go from somewhere to (and through) somewhere else. There can be no compression without the bringing together of places and their occupants. A 'scape will not manifest in the absence of a physical landscape where a rug is woven or a television broadcast is received. Globalization has distinctive spatial correlates, spaces that are hybrid sites (Nederveen Pieterse 1995). The export production zone (EPZ) is one such site, a massive industrial district where captive (sometimes quite literally) local labor assembles commodities under "favorable" terms for offshore transnational corporations. Banking havens (a.k.a. "fiscal paradises") are another example, states comprised largely of banking institutions where white-, gray- and black-market profits may be sheltered from taxation and even laundered: Luxembourg, Vanuatu, or the Cayman Islands, the latter with more registered banks and companies than full-time inhabitants (Chossudovsky 1996). But the most prominent of these sites is the world city. Indeed, globalization seems consistently to occur in tandem with urbanization, and deglobalizations historically appear to coincide with the collapse of urban societies. This latter point is not just an academic observation, but a demonstrable (and potentially prescriptive) phenomenon with heavy consequences. By way of example, in attempting to sever Kampuchea from the contemporary system of colonially influenced global trade, the Khmer Rouge made the near-instantaneous depopulation of the country's urban centers an immediate priority. (For a balanced discussion of this see Vickery 1984.)

Happily, these lacunae in global theorizing are remediated by a growing body of theoretical and empirical investigations into colonial and contemporary cities' centrality to worldwide material and symbolic exchanges. Much of this work falls prey to assumptions that world cities are epiphenomenal creations of larger processes and convenient sites for observing globalization symptomatically. There is also, however, a consensus that global formation is to be sited in the growing concentration of the world's wealth and population into an emergent network of globally interoperating cities. To this I add that it is not just the population but their everyday undertakings that underpin such global interoperation. This last point opens the possibility that globally formative processes are ultimately to be found in everyday urbanism (Chase, Crawford, and Kaliski 1999), and in the practice of everyday life.

Into the City

Not long ago I initiated a classroom discussion with a score of students in an effort to discover how they understood their nationality. To do this I informed them that I commanded a massive military force graciously provided by a hostile foreign power, and needed to know where to invade so as to best rile up my students. The responses I elicited were surprising. Rather than indicating the students' perceptions of their nationality, I elicited responses that revealed how thoroughly my students had supplanted national identities with urban ones.

One student, of Indian descent but born in the San Francisco Bay Area, exemplified the general sentiment. He stated that were I to invade the Bay Area, he would fight me. Were I to invade Los Angeles, New York, or Chicago, he would fight me, as he'd been to these places and felt a part of them. Were I to invade London, New Delhi, or Mumbai, he would take up arms against me as he had family in these places. And were I to invade Paris, Mexico City, or Tokyo, he would still consider entering the fray. Despite having no personal connection to these latter locales, he perceived them as being vital in differing ways to his material and cultural well-being. However, were I to invade rural Guajarat; Omaha; *anywhere* in the southern United States (with the possible exception of Atlanta), or even Bakersfield, California, he "wouldn't give a shit, you can have 'em!"

As I considered these responses, I realized they were similar to my own sensibilities. I too would consider fighting for places like Manhattan or, if not Mumbai, then probably Helsinki or the Tokyo-Osaka corridor. But I cannot honestly say that I would take any personal risk in defense of the good burghers of Bakersfield, just up the freeway. As people, our lived experience has situated more and more of us firmly as urbanites and, more extensively, within a globalized urbanity. But what does such an urbanity look like, and how has it come into being? The answer to these questions can be found in the production of the world city as both a discursive representation and an evolving material reality.

Urbanities through the Looking Glass: Megacity vs. World Class City

As late as the early eighteenth century there existed numerous regions of the world with comparable levels of urbanization. Further, the predominant city of the most urbanized region of Europe (Britain-Holland) ranked fourth in size, overshadowed by the primate cities of China, Japan, and the Ottoman Empire (Berry 1990). This changed with the hegemonic political and economic ascent of Europe, culminating in the British Empire. Nor did levels of urbanization outside Europe decline only in relation to Europe's northwest. Many of these urbanized regions experienced absolute declines as colonialism restructured these "city-centered world economies" (Braudel 1984, 22) for incorporation into colonial dependency. Great cities of the world previously central to their own domains were either incorporated as centers for occupational administration, or bypassed entirely with the elevation of previously marginal settlements to entrepôt status.

From this newly imposed urban hierarchy (King 1990) emerged the highly unequal interdependency of colonial city to metropolis, an asymmetry replicated microcosmically in the contrasts between the physical and social conditions of the colonial city's native and colonizers' quarters. It is in the popularly perceived differences between the instrumentally impoverished colonized city and the imperial metropolis, enriched by its dominant position within colonial exchange relations, that contemporary conceptions of the megacity and the world city are rooted.

The megacity, commonly prefixed by a pejoratively deployed "third world," descends from the colonial city, particularly its so-called native quarter. It is popularly conceived of as a city swelling with an impoverished population of commonly rural-to-urban migrants. This population challenges the capacities of an allegedly inept, often corrupt administration and antiquated technology to provide a quality of life comparable to implicitly Western metropolitan material standards. The result of the megacity's inability to care for its own is unemployment and underemployment generating a large, informal, sector economy (a highly debatable classification in its own right), environmental degradation, and associated health problems. Such urban ills are specifically attributed to a host of interacting causes: failing infrastructure, lax to nonexistent health and safety standards, housing shortages generating pavement and squat dwellers, and a polarization in living standards between the entrenched and educated urban elite versus the bulk of city residents (Gilbert and Gugler 1990).

The world city was first defined in 1915 as the metropolis' direct descendent, a city where a disproportionate share of the world's business is transacted (Geddes 1997). It was primarily a major center of political administration, housing the most powerful state institutions, but with corollary stipulations that it also serve as the leading banking and finance center. Critical to this is the seamless provision of physical and cultural infrastructure requisite to accommodating persons trained and experienced in maintaining the world city's political and economic transactions (Hall 1966, 1984).

This conception of the world city, and such affiliated sine-qua-non trappings as major department stores and opera houses harking back to the height of imperial European society, serves as the model of world cityhood. This model in turn drives various cities' ongoing efforts to become world cities through municipal makeovers. One obvious instance of this is Los Angeles's attempt to turn itself into a "world-class" city through the subsidization of a high-rise central city skyline (CRA/LA 1987; Davis 1990) and attendant subway systems. More broadly, one can point to the global rash of museum building in the past decade. Los Angeles has seen the installation of two highly celebrated new art museums and the complete remodeling of a third. San Francisco has recently opened its own Museum of Modern Art (named in self-conscious emulation of New York's museum of the same name). The city of Frankfurt (a.k.a. "Bankfurt") am Main has constructed a museum row consisting of more than a dozen new museums on the banks of the Main river. Bilbao has become most recognized for its Frank Gehry–designed outpost of the Guggenheim Museum. And in a bid for recognition as the European cultural center of the new millennium, Helsinki has just completed its own modern art museum. This last is sited so as to claim pride of place by controversially overshadowing the centrally located monument to Finnish civil war hero Marshal Mannerheim. (Helsinki was only partially successful in its bid, having been declared cultural capital of the millennium conjointly with seven other European cities competing for the same honor.)

Megacity and World City Convergent

Ironically, it was during (and, as will become apparent, due to) these makeovers of numerous cities from the 1970s onward to attract global enterprise that other, less boosterish aspects of the world city were revealed. The world city's new wealth, logistical centrality, telemediated valorization and historical prominence acted as a magnet that pulled in the most skilled and/or desperate migrants, both foreign and domestic. The corollary rise in both population and high-end investment served to swell the built environment to the point of outstripping the capacities of existing physical and administrative infrastructure while putting upward pressure on land prices. Deindustrialization was followed by low-wage reindustrialization (or, more colorfully, "industrial reflux"). This was concurrent with the appearance of high-wage information services and part-time commercial/retail support, polarizing urban income between an educated elite versus the bulk of city residents. These factors in turn created affordable housing shortages and displaced the most vulnerable residential populations (Wolch and Dear 1993). Municipal administration, capital-starved by a range of tax revolts, national desubsidizations, and the provision of incentives to business, became increasingly ineffectual. Meanwhile, flight from the world city's burgeoning ills accelerated processes of exopolitanization (see, e.g., Soja 1996a), the formation of sprawling edge cities commonly administered by owner-operated privatized proto-governments (Garreau 1991).

Many of these ills are claimed to be a by-product of the effects of global economic restructuring. The spatial disaggregation implicit to disorganized capitalism's informalization and dispersal of production (Skorstad 1991) creates the need for tightly coordinated command and control. By reason of historic and current patterns of population and resource agglomeration, this command and control is best exercised by "finance and specialized service industries" preeminent in the world city (Sassen 1991). World cities thus act as "centers for global communication and management," housing the "vast range of highly specialized services and top-level management and control functions" operating as the "global control capability" for the world system (Sassen in King, 1996). The corollary collapse of Fordism and valorization of top-level managerial functions leaves little call for the organized industrial work long central to supporting a relatively affluent working class, but a pressing need for retail salespersons, janitors, and fry cooks. Therefore, restructuring supplanted middle income production jobs with both high-wage symbolic and low-wage service work, simultaneously and in the same locales.

Thus, determination of world-city status and rankings of world cities continue to rely upon such traditional factors as trade, wealth generation, and the presence of major national-cum-transnational enterprises.

But these indicators may also be taken as positively correlative with a host of urban dysfunctions formerly associated with the absence of these same indicators (Sassen 1991). More waggish observers of this conundrum's urban outcome took to bandying about the term "third world class cities," a gallows-humored nod to the list of ills that had became endemic to world cities: homelessness, infrastructure failures, preventable diseases (previously limited in popular imagination to the "unhygienic native cities" of the tropics; see King 1991, 41), and the relative immunity of new classes of well-recompensed symbolic workers. Urban physical environments both reflected and abetted these trends (Davis 1992a). The denigration of street gatherings and neglect of existing "public" spaces (Sennett 1990), coupled with their replacement by privately owned and maintained secured spaces for "public aggregation," turned many urban populations into a distinctly incivil society segregated within two distinct urban landscapes. Of these two landscapes, the more overtly dystopian is the polyglot "third world at home" (Koptiuch 1991) or, as I call it, the *in-beyond*—the internally contained microperipheries of the world-system's core regions (I have adapted the term from *near-beyond*, a Soviet descriptor applied to that empire's central Asian possessions). Its counterpart is the tightly controlled theme-park commercial and residential developments targeted towards affluent consumers (Sorkin 1992), glitzily packaged commodified communities that I call, more simply, *commudities.*

This segregative dynamic is an unavoidable presence in the world city. It is visible in the privately owned and administered pocket parks and through-block atria of corporate Manhattan (Schiller 1989). It can be found at Universal CityWalk's militantly policed simulacra of world citified Los Angeles (discussed in greater depth in chapter 4). And it is plainly apparent in the high-priced cozy neotraditionalist (also known, dubiously, as "new urbanism") town planning of Robert A. M. Stern, concretized by others in the Floridian suburbias of Seaside and the ex-Disney Celebration. Such spaces in turn articulate new and disturbing social relationships. Consider, for example, the visitor to a luxuriously appointed restaurant who, wishing to avoid walking through the decaying streets, drives to the restaurant's entrance and hands the car over for valet parking to an underpaid recent immigrant (Crawford 1988). Further, it should be noted that such social articulations and their corollary segregative spaces are not original to the world cities of Europe or the United States, having existed previously in such locales as São Paulo and Manila (Caldeira 1996).

The redefinition of the world city is complemented by the redefinition of the megacity. Modernization theory of much of the previous century assumed that the problems of scale and management adhering to the megacity were a by-product of 'catch-up' development. Such problems were supposedly akin to those experienced in European locales like London from the fifteenth through eighteenth centuries (Gillis et al. 1996). By corollary, it was thought that the application of Western techne to the megacity would permit it to 'evolve' beyond these dysfunctions (see, e.g., the United Nations HABITAT annual global reports). But as these urban ills have reemerged in the well-technologized bastions of Western urbanity, the term megacity has been increasingly disassociated from notions of "third world underdevelopment." Rather, the notion of the *megacity* has broadened into a kind of performance standard including such factors as a population approaching ten million, significant income polarization, and the presence of at least one "ethnic" group (Grigsby 1995; the term *ethnic* was here used to indicate a numerically significant minority population).

The world city has thus become essentially a megacity with money. And, as many megacities in the decolonialized (or neocolonial) world have increased their take of globally circulated capital, the distinction between the two withers away. The remaining difference becomes a historical one, an artifact of the megacity's role as a conduit for asymmetrical resource flows to and from the metropolitan predecessor of the world city. Hence the appearance of what could be called the world megacity, a place informed by the simultaneous presence of "the corporate city of high-rise office buildings, the old dying industrial city, the immigrant city. A space of power; a space of labor and machines; a Third World space" (Sassen in King 1996, 23).

The Place of the World Megacity: Is There a *There* There?

World megacities entail novel consequences for the city as an entity, cities as a whole, and the very conception of city-ness. Deyan Sudjic acknowledges this in his interpretation of world megacities, or "hundred-mile cities" from a cartographic perspective, as "force fields" of mobile capital and people that "stretch a hundred miles in each direction, over towns and villages and across vast tracts of what appears to be open country, far from any existing settlement that could conventionally be called a city" (1992, 305). These force fields give off flashes of investment that precipitate the appearance of office parks, target-marketed commudities, and giant shopping centers. Such facilities appear with seeming indiscriminacy, whether in what used to be an outlying field or behind the facades of old central-city brownstones. So the city becomes a crazy quilt of inner-city export production zones and exurban postindustrial technopoles (Scott 1993), fortified gentrification in old urban cores (Smith in Sorkin 1992) and abruptly constructed residential edge cities (Garreau 1992).

Further, these locales are linked together ever more tightly across geographic distances by advances in electronics and telecommunications. In so being they come to jointly dominate world affairs, evinced by the financially preeminent triumvirate of New York, London, and Tokyo (Sassen 1991). Such widespread integration has fused hundred-mile cities into a thousand-mile city or, per my preference, a *metapolis:* the nonlocally articulated city of cities, a planet-spanning but spatially discontiguous urban sprawl that is coupled ever more loosely with national space (Holston and Appadurai 1996). This entails that the world city be reconceptualized as one of a number of addresses in a single, spatially diffuse city spanning much of the globe (Sudjic 1992). In the process, the logics of urban spatial agglomerations, each driven by its own center, has given way to a new, more dissonant international geographical order. In the decline of long-standing limits upon communication and transportation that have mandated propinquity, nested hierarchies of central places are supplanted by a seemingly haphazard juxtaposition of land uses scattered across space. At the planetary scale, multiple distant continents are stippled with genetically identical landscapes of strawberry or broccoli, all for export to a select subset of consumers in similarly select locales. Amid these landscapes, identical assembly lines produce the same brand of automobile, supplied with parts and managed from distant continents. Expensive condominiums appear among squatter slums, indistinguishable in form and occupancy from (and often in direct communication with) luxury housing built atop homeless encampments elsewhere in the world. Thus, what in close-up appears to be a fragmented and polycultured landscape is, from a wider perspective, a collage of elements selected from a limited menu of monocultures: an assemblage of dislocalized but nearly identical facilities spawned from often quite distant flexist investment initiatives. In turn, these built monocultures are widely strewn among adaptive and persistent local variations that have proven similarly adept at dislocating themselves to propagate globally, thus creating the geographically diffuse polycentric hub that is the metapolis.

The implication of the metapolis is therefore not that of a homogenized and harmoniously operating urban monolith. Each city node in this global urban field is made of a different selection of ingredients, and each rises and falls in relation to every other. As a result there are intermittent eruptions of interurban rivalries, battles to differentiate one's own city as a superior product (White 1995) and to secure positions of competitive advantage. This is a strategy of urban entrepreneurship that entails robbing Saint Petersburg to pay Minneapolis-Saint Paul, concurrent with a social Darwinian reconceptualization of cities as animals fighting against one another tooth and nail for survival in a global marketplace-cum-jungle. It also provides another explanation for the obsessive building of museums and high-rises. Such construction is indicative of a belief that to install the de jure signifiers of world cityhood is to attract the resources and personnel that confer the de facto status of world cityhood. In the process, cities struggle to fund basic services while diverting hundreds of millions of municipal dollars to lure outposts of flexibly transnationalizing cultural institutions and clad them in the latest high-style architectural fashions (for example, the proliferating chain of Guggenheim museums; see Friedman 2003).

"The city" as we have known it, and cities in general, are undergoing radical transformations in their internal relations, their mutual interoperation, and in their cultural and economic coupling to the surrounding nation-state. At the very least, such transformations highlight the growing prominence of centrifugal and centripetal urbanization mechanisms. In considering global urbanization centrifugally, the image of classical and medieval city-states has reemerged. Such recovered urban images have taken the form of "citistates," sprawling urbanized regions mustering their resources and citizens to compete entrepreneurially for larger volumes of global economic flows (Peirce 1993). Looking to the centripetal forces maintaining a global urban system, established diasporas (e.g., Jews, Chinese) and newer nonlocally generated cultures (e.g., arbitrageurs, Anglophone air-traffic controllers) constitute a central fixture. Such dislocalized communities have woven themselves through the body politic of all the world megacities, and act as mediums of global exchange that some have asserted are in intense competition with one another (Kotkin 1993). Thus, the struggle between citistates may be recast as low-level tribal warfare in a thousand-mile city of tribes.

Yet the lived reality of the metapolis is far more complex, affecting tribes as much as it is affected by them. In Mumbai, for instance, distinctions among religion, regional origin, and class/caste determine distinct identities among inhabitants, precluding any number of identity groups from interacting at work or leisure. In Los Angeles, on the other hand, these same persons reclassify as *desi* within the "host" society. The internalization of this classification does not make established fissures disappear, but it does produce a new sense of broader collective identity. It is plainly visible in such places as "Indo-Paki" grocery stores, where one finds devotional placards of Shiva hung between landscape portraits of the Sikh's golden temple at Amritsar and calligraphic supplications to Allah.

The thousand-mile city as object suggests an even more radical reconceptualization of the urban in light of world city formations. The eccentric interconnections forming the unified urban field of the metapolis, and the peculiarities of how places are so interconnected across vast distances to form that field, may signal the end of the city as we've known it. Models of village-to-town-to-city settlement hierarchies with corollary market catchment areas (Christaller 1966), and their scalar extension to contested urban hierarchies within a world system of cities (Knox 1995), are losing relevance as urban representations. Rather, "all boundaries are shifting . . . in the city, of course, but also in all the technologies that define the space of the city," leading to a condition wherein "the city" ceases to exist as an object. Instead, the city becomes a spatial nexus of ever more diverse "historically and geographically specific institutions and social relations of production and reproduction" (Douglas in King 1996, 1).

The worldwide integration of these nexuses, some into dominant and others into more dependent roles, has engendered the model of a hierarchically ordered world city system. Not surprisingly, this hierarchy privileges transnational flows of capital as its prime mover, and from this derives a new world urban order in which New York, London, and Tokyo sit on top, cities like Frankfurt and Singapore reside one or two tiers down, and far below them are nationally significant cities with global connections like Mexico City and Lagos. This view, however, is one that remains focused upon that "corporate city of high-rise office buildings" (Sassen in King 1996, 23), and regards the densifying matrix in which they are embedded only as unintended consequences. Such fetishization of tower-studded skylines and the transnational capital they channel leaves us fixated upon counting head-office locations so as to determine which conurbation to elevate closer to New York, London, and Tokyo's holy trinity of world citydom. And admittedly, head offices are easily counted. This hardly entails, however, that they are all that counts, and counting different indicators yields some very different world cities.

Not every node within the world city system fulfills the same function or exerts control over the same spheres. By way of example, Tokyo prodigiously includes the corporate city, but it certainly isn't much of an immigrant city. Further, beyond such niche genres as anime and video gaming spinoffs, Tokyo's mass-mediated cultural product hardly plays the lead role on the world's stages. Conversely, Mumbai is not much of a global financial capital (although it is certainly a prime regional recipient of global capital; see Grant and Nijman 2002). But as a place of cinematic production and dissemination Mumbai's annual output exceeds not only that of Tokyo, but Los Angeles as well, and that product disseminates throughout the world. Other cities are "worlded" not on account of their economic control, but because of their labor power (Manila), technological capacity (e.g., Seattle, and Mumbai again!), or realpolitikal muscle (e.g., Washington, D.C.; see Hannerz 1992). Each of these spheres, in turn, defines a radically different perspective from which to assemble a world city system and rank its constituent cities. For instance, were we to deemphasize capital flows and head-office counts so as to foreground flows of metaphysical belief and count worldwide adherents, a very different listing of primate world cities emerges: Madinah, Vatican City, perhaps Dharmsala and Salt Lake City, and, for those who regard neoclassical economics as one of the planet's preeminent theologies, Chicago. Certainly,

Madinah isn't a center for foreign investment in any sense of the word. Beyond this, unless one is part of the Umma (the Muslim community), it may be difficult to even place Madinah on a map. But to the Umma, especially its Sunnite congregants, Madinah is crucial. And that congregation is present worldwide, increasingly so due to active missionizing.

Thus, the metapolis is not simply a world city system but a system of world city systems or, more aptly, a landscape of world cities that systematizes differently depending upon how one looks and what one looks for. Additionally, the disjunctions between these different systematizations are not just an artifact of how we see, but also an impetus to how we act: consider, for instance, the currently escalating tension between Madinah and Washington, D.C. So while it remains the case that being a place where disproportionate shares of the world's business are conducted determines world cityhood, the world's business takes many forms indeed. Rather than enumerate corporate offices and high-volume international air routes to ascertain *whether* a given city is a world city, it is necessary to ask in which spheres of influence is a given city a world city, to whom that city is a world city, and so what different world city systems are out there and how do they intersect one another. By redirecting our gaze away from the heavens of capital circuits, we discern a plurality of world city criteria and world city systems. But simultaneously, this shift also enables us to discern how different sorts of world cities all manifest themselves within any single metropolitan area.

Lifeworld(s) of the World City

Cross-cut by restructuration, intensifying long-distance interoperations and increasingly rapid point-to-point connectivities, the city has come unbound. The very idea of a world city as an object of analysis thus becomes problematically incomplete. Alongside it can be posited a transnational urbanism with nodes comprised by intersections of "the transnational flow of ideas, goods, images and persons" (Smith 1999; also see Smith 2001 for an explicitly social-constructionist take on transnational urbanity's formation). I, however, prefer the simpler term *transurbanism,* given that these nodes are unique articulations of multiple global identities (Massey 1993) that are as much translocal, transmunicipal and transregional as they are transnational. Saskia Sassen is similarly attuned to such eccentric geographies of the emergent global. Diversifying common definitions of the world city, she points out the existence of places that are "sites not only for global capital, but also for the transnationalization of labor and the formation of transnational identities . . . the terrain where people from many different countries are most likely to meet and a multiplicity of cultures come together" (1996, 217). Not surprisingly, then, the inhabitants of these sites can be highly polyvalent, including elites who "think of themselves as cosmopolitan," members of "localized" cultures "as cosmopolitan as elites," an assemblage of "unmoored identities" engaged in the invention of new transnational politics (Sassen 1996, 217–19; see also Sassen 1999, 101–2).

Of course, such sites and identities here remain outcomes of global processes, the minutiae of global formation. But what if that minutiae were approached as the underpinnings of globalization, rather than as the result? To accomplish this task of reimagining, we must close the analytical and operational distance between the global and the world city on the one hand, and ourselves on the other.

3
The World on the Street

I have thus far been talking *about* global formation rather than talking from *within* it. This tends to devalue the lived world and the mundane, bolstering the privilege of academia's critical distanciation that inhibits development of a "science of the particular" (Fiske 1992, 159). It also reveals the dogged persistence with which the *global* and the *local,* discursively produced scalar categories, are taken for granted and inscribed back onto lived worlds themselves. Together, these operations can only serve to reproduce precisely the lacunae in globalization theory I have been criticizing.

This impulse toward comprehensive description, most commonly of a political economic bent, enforces a predilection for the synoptic. Such a tendency among those of us who take the world and its cities as objects of investigation is hardly surprising given our embeddedness within the arguably logical positivist realm of the social sciences. Simply, *how you see determines what you look for, which in turn is what you get.* But it also underscores the question of who holds (or, perhaps more appropriately, arrogates) the authority to define the planet and its places.

This is no mere academic question. Mindful of the supposition that a thing becomes what it is through how it is inhabited and utilized, not only is how we see what we get, but what we get both informs and is informed by how we act within it (Certeau 1984). Thus, in the tacit definition of the world as something of a higher-order politicoeconomic circulatory system, academicians and allied decision makers act within and upon the world in ways that reinforce it as a circulatory system. In so doing they run the risk of inadvertently rendering conditions on the ground increasingly unamenable to the material exercise of other visions and possibilities.

This is not to say that explications of the world and the world city as a politicoeconomic system are either mistaken or without utility. The problem, rather, is this: can anyone authoritatively assert that globality *is* an apprehensible politicoeconomic circulatory system? Can it be authoritatively asserted that there is *a* world to speak of at all? Harking back to Gertrude Stein's commentary on Oakland, is there a *there* here? The univocality implicit in efforts to authoritatively define globality suggests that there is indeed, and that it is to be found in gross aggregate data on migratory demographics, capital circulation, ethnonational composition and the like. But in so assuming, everyday occurrences become either colorful anecdotes or residual cases of how the global is divergently received locally. The places in which the everyday occurs all too often become abstract surfaces, substrates that undergo (and resist) subordination to new transport and communication technologies.

This bird's-eye perspective, however, conceals the extent to which globalization is emplaced, and the extent to which emplaced persons and collectives conduct and concert globalization at the same time as they are conditioned by it. Thus, globalization takes on the aspect of a juggernaut, traveling at warp speed with nobody identifiable at the helm, leaving only the options of assimilation or resistance. Saskia Sassen underscores this problem in her claim that "the dominant narrative concerns itself with the upper circuits of capital, particularly the hypermobility of capital, rather than with that which is place bound." In response, Sassen advocates recovering "the noncorporate components of economic globalization and to inquire about the possibility of a new type of transnational politics" (1999, 101). This counterproposal, however, can be carried even further. We must look at globalization beyond economics, and work from the inside out to recover the global implications of our everyday life worlds from categorization as noncorporate economic components. This recovery may be accomplished by means of our own experiences of the world city itself.

Worlds and Cities, Hard and Soft

There may be much consensus that the world city is a built landscape that operates as a politicoeconomic machine. But the experiences and perceptions constituting our lived realities of the city are seldom (if ever) so univocal. Jonathan Raban (1974) provides a way to make analytical use of this discrepancy. According to Raban, the city is divided into hard and soft elements. The former refers to the material fabric of the built environment, the streets and buildings that frame the life of the city dweller. The latter, by contrast, is an individualized interpretation of the city, a perceptual orientation created in the mind of every urbanite over time. The relationship between the two is complex and indeterminate. The newcomer to a city first confronts the hard city, but soon "the city goes soft, it awaits the imprint of an identity. For better or worse, it invites you to remake it, to consolidate it into a shape you can live in. You too. Decide who you are, and the city will again assume a fixed form around you. Decide what it is, and your own identity will be revealed" (Raban 1974, 11).

So within the material framework of the city itself, the "hard city," are a plethora of overlapping and interpenetrating "soft cities," subjectively apprehended cities built of each urbanite's experiential perceptions of the hard city. Further, these soft cities need not remain subjective, individualistic interpretations. In that the soft city *is* the city to any given inhabitant, these soft cities divergently inform each urbanite's expectations, beliefs and actions. As a result, soft cities are operationalized and externalized within the hard city, materially enacted by means of distinctly spatial practices, visions and agendas (Purcell 2001).

Michel de Certeau's consideration of how place and daily life intersect provides a means to understand how soft cities are so enacted. Place, according to Certeau (1984), is an arena. It is the structuring of terrain by the dominant, the authoritative determination of what terrain should and will be. Space, on the other hand, is what is made by those who must live within place. It is the setting, the habitus carved out of place through the creative practice of everyday life. It is the product of place being poached, subjected to reappropriative detournement, adapted by the others who live within it to meet their more-or-less unauthorized needs and desires. In the process, place as authoritatively defined is *dis*placed, giving way instead to (relatively) liberated space. And should the poachers persist, the social relations they produce within such liberated space may resolidify that space into a counterplace that is, for all intents and purposes, a new place in its own right. Thus the hard city, whether world city or otherwise, is gradually and irregularly reforged in accordance with intersecting soft cities.

In considering the world city, then, there is not *a* there there, or at least not a consistent one. Rather, there are a multitude of coexisting and frequently conflicting theres, producing a world city that is fluid, contingent, and panoptically indescribable. Thus, examinations of the strategic operations of world city formation must be balanced by a complementary foregrounding of urbanites' interventions within the world city, interventions that strive to render various soft cities concrete and thus remake the hard world city itself.

This perspective also provides a way to contextualize conventional notions of globalization, and a new way to think about global formation. Globalization becomes the process of determining the arena at the broadest geographical scale currently imaginable—that of the earth as a whole.

It is how, to adapt Raban's terminology, the hard planet is brought into being. As globalization's supposed antithesis, localization becomes the process of carving lived and meaningful space out of that arena. This may be accomplished through acquiescence, adaptation, piecemeal appropriation, resistance, reaction, or any combination of these tactics. Such contention between place makers and space takers may even be meditated by institutions charged with harmonizing the impacts of the global arena upon local settings, a process that Eric Swyngedouw (1997) reads as the best definition of glocalization. But whichever the tactics, localization is the practice of poaching settings for everyday life from within authoritatively imposed global place. Together, this dialectical process constitutes global formation's top-heavy vertical circuit or, more simply, Globalization (with a capital *G*).

This vertical circuit has, to date, been conscientiously explored and theorized (e.g., Morley 1991, 1) to yield much needed critical insight into the reciprocity of imperfect global control and the contingent ambivalence of local resistance. Such investigations are, however, necessarily partial. The globe may well be the place of an incomplete dictatorship of the dominant, one that in its present configuration takes the form of a haphazard dictatorship of the market. But it is also much more. To reduce global formation to Globalization is to take global formation for a one-way process proceeding from the dominant to the seething impacted, and to depict globality as a dialectic between the big global and innumerable little locals. Further, this reifies the scalar divide between 'global' and 'local,' and so neglects the insight that "scale is . . . a way of framing conceptions of reality" (David Delaney and Helga Leitner, quoted in Towers 2000, 27; see also Siderov 2000, 552). Such framings are politically purposeful strategies, and the contraposition of gigantic global and miniscule local clearly has severely disempowering implications for the latter.

From the perspective of the world city, however, there is something else at work in the world besides (and within) Globalization. Given that Globalization is manifested materially by, among other things, cities' world citification, then soft cities are ever more a localized softening not just of the hard city, but of the metapolis and thus of the hard planet as well. The soft city so becomes the everyday appropriation of both urban space and global space. Further, those who poach the place of the world city increasingly live their everyday lives, and so practice their everyday tactics of spatial appropriation, both within and across world cities. Thus, the localized spaces carved out from the world city's place are increasingly dislocalities as well, and so are enacted on a planetary scale. In short, soft cities in the world city are soft world cities. Soft world cities, through their hyperextension and attenuation within systems of world cities, are simultaneously soft planets: cognitive depictions of the world as experienced and understood from the partial perspectives of those who inhabit given dislocalities. And through their everyday practices such inhabitants necessarily act upon their soft planets, enact them materially, and so render their own soft planets hard within the hard planet itself. How could Globalization possibly be immune to these proliferating everyday tactics of appropriation? The hyperextended enactment of numerous soft planets constitutes the fundament of a lateral circuit of global formation, or simply globalization (with a lowercase *g*). It is this globalization, this widespread production of and interaction between commonplace settings, that must be concretely explicated. Such explication entails taking globalization in the everyday seriously. It means recognizing that just as Globalization feeds down to restructure daily life, the hyperextending practices of everyday life in turn form globalization and, in so doing, feed back up to revector Globalization. Thus, everyday life does not just respond to Globalization, it also redirects it.

The distinction between Globalization and globalization is useful for representing processes of global formation at broad and fine scales of resolution, respectively. But no less than the scales of resolution they refer to, artifacts of where we chose to put our eyes, the division between Globalization and globalization is artificial. Globalization may be the realm above wherein reside capital and information flows, an international division of labor, cultural relativization, mass-communications media, and transnational corporations. But these phenomena are themselves descriptors for aggregate processes and institutionalized organizational patterns. Such processes and patterns are themselves comprised of certain subsets of hyperextended practices, practices that can only occur in the course of everyday living. Such emplaced practices could thus be seen as the local holes through which global flows percolate. Without such holes, a flow could not flow, and the "upper circuit" would become to "local (historical) stickiness" as irresistible force is to an immovable object.

Yet the implications run deeper than this. In recasting global flows as aggregates of everyday practices, their constituent elements become discrete localizable instances. Thus, the flows cease to be flows at all, and the very characterization of nonlocal interactions as flows is revealed to be an obfuscatory metaphor that confers a false inevitability. And by correlate, the holes cease to be holes, passive conduits that through the happenstance particularities of their positionality facilitate global passages. Fully acknowledging globalization's everydayness therefore problematizes Globalization, repositions it as an arrogative discourse that valorizes particular privileged globally formative practices of a markedly plutocratic sort, institutionalizes them, and so secures their hegemony (Dicken, Peck, and Tickell 1997; McMichael 2000). Or, more simply, Globalization becomes the worldview of a soft planet that got the upper hand.

Thus the hard planet of Globalization is not *just* there, nor did it simply happen. It was and is produced through its material enactment within the control centers of the world city, upon the metapolis, and outward from it. In the process, the presumptive dialectic of global and local, and even the elegant reciprocity of Globalization and globalization, collapses to become something else entirely: a complex and asymmetrical assemblage of globally formative everyday practices, practices that accrete in diverse and peculiar ways to turn cognitive soft planets into concrete alternate globalities.

Respatializing this argument, it becomes apparent that the transurbanism of the metapolis constitutes not just how the global meets the local, but a means and place whereby the local constituently *is* the global. Such reciprocal reproduction of globals and locals occurs at various scales, all in the course of urbanites negotiating their everyday lives. It is made by the community effects of, and responses to, impacts of traffic bound for swelling international airports. It is made by protests against far-away events held in diversifying immigrant neighborhoods (Massey 1993). It is made by peddling expired imported antibiotics on the sidewalks in front of urban hospitals to those too poor to afford medical services (Banerjee 1993). And it is made in such specific, amicable day-to-day interactions as my own recent conversation in Los Angeles with a self-identified Guatemalteca Mayan. Dressed in Levis and carrying a boxed Sanyo stereo balanced precariously atop her head, she approached me with great excitement to let me know that the aloha-style shirt I was wearing was made of cloth woven in a pattern indigenous to a village neighboring her own.

PART II

Hard City, Soft Planet

ChalDaq, ghorDaq je law'bej Doch, Horey'So.
'ej puS Doch'e' neH najlaHbogh je QeDlIj.

There are more things in heaven and earth, Horatio,
Than are dreamt of in your philosophy.
—Nick Nicholas, Andrew Strader, and Mark Shoulson,
Hamlet, Prince of Denmark, the Restored Klingon Version

We have now moved from broad and generalized characterizations of glob-alization as object to some suggestive notions of globalization as an articu-lation of processes embedded in everyday practices. Further, those practices are situated in space, particularly the spaces of metapolitan dislocalities, to embody an assortment of nonlocal fields and their attendant globalities. But in what particular ways are such dislocalities manifested, and manifested so as to produce which differing globalities? Answering this necessitates a shift in perspective from one of detachedly talking about world cities to one that is within a world city, moving beyond the metapolis as a categorical object and into a real city of real buildings, real streets, and real people.

To do this I take up Dorothy Smith's admonition that my "process of inquiry is one of exploring further into those social, political and economic processes that organize and determine [and, I would add, are organized and determined by] the actual bases of experience." Such an exploration requires that "we must begin from some position in the world," that our method "begin from somewhere." And that somewhere is our own position: "We begin from where we are" (Smith 1987, 177).

So I begin with where I am: in Los Angeles. Los Angeles is a place I know to have a concrete existence. And I know this place well—it has been my home for much of my life. It is thus a better place than any to serve as my own point of entry into this exploration. But my own familiarity with L.A. is not the sole rationale for beginning here, nor need it necessarily be the primary one. L.A. is also an example of a world city, and an excellent example at that.

Even by the most canonical indicators of world-cityhood, L.A. inarguably matches the criteria. It is a global financial and administrative capital, in sheer dollar amounts and transnational transaction volumes the predominant U.S. city on the Pacific Rim. In light of this, L.A. sits high in the rankings of the fifty-five cities constituting the world city hierarchy, well within the top ten constituting the "alpha" cities. L.A. is not, however, an extreme instance or stand-out anomaly within this hierarchy. Operating within the shadow of its prominent East Coast counterpart, New York City, from financial and office-location perspectives L.A. does not inhabit the rarified pinnacle occupied by the triumvirate of New York, London and Tokyo (Beaverstock, Smith, and Taylor 2000). Rather, L.A. shares a less primate status with such cities as Frankfurt, Milan, or Singapore, and thus constitutes a more typical instance of a world city. But on some other axes germane to global formation, L.A. is indeed primate. Most notably, L.A. is a major center for television production, and *the* center of command and control for film industry and related multimedia production, distribution, and administration (although for sheer volume of films produced, Mumbai remains number one). Further, industries predicated upon flexible contract-by-contract employment like film and aerospace have been present in L.A. as far back as the first quarter of the twentieth century, suggesting that L.A. may have played a prefigurative role in the emergence of flexism. Also symptomatic of L.A.'s world city status is the city's self-representation as a world city, through the construction of such signifiers as high-profile cultural institutions and a new of-a-piece high-rise central business district. Indeed, L.A. subsidized this district with tax dollars gleaned from the East Asian trade surplus, a kind of nonlocally articulated "municipalized land speculation" (Davis 1992b, 26) wherein what happens in Los Angeles results from what happened the day previous on the opposite edge of the Pacific Rim. Other less glamorous facilities reinforce the point. As of 2000, L.A.'s primary international airport ranked third in the world for volumes of passengers and cargo, with both up over 5 percent from the preceding year (ACI 2000), and in 1998 "Worldport L.A." ranked eighth worldwide in volume of containerized traffic (AAPA 1998).

These latter statistics point strongly to L.A. as a prodigiously agglomerated market and a megacitified population. As of the 2000 census, that metro population was approximately nine and a half million, placing L.A. well into the ranks of the megacities. And much of this population is globally connected through more than just transnational capital flows and their management. L.A. is an immigration magnet and immigrant entrepôt into the U.S. Latest census data indicates that over 20 percent of the city's population is foreign born, and this population is increasingly drawn from every continent of the world. Although a gross aggregate statistic, this statement points to the presence of the planet on megalopolitan L.A.'s streets. There are more Iranis in L.A. than in any city outside of Tehran, and more Cambodians than anywhere outside of Phnom Penh. Armenian is the first language in large areas of the abutting cities of Glendale and Burbank, and in pockets of eastern Hollywood, where the boundaries of Little Armenia overlap those of Thaitown. Not far southwest of this conjunction, a three block stretch of Fairfax Boulevard has been granted formal recognition as Little Ethiopia. But it is the geographical links to Latin America and East Asia that are reconstituting the region's demographics. It is said (although difficult to verify, not least of all for reasons of immigration status) that the region boasts more Mexicans than any city outside Mexico City, and 10% of the global population of El Salvadorans. There has emerged a little Saigon spread across an area half the size of Ho Chi Minh City itself, and a roughly seventy-block (and growing) swathe of Mid-Wilshire rechristened Koreatown in the map books and street signs throughout the 1970s and early 1980s.

Los Angeles is thus a capital of capital, of communications, and of immigration. It is a more than sufficient point of entry into this inquiry, a real world city where this exploration can begin. But such a statement, predicated upon detached observations of statistically and empirically demonstrable conditions, conceals a deeper question: what exactly does *real* mean in relation to the world city of Los Angeles? This question in turn has many heads. What does it mean to say Los Angeles is a real city? What is the reality of Los Angeles? And is the reality of Los Angeles a singular, unitary thing, or is it a product of numerous realities in continuous flux?

At their most superficial, these questions hearken back to H. L. Mencken's statement that Los Angeles is nineteen suburbs in search of a metropolis (a quote later retooled and attributed to Dorothy Parker, as "seventy-two suburbs in search of a city"). Within the classical definition of cityhood, Los Angeles has long been either exceptional or outright excluded. Throughout its development, Los Angeles has emerged as an annexed and infilled sprawl of outlying speculative developments. The bulk of this sprawl did not extend concentrically from Los Angeles' historic center and, indeed, that center was largely irrelevant to and subordinated by outlying locales for much of the twentieth century. Such peculiarities have resulted in a metropolitan region comprised of 177 cities, and numerous former suburbs in secessionist search of their own cityhood. From this has emerged a general prejudice that Los Angeles is not a real city. It is not a city that has, Chicago style, grown outward with decreasing density from a singular dense core cum central business district. Simply, if models of the city as an expanding organism are the paradigm of cityhood, then Los Angeles does not fit the paradigm.

But in the field of urban studies, paradigms are indeed shifting. With the hyperextension of urban economic and social relationships, city centers bifurcate again and again into multiple business, commercial, and residential centers, each diffusing to accommodate new sectors and niches both socially and spatially. The map becomes scattered with quasi-centers. Eventually, this "route to chaos" (Peterson 1988, 155) passes a threshold at which a phase shift occurs, and old urban logics no longer obtain without being buried beneath mountains of addenda and qualifiers. This process is visible in major urban centers throughout the world, but it is precisely the condition that disqualified L.A.'s "cityness" under the old paradigm. Thus L.A. has become not just a real city, but a really significant one, a place in which transurban restructuring is prefigured and particularly evident.

But as Paul Feyerabend points out, paradigms do not shift in smooth succession, no matter how vehemently their champions may claim otherwise. Rather, new paradigms overlap with only a small subset of their predecessor's problems and facts, and twist them to fit a radically different framework (Feyerabend 1978, 178). Such a radically different framework does not emerge endogenously from detached contemplation of the prior paradigm's paradoxes. Instead, it results from new tools, new technologies, new findings and new ways of seeing that more often than not have been raided from other fields. This conceptual and methodological booty determines not only what should be investigated, but what is visible and, thus, what is investigateable. Therefore, knowledge advances (although not in any linear sense) by breaking the established framework defining the problems at hand. This fracture is produced through engagement in such supposedly "irrelevant activity" as "outrageous hypothesizing" so as to construct new frameworks in which the previously irrelevant takes on new significance (Feyerabend 1978, 176). Such activity is akin to what Jacques Derrida (1976) refers to as rehearsing a radical break, a rehearsal that constitutes the break itself. The worlding of the city, in practice and as an analytical focus, is one means to construct this break. It challenges long-standing mechanistic models of the city as a centralized and self-contained cellular organism, and so foregrounds precisely the characteristics that established paradigms "set about to eliminate and, failing that, conceal" (Bauman 1992, 189). The articulation of everyday urban acivities into nonlocal fields creates new ideas of what makes for a real city—its reconstitution as a postmodern habitat "free from constraints of deterministic logic" that "no longer lends itself to the organismic metaphor" (Bauman 1992, 192; see also Dear 1988).

Los Angeles provides a solid example of this disordered and disordering break. By the old paradigm, L.A. long appeared as the land of flakes, nuts and lotus eaters, a city without rhyme, reason, or a common narrative (McWilliams 1946; Fogelson 1967) except perhaps the depiction of freeways strung with an iconography of the bizarre (Banham 1973). According to Edward Soja (1989), however, by the last decade of the twentieth century Los Angeles presented itself as a decentering metropolis powered by the insistent fragmentation of flexism. Its urban structure became that of a complexly fragmented mélange of wedges, citadels and corridors bound to an overarching rationality of panoptic social control and accompanied by a postmodern consciousness that constituted a cultural and ideological reconfiguration of how social being is experienced: "With exquisite irony, contemporary Los Angeles has come to resemble more than ever before a gigantic agglomeration of theme parks, a lifespace composed of Disneyworlds" (Soja 1989, 246), a place where "it all comes together."

This perspective resituates L.A. in a newly emergent world context to articulate the links between political economy and postmodern culture, and so reveals that the city's fragmented and socially differentiated physique is not particularly exceptional at all. Rather, changing circumstances have rendered the exceptional qualities of L.A. increasingly consonant with a lengthening list of new and expanding cities. But this perspective also remains a studied and detached one that seeks to discover the rationality inherent in the cityscape from a singular, overhead vantage point. Against this the polycentric, polyglot, and nondeterministic postmodern habitat demands to be explored from within as numerous intersecting fragments and facets.

How we see, and its concretization through how we do, may well be what we get. But in that there are many ways of seeing and doing, the corollary demotion of detached statistical observations and of any one metanarrative's (Lyotard 1984) totalizing paradigm obliges us to grapple head-on with how the city in general, and Los Angeles in particular, is different things depending upon how one looks, and upon what one looks for. The L.A. of worldwide mass communications differs from and articulates with the L.A. of diasporas, which in turn differs from and articulates with the L.A. of capital valorization and conspicuous import consumption or the L.A. of municipal administration. L.A. becomes not a prefabricated setting for people's relations, but a haphazard weave of cities, of overlain and disjunctive cities. The boundaries constituting the object that is Los Angeles collapse, presenting the problem of which L.A.(s) is/are the real one(s).

So, how many L.A.s are there? How do we make them, and they in turn make us? The answers, of course, are contingent. They depend very much upon our own bodily situatedness, whether we are in an affluent neighborhood or a deeply impoverished one, a dense apartment complex or a sprawling suburban ranchburger house, whether we make executive decisions or clean the offices of executive decision makers. And while many of these differing L.A.s will share enough common features and underlying formative experiences to harmoniously converge, others will be so wildly divergent as to be incommensurable.

All these versions of L.A. therefore have their own validity, all are true from their respective perspectives. Thus, L.A. is a palimpsest of innumerable overlays of many different L.A.s, each with its own experiential reality and validity. And yet, we understand implicitly that some of these versions of Los Angeles are more equal than others. There is more at work here than relativistic difference; these differences exist in some relation to one another. They are, in short, relationalist, they do not just differ from one another, but defer to one another as well (Derrida 1976, 1978). Some have attained positions of hegemony while, in the process, others have been othered, subjected to devalorization, maltreatment and instrumental disempowerment. Further, this othering is not something that merely occurs discursively and in our heads. It is something realized by means of material practices in the everyday. In the city it is felt concretely: in the layout of streets as social spaces or traffic sewers, in the design of buildings to welcome or disinvite, in the administration of property rights that tell us where we may be and what we may do there.

This othering constitutes one of the most critical dynamics of L.A.'s world citfication: the intensification of economic and cultural difference within the city. Corollary with this is a disordering of the city and its social milieus as we knew them, the importation and proliferation of innumerable (and frequently incommensurable) versions of what L.A. *is*. In response, this new and continuous disordering of Los Angeles is met with forcible reordering and regulation through the installation of physical infrastructure configured to discipline (see Foucault 1979) and exclude. As a result the built ecology of metapolitan Los Angeles becomes an increasingly heterogeneous and heterogenizing one and, conversely, an increasingly suspicious and segmented one, rife with spatial injustices targeted toward keeping the city's others both othered and contained.

But Los Angeles, whether world city or otherwise, is not an object that heterogenizes and reorders itself like some sort of cognizant organism. Rather it is the people in and of L.A. who so reforge its spaces, who experience heterogenization as pleasure or peril and reordering as comfort, repression, or a bit of both. And it is these same people who elide and even resist this tightening of L.A.'s discursive and material regulation in unforeseen, highly creative and, despite their apparent marginality, often effective ways that are no less central to the reformation of L.A. as a world city. To see this, however, we must move beyond discourse *about* the world city, and *about* the city of Los Angeles. The time has now come to move *in*.

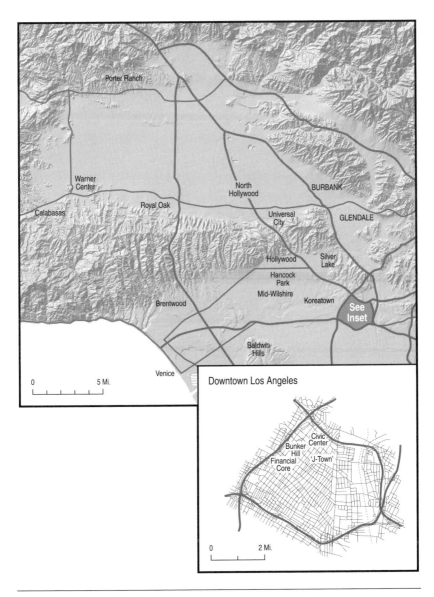

Metapolitan Los Angeles: places referenced.

4.

The City Hardens

My first vision of the metapolis's iron undercarriage came to me almost thirty years ago, as a kind of souvenir. My grandparents visited our house, in what was then the far western exurbs of Los Angeles's San Fernando Valley, after returning from a cruise to Rio de Janeiro. And they brought with them stories that would have seemed unbelievably dystopian were it not for the fact, as I then believed, that grandparents do not lie. They spoke of how the houses of the rich Brazilians were surrounded by high walls topped with broken glass. The concierges of apartment buildings carried automatic weapons. The city's outskirts were packed with cardboard and corrugated metal shanties. Children in ragged clothes slept on the sidewalks and ate out of garbage cans in alleys.

My parents still live in that same suburban house, purchased thirty-five years ago. For 18 of those years, the house remained much the same. I would pass through a front yard open to the street, unlock and rotate the doorknob, and walk in.

Over the past decade and a half, however, the simple act of entering the residence has grown dauntingly complex. Next to the door is a small metal plate with an illuminated red L.E.D., warning of the presence of an activated alarm. Upon disengaging the deadbolt and opening the front door, I have thirty seconds in which to disarm the alarm by entering a sequence of digits into a small keypad in the entry hall. Should I forget the number, or should the hall be too dark to work the keypad within the prescribed time, a shrieking siren wakes the neighborhood. Next, the deadbolt must be reengaged and a separate switch, located elsewhere in the house, must be tripped to deactivate pressure pads strewn beneath the floor and contacts embedded

Regulating Metapolis—a security camera in the plaza of a Bunker Hill citidel, Los Angeles.

into the interior doorways. At that point the house's interior becomes safe for passage and the alarm may be safely reactivated as a perimeter defense. At any time, the alarm may be intentionally activated by hitting "panic buttons" sprinkled throughout the house at strategic locations. The exterior of the house, once illuminated only by a porch light, now basks in the glare of multiple 150-watt security lights in the back and side yards, switched on from dusk to dawn by photoelectric sensors.

My parents' house is one of the neighborhood's less obtrusively secured. Many other houses feature lawn signs cautioning passersby of armed response. Some include security lights in the front yards controlled by motion detectors, set to blind anything that moves on the adjacent sidewalk and street. A few have installed spike topped perimeter fences with remote-controlled chain-driven gates, facilitating automobile access without having to exit the vehicle. Patrol cars carrying private security officers pass through the street late at night, watching over only those homes whose owners pay an additional service fee.

This neighborhood transformation did not occur all at once. It was a long, incremental process that only after a decade or so became obvious. A few residences took action in response to specific incidences. Most, however, are reactions to a pervasive sense of insecurity. It is an insecurity at odds with the neighborhood watch maps showing this portion of Police Reporting District Number 1091 largely free of the *X*s and *R*s marking sites of residential and street burglaries.

Meanwhile, three blocks away, people in ragged clothes sleep in the bushes by the side of the freeway and eat from the dumpsters behind the super-market.

Interdiction's Components

Blockhomes, my term for secured residences like that of my parents, are one component in the ongoing production of the new world bipolar disorder in Los Angeles, rendering the urban landscape an intrusively nervous place. Nor is this landscape an exclusively Angeleno phenomenon. Blockhomes of various forms can be found increasingly in Moscow, São Paulo, and Manila—indeed, in any of the emergent locales of the metapolis. Thus, my exploration of the paranoiac urban landscape of L.A. will yield intimate analytical encounters with globally proliferating forms of interdictory space, space designed to intercept and filter or repel would-be users. Such spaces are a response to the presencing of particular nonlocal fields as dislocalities in particular world cities, strategic modulators of globally formative processes, and generators of spatial inequities that themselves project globally.

The cityscapes of the metapolis are therefore critical to, and complicit in, the articulation of the new world bipolar disorder through the enactment of strategies that reduce disorder through the enforcement of polarization. This is a problem of vital importance not just academically but, even more so, eth-ically. The new world bipolar disorder, after all, entails within the metapolis the simultaneous presence of an overvalorized dominant corporate culture and a multiplicity of corollarily devalorized others (Sassen 1999, 110–11). And such an inequitable ordering of difference is no happenstance occur-rence. In a rapidly changing urban milieu with strong tendencies toward disorganization, this ordering of difference is essential. Social difference is requisite to social change, and it is in the control and ordering of said difference that the systemically assured perquisites of the dominant can be preserved and expanded.

Given that the maintenance of social organization requires the ordering of bodily behavior, devalorization and discursive othering can therefore only exist insofar as they have concrete effects, and are thus manifested concretely. So interdictory space, in the words of a colleague working in public/private urban design, becomes an inevitability, since "those who have need ways to make sure those they took it from can't come and take it back." Thus the new world bipolar disorder and its subsequent permutations are produced on the ground, and in the everyday, through practices and built forms that render it a material reality and so bring it into being. It must be made in the streets of metapolitan Los Angeles, as in those of the rest of the metapolis. And it must be made stable, static and, above all, secure. Spatial interdiction, and interdictory spaces, are the means to this end.

I find it fruitful to classify interdictory spaces into five flavors:

- Stealthy space: space that cannot be found. Such space is camouflaged or, more commonly, obscured by such view impediments as intervening objects or grade changes. The Poets' Walk garden of Citicorp Plaza, in the heart of downtown L.A.'s central business district's financial core, exemplifies stealthy space. It is concealed behind an office tower, a department store entrance kiosk, and a flight of escalators. Despite developer's brochures touting the plaza's areas as "public spaces" (Prudential Property Company 1992) the project includes no public easements and discourages access by hiding behind a "corporate 'front door' [that] is an empty, undistinguished space" (CCACOSTF 1990).
- Slippery space: space that cannot be reached, due to contorted, protracted, or missing paths of approach. This strategy is costly, as it may require obfuscating numerous routes of access extending well beyond any single site. Justifying this expense, slippery space provides public relations benefits: in the event of criticism, the exclusivity of slipperiness can always be depicted as an unfortunate and unintended by-product of preexistent topographical constraints. California Plaza's Watercourt, atop Bunker Hill just north of the financial core, exemplifies slippery space. It looms over downtown L.A. with highly convoluted means of access from the streets below.
- Crusty space: space that can not be accessed due to obstructions such as walls, gates, and check points. The Los Angeles County Museum of Art's grounds and sculpture garden at Hancock Park are riddled with crusty space. Once open to one another and the

Interdicted bodies—the prickly space of "bum proof" benches, eastern edge of Bunker Hill, Los Angeles.

surrounding greenswards, these facilities were encircled within a nested series of high wrought iron and chain link fences through-out the 1990s. In all fairness these interdictory layers were largely removed by mid-1999, but only because a new fence of eight-and-a-half-foot-high vertical steel columns, painted green to blend with the park's verdant environs, was installed to completely encircle the park's perimeter.

- Prickly space: space that cannot be comfortably occupied, defended by such bedeviled details as wall-mounted sprinkler heads activated to clear loiterers, or ledges sloped to inhibit sitting. The park wedged into a southwest facing pocket between the sidewalk and the Ronald Reagan State Office Building, at the farthest southern outpost of the downtown civic center, is a willfully prickly space. It "boasts" sparse shade, highly reflective pavement, and backless benches with seats at a leg-numbing height of twenty-four inches above the ground.

- Jittery space: space that cannot be utilized unobserved due to active monitoring by roving patrols and/or remote technologies feeding to security stations. The Biddy Mason pocket park in the Broadway-Spring Center, just west of the Reagan State Office Building, caricatures jittery space. A through-block connection "offering direct secured passage" (Yellin Company, n.d.) to an adjacent parking structure, this park features guarded restrooms and seventeen video cameras monitoring the park's sitting areas, elevator landings, and even the public sidewalks abutting the park entrances.

In the field, of course, it is rare to encounter these spaces in isolation. Rather, they tend to be deployed in conjunction so as to form distinctly unfriendly mutant building typologies.

A Built Typology of Paranoid Urbanisms

The aforementioned *blockhome,* for instance, is a residence with a crusty inner core of thick blank walls, often embedded in an extended jittery perimeter of alarms, video observation cameras and hypersensitively triggered security lighting. Fast becoming the Angeleno residence of choice, blockhomes are most apparent in gentrifying areas, where new wealthier residents feel threatened by the established poorer community. Venice Beach is dotted with blockhomes forced into compact bunker and tower forms by the constraining expense of beach property. The high style architectural tastes of the area's maturing bohemian residents have resulted in oddly angled concrete walls, cor-ten steel gates and tall tilted courtyard enclosures collaged of stucco and frosted glass. Witty references to the preexistent community abound; a miniature white picket fence set before a windowless studio house sheathed in corrugated metal, an opulent home stealthily retrofitted into the dilapidated shell of an existing house (complete with an address number spraypainted graffitiesque across the housefront). This trend, however, is not confined to locations in flux. In established affluent foothill neighborhoods like Royal Oak, neighborhood homes sprout such features as crenellated walls and fences comprised of unscaleable vertical piping. Some homes include exterior video cameras to communicate the identities of visitors prior to admission through remotely controlled driveway gates. Others employ prickly plantings in "security-oriented gardens" beneath windows and surrounding the property. In areas such as this, the entire neighborhood may be rendered slippery and jittery; the streets often have no sidewalks, and police may be augmented by private security hired as street patrols (the entire Royal Oak neighborhood has contracted with Westec for security services).

Just five blocks from my parents' house, immediately beyond the western pale of the San Fernando Valley, is Calabasas. Calabasas is an incorporated affluent residential community priding itself on its "Old West" charm. Most of publicly accessible Calabasas, though, is not somewhere to linger in but to pass through, as the streets are a pointedly inhospitable place to sojourn. Throughout the past two decades, these hills have been covered with over eight hundred homes contained within multiple walled and gated residential commudities. Such commudities are perhaps the most remarked upon feature of a globally disseminating Angeleno urbanism, the so-called gated community (Blakely and Snyder 1997) or, from my perspective, *luxury laager*. Most public roads of Calabasas are now confined within a continuous lining of cinderblock walls punctuated only by occasional guardhouses or remotely activated gates. As these luxury laagers face private internal streets, little effort has been made to landscape the public rights of way, leaving the spaces between the laagers very prickly; unshaded, hot, and forbiddingly barren. Similarly forbidding streets are now the norm throughout the new hillside developments ringing the L.A. basin.

These developments sell exclusion. Advertisements tout interdictory features with the *Dragnet*-like brevity of "Gated with 24 hour Drive-by Security" (Mountaingate at Brentwood, n.d.; note the entirely novel use of the ominous "Drive-by" moniker) or florid prose like "As you drive through the wrought iron gates, past the uniformed guard, and over the rushing stream, you will be transfixed by. . . ." (Summit at Warner Center, n.d.). And there is also the appeal to novelty, like one moated development's "deep 25 acre lake [that] provides total security for the owners of the spacious high-rise condominium homes" (Palm Springs Life 1993). Jittery beneath a crusty shell, sealed luxury laagers with checkpoint entries and private internal security patrols may now be found throughout the L.A. area and beyond. This proliferation has lead to an explosion of typological permutations providing residential units in a wide range of prices. At Park LaBrea in the Mid-Wilshire District, a complex of high-density apartment buildings has been refitted with metal fencing stretched between the structures to block access to internal streets. At Summit at Warner Center, medium density stealthy suburban townhouses are set atop tall berms, landscaped so heavily as to obscure the fact that there are residences atop the hill. And back in Calabasas, low density clusters of exurban mansions are accessed by passage through sentried forecourts augmented by video cameras to record visitors' license plates.

One constant of the spaces between luxury laagers is an eerie absence of people, and a similar dearth of open public spaces. "Public space," space held by the state and administered as more-or-less freely accessible to any would-be visitor, has long been subjected to privatization as a response to local state penury. The Proposition 13 property tax "revolt," declines in sales tax due to consumers' loss of purchasing power, the deep recessions of the early 1990s and 2000s, and reduced federal assistance have engendered a retreat of the local state (Fulton 1992, 8). In the process, the fiscally burdensome functions of public space have been divested, and potentially profitable functions transferred to the private sector. Such facilities as parks and libraries have thus been cannibalized by shrinking tax revenues and declining income from user fees, first losing programs, then maintenance, and in many instances closing entirely.

Canonically defined public spaces are thus increasingly supplanted by privately produced (although often publicly subsidized) "privately owned and administered spaces for public aggregation" (Schiller 1989). That is, spaces of consumption or, most commonly, malls. In these new, "postpublic" spaces, access is predicated upon ability to pay. People, goods, more-than-passive activities and ideas narrowly perceived as inimical to the owner's sensibilities (and profit margin) are unaccommodated or ejected by private security as quickly as they are manifested. Exclusivity rules here, ensuring the high levels of control necessary to prevent irregularity, unpredictability, and inefficiency from interfering with the orderly flow of commerce.

But the mall, too, has taken on a paranoid cast. Commonly, malls now include running fences to enclose the mall parking lot, limiting points of access. Spaces of consumption cannot seal themselves off completely, being dependent upon customer access for sustenance. Even so, they have imposed tight controls over use, becoming *strongpoints of sale.* The smallest strip mall has become a tightly nested series of crusty, jittery, and prickly spaces. The fenced parking lot itself is watched over by armed security guards. Pay phones have been removed to discourage vagrants, and some convenience stores have installed exterior speakers blaring Muzak to drive away adolescent head-bangers. Fast food outlets, equipped with video cameras at pay stations and drive-through windows, feature outdoor eating and playground areas surrounded by outward curving steel bars. Loading docks large enough to swallow delivery vehicles whole are accessed through steel doors set into concrete parapets and watched over by guard towers. The interior promenades of some larger malls are unremittingly jittery, remotely monitored by both private security and police in onsite substations. One mall substation in Baldwin Hills serves as a base for two hundred police officers, coordinated with another bay immediately across the promenade that houses a municipal courthouse. These substations have become central institutions in affluent suburban malls, where the role of shopping as community social focus has provided a site for police contact with the civilian populace. Here, the substations serve as the local hub for community policing and neighborhood watch operations.

This "make-my-day" shopping has undergone accelerated research and development in the decade since L.A.'s 1992 "civil disturbance," paying special attention to thwarting looting and arson. This is most notable in Koreatown, one of the hardest hit locales. Wood-frame structures, flammable and easily breached, have been replaced by single or double walls of concrete masonry. Rooflines have been raised to deflect fire bombs thrown from street level. Display windows have been filled in, or set into concrete bulwarks three feet above sidewalk level to prevent automobiles ramming through to the interior. Glass entries have been replaced with armor plated roll down doors, often pregraffitied to discourage taggers.

A few blocks east of this persistently smoking wreckage of L.A.'s multi-cultural mythos is Bunker Hill. Bunker Hill is the crown atop L.A.'s central business district, covered in high-rise office towers over the past two decades in no small part to provide L.A. with a skyline signifying world class city status. Getting up Bunker Hill is no small task, as the hill's property holders prefer to keep their distance from the populations down below (except when they're required for janitorial tasks). The entire hill is slippery, separated from the surrounding city by an obstacle course of open freeway trenches, a palisade of concrete parking garages, and a tangle of concrete pedestrian bridges linking citidel to citidel high above the streets. The streetscape here consists of the blank undersides of vehicular overpasses, towering walls studded with giant garage exhaust vents, and seating cleverly shaped like narrow sideways tubes so as to be entirely unsittable. Readily attaining the summit from the south necessitates climbing a narrow, heavily patrolled stairway plaza, studded with video cameras and clearly marked as private property. As of 1996, a staircase and a twenty-five-cents-per-ride historic funicular (the Angel's Flight) were installed on the hill's eastern face, but this only after the city redevelopment agency's protracted negotiations (and ultimately, intense arm twisting) of the hill's property holders. Prior to this, and speaking from personal experience, walking onto the hill could easily entail inadvertently walking onto a freeway offramp.

The plazas atop Bunker Hill reflect both a shared consciousness among developers and state institutions of the value of user-friendly urban design, and a differing conception of to whom those benefits should accrue. These citidels are the financial control centers of the metapolis; but they are also properties administered by management companies, competing with one another to attract corporate tenants. Attractive site amenities are seen as integral to this competition by providing spaces where "office workers will find outdoor areas for noontime relaxation" (Metropolitan Structures, n.d.). Municipal agencies, meanwhile, see plazas as developer-funded additions to the city's open-space inventory. Thus attempts are made to extract plazas from private developers in exchange for subsidies provided through below-market-rate land sales or leases, tax abatements, and density bonuses. In negotiations with developers, municipal agencies have been successful in linking public subsidies to the provision of habitable open spaces, in no small part because such spaces enhance the value of the project to the developers.

Interdicted city—the slippery space of a citidel's elevated plaza, Bunker Hill above Grand Avenue, Los Angeles.

Municipal agencies have not, however, been particularly successful (or, in some instances, terribly concerned) with assuring right of free access to these spaces. Thus, public subsidies have often been expended to create plazas that are stealthy behind hedgerows and grade changes, jittery with blue-blazered private security, and accessible only at the discretion of private owners. Most have small bronze plaques at the property line reading "PRIVATE PROP-ERTY. RIGHT TO PASS BY PERMISSION, AND SUBJECT TO CONTROL, OF OWNERS. sec 1008 CIVIL CODE." Inside the plazas are malls uniformly equipped with Italianately named eateries, express mail posts, drycleaners, and gift shops—compact business arcologies that relieve office workers of the need to leave the premises. They are lushly planted, and ornamented with water features. They are graced with high-art plaza turds signed by some of the best plop artists. And, once again, they are circumstantially off limits to much of L.A.'s citizenry.

Toward a Piecemeal Police State

In concentrating upon the more dramatically visible features of the built environment throughout this tour, there are equally significant interdictory elements in the landscape that escape ready notice. By far the most common of these is the intermittent whir of helicopter rotors. Across the city, police helicopters maintain a continuous vigil overhead with the aid of gigantic block numerals painted atop select buildings and busses. One helicopter keeps watch over each of the city's three patrol areas at any given time. These helicopters, mostly Aerospatiale/Eurocopter AS350 B-2 Aerostars, were originally developed for military applications. They can cross the basin in eleven minutes at a speed of approximately one hundred forty miles per hour. These helicopters are equipped with Boeing/Spectrolab's SX-16 Nightsun illumination system, producing thirty million peak-beam candlepower, and the Forward Looking Infra-Red (FLIR) sensing system capable of detecting body heat at a distance of one thousand feet, a lit match at four thousand feet.

Similarly inconspicuous are the lampposts and roadway signage, despite the fact that we are ever more conspicuous to them. Video cameras have become standard equipment at major intersections across the city. Set in bulletproof casings more than forty feet above street level, the cameras are equipped with remotely controlled pan, tilt, and zoom capabilities. They feed to a control center beneath Los Angeles City Hall. These cameras are part of the three-hundred-million-dollar Automated Traffic Surveillance and Control system now ensconced citywide. ATSAC cameras are presently used only to determine the specific cause of traffic delays indicated by in-pavement sensors, but similar systems for keeping eyes on the street are now in systemic use throughout the United Kingdom (Graham and Marvin 1996) and are rapidly spreading throughout the European Union. Further, spokespersons for the Los Angeles Police Department and for the mayor's office have been careful not to deny an interest in using the cameras to keep watch over the streets, sidewalks, and adjacent properties; nor is this surprising given that the city's police department increasingly shares the rest of the city's love affair with electronic media. Cameras, video recorders and computer terminals can now be found in LAPD patrol vehicles, enabling mobile street level surveillance and the instantaneous gathering and transmission of such intelligence as still video images. In essence, the entire city region has become jittery space.

Interdicting Globality

How are these instances of interdictory spaces and practices to be read in conjunction with the transurbanity of global formation? I have previously sketched an answer to this question, but before this answer can be fleshed out it is necessary to dispel another—that of *criminality*. Over the course of its heated emergence, interdictory space has been legitimized beneath the rubric of crime waves and a reciprocal war on crime. And indeed, crime in Los Angeles has looked bad. We hear continuously about the accessibility, miniaturization, and increasing potency of offensive weaponry, about such new forms of crime as carjacking, classroom shootings, and home robberies, and about the alleged local presence of such supposedly bloodthirsty syndicates as Hong Kong Triads and ex-Soviet *mafiyas*. We *hear* about them largely because they are held aloft as lurid symbols of social disintegration by ratings and circulation hungry local media (e.g. Glassner 2000; see also the *Los Angeles Times T.V. Times*, 1993, for a priceless example). The resulting portrait of Los Angeles as a war zone has been uncritically presented, and accepted, as confirmation of urban dysfunctions being both out of control and uncontainable. But the FBI's Uniform Crime Reports and the National Crime Survey tell an entirely contradictory story. For the period when lurid crime stories and proliferating interdiction burst onto the local scene, 1985–1995, real crime rates fluctuated within relatively stable levels. They remained well below the highs of the late 1970s, and even dropped throughout the latter half of the period. Further, L.A.'s crime rate per 100,000 people throughout the period had been among the lowest of all major American cities. While these aggregate statistics conceal the fact that some areas of L.A. suffered startling high crime rates indeed, it was the areas at lowest risk where interdictory space could be most readily afforded, and was most enthusiastically instituted.

Beyond this, the efficacy of interdictory spaces in stopping crime is itself questionable. Consider, for instance, the luxury laagers. I have examined crime incident maps and quarterly crime reports for the period 1988–1996 in six police reporting districts. I selected these districts because they are comprised largely or entirely of gated developments, and have adjacent reporting districts of similar, ungated properties. My working hypothesis had been that I would see lower instances of crime in the luxury laager districts than outside, and could then proceed to investigating crime-displacement effects. But instead I found that crime rates, and fluctuations of those rates, were little different inside and outside the laagers for all categories of crime. This held true even in the case of tightly secured laagers comprised of single-family homes, like those in the Porter Ranch area of the far northern San Fernando Valley. Here crime rates rose with the construction of new laagers to mirror crime rates throughout surrounding ungated areas with comparable population densities and building stocks (e.g., LAPD Reporting District Number 1701, newly gated between 1989 and 1999, in comparison with adjacent reporting districts). Further, crime rates throughout such affluent suburban areas were negligible to begin with, both within and outside luxury laagers.

Further, in cases where existing developments have been subsequently gated I was able to compare crime rates prior to and following gating, and here again results proved counterintuitive. Initial drops in crime rates as a result of gating, relative to adjacent ungated areas, either failed to occur or returned to pregating levels within one to three quarters after gating. Finally, one high density urban laager (LAPD Reporting Districts 714–715, the area comprising the Park LaBrea apartments) showed a significant rise in residential burglaries, residential robberies, and street robberies just *after* it was gated.

Despite these facts, a palpable sense of insecurity remains. Police chases and neighborhood tragedies are reported with ever increasing vehemence and frequency. As I write this I can step onto my balcony overlooking the Los Angeles basin and see two police helicopters circling over Silverlake, the little piece of the in-beyond I consider home. These are accompanied by twice as many television news choppers, circling overhead, feeding images of I've no idea what directly onto my television screen. And popular consensus, of course, reflects this reportage. During a radio interview in which I presented FBI statistics demonstrating the nonexistence of L.A.'s crime wave, a listener called in on his car phone to angrily insist that I was a liar and had made up the numbers. I *must* have. The extent of change in L.A. over the preceding decade, his sense of it as a palpable threat, and the increased presence of graffiti proved it! And as he spoke, he was en route to the luxury laager he had moved into precisely to escape this threat.

The extent to which this paranoia has penetrated into everyday consciousness must not be underestimated. By way of example, the long-standing greeting "Happy Holidays" has been supplanted around L.A., in both public signage and personal discourse, first with "Happy and Safe Holidays," then with "Safe and Happy Holidays," and now simply with "Safe Holidays," dropping joy out of the equation entirely—or, perhaps, collapsing joy into safety. Such changes in consciousness correspond with changes in practice. The shift from "Happy Halloween" to "Safe Halloween," for example, finds practice in injunctions against children's trick-or-treating in their own neighborhoods. Instead, those with access to disposable income have relocated such activities into such privatized spaces of consumption as shopping malls or, this past year, into one regional amusement park advertising itself as "The Safe Place to Trick-r-Treat" (and offering parents of the aforesaid Trick-r-Treaters a special "reduced" admission fee just over twenty dollars). This panic-driven privatization process helped render Halloween a $2.5 billion revenue generator by 1996, and has generated a trade magazine devoted to marketing the holiday, *Selling Hallowe'en* (Hannigan 1998, 76, 203). Thus, many urbanites' inflated fears of the world beyond their property lines impel interdiction and ensure its profitability. In the process, spatial interdiction comes to entail more than just the exclusion of multiple populations and a wide range of associated social practices. It entails taking such exclusions for a social good. And as a further result, questions of interdictory space's sociospatial injustices and resultant social dysfunctions are pushed ever further into the realm of the inconceivable.

This is not to imply that interdiction is a source of civic pride. To the contrary, what is fast becoming most noteworthy about interdiction is its near unnoticeability, a result of interdictory spaces' continual evolution into subtler and more systemically pervasive forms at the scale of the everyday. Innumerable, smaller interdictory spaces have been appearing throughout Los Angeles. When considered in the aggregate, such infill interdictions suffuse spatial exclusion into the fine-grain interstices of L.A.'s everyday landscape. And they have done so silently. By way of example, roughly a half mile away from where the aforementioned helicopters are circling their prey is the studio complex of the local public television station. In 1999, the studio completed construction on a dramatic arched entranceway to their facility, fitted with massive swinging steel gates. This edifice comes complete with a preciously venerable name, emblazoned across it in antiqued bronze letters: "Gateway to Knowledge." And between the arches of this gateway to knowledge is a new sentry booth with smoked-glass windows, staffed by guards charged with the responsibility of preventing passage through the gates. Enhancing the irony, the walkway immediately behind the secured gate has been renamed the "Pathway to the Future."

The unremarked appearance of this cutely monikered gate is starkly emblematic of how interdictory space has become a staple of the metapolitan landscape, a positive presence, and even a source of fun. This sea change in attitudes is attributable to an ongoing dual process functioning to render ever higher levels of surveillance and physical control, and their recipients' corollary social peripheralization, popularly acceptable. The first component of this process is naturalization, in which surveillant control becomes so deeply embedded in our daily lives that we simply fail to notice it. The second component is what I term *quaintification,* the design of interdictory technologies so as to render them innocuous and even charming. Through quaintification, forms of surveillant control that are too harsh to fade into the background are symbolically rehabilitated as both unthreatening and even laudatory by civic authorities, private developers, and their targeted clientele.

Naturalization is an unsurprising part and parcel of the protractedness of the urban "forting up" process, a tendency to grow accustomed to, complacent about, and even welcoming of the presence of surveillant control. This naturalization of interdictory spaces and practices has been accelerated by efforts to render the increasingly pervasive technologies of security relatively invisible. Thus, as the world city has rushed headlong toward panopticity, it has simultaneously dissimulated that panopticity. It is in such dissimulation that naturalization comes into its own. With newly emergent control

Quaintified perimeter fence at the Los Angeles County Museum complex, Hancock Park.

technologies, the dissimulation of panopticism is implicit to the design of interdictory technologies themselves, as evidenced by the stealthy telematics of consumer preference databases, wafer-thin leg-band transponders for criminals and peripatetic elderly alike, and carefully camouflaged micro-miniature closed circuit television cameras (Graham and Marvin 1996).

Yet many control technologies resist the impetus to invisibility. A wall around an urban amenity remains, both materially and perceptually, a hard barrier. Security guards continue to be clearly identified, in dress and equipment, as security guards, lest they be deprived of the capacity to fulfill their primarily deterrent role. This problematic is underscored in spaces targeting the affluent: on the one hand, users demand the reassuringly visible presence of protection from unpredictable and potentially unpleasant encounters with otherness but, on the other, balk at living, socializing, and spending their money in the hostile antiaesthetics of something resembling an armed camp. In response to the conundrum of rendering security simultaneously apparent and palatable, quaintification becomes a means of rendering interdictory spaces and practices aesthetically pleasing, quaint policing for what Edward Relph has called quaintspace (1987, 252–58).

It would seem that cute repression should be an intolerable oxymoron. Despite this, we increasingly tolerate it. Richard Sennett's insights into the urban start to approach the heart of this seeming contradiction. According to Sennett, cities are exciting. They are places in which diverse populations both experience, and by their very presence constitute, unforeseen encounters and expanded opportunities. That's why so many of us are attracted to cities. Conversely, however, excitement and unforeseeability necessarily entail risk and even menace: implicit to the notion of unpredictability is the possibility that encounters in the streets will not transpire as you might wish (Sennett 1990). And as we have seen, as Los Angeles has merged into a metapolis over the past fifteen years, the encounters in the streets have become markedly less predictable. Crime rates may not be up but diversity and polarization certainly are, rendering L.A.'s streets rife with the coexistence and collision of innumerable cultural and subcultural practices, and a fair measure of financial insecurity.

There are numerous factors to account for this; one is population increase. L. A.'s willful presence in the global arena has attracted a mushrooming population, with estimated residential densities in some areas exceeding those to be found in parts of Midtown Manhattan. This has escalated demand, and rendered real estate prohibitively expensive for a majority of Angelenos. Resulting land pressures have crowded higher density development into neighborhoods of traditional, albeit less affordable, suburban homesteads previously isolated along quiet avenues. In addition, this development swallows portions of the mountains, nibbles at the beaches, and presses in against the few major regional parks.

This impact of increasing demand for limited real estate is exacerbated under flexism. In the first half of the 1990s, Los Angeles lost half a million well-recompensed jobs, owing largely to the continued outmigration of industrial investment for more easily exploited locales and to the post–Cold War desubsidization of the area's warfare industry. This collapse of the labor market's demand side exacerbated the impoverishing effects of more than a decade of upward income redistribution under "trickle-down" economic policy and the corporate capture of mobile capital. Corollary with this was expansion of low wage/low skill service work and temporary employment arrangements. Such shifts in the labor market increased already substantial differences in quality of life between the city's highly visible elite and expanding poor, deforming the geography of resource flows within the city to harmonize with the distributional inequities of the emergent world economy in general. Further, in the absence of affordable land and opportunities for significant economic advancement, the parks and streets of neighborhoods in L.A.'s in-beyond took on new functions: rent-free open-air markets for the exchange of narcotics and sexual services, for instance, or unauthorized sites for homeless encampments (see, e.g., Wolch 1996).

But an equally vital rationale for interdiction is that of migration itself, crossing economic with cultural difference. Los Angeles is the affluent world city most frequently and widely represented (and misrepresented) in electronic media, and the fastest growing on the American West Coast throughout the 1980s. It has thus become a destination of choice for a disproportionate slice of the planet's estimated one billion immigrants. Nor have these immigrants been segregated out and ghettoized, left to settle only in demographically homogeneous low-rent locations. Rather, fair housing ordinances, the affordability of age-depreciated commercial and residential clusters, and the comparative mercantile affluence of some new immigrant communities have enabled them to relocalize widely across the L.A. basin.

Rising population in a limited area, concentrating wealth and poverty, and increasing cultural segmentation at regional and neighborhood levels are producing in Los Angeles, as in the metapolis at large, a densely packed heterogeneous population manifesting dramatic juxtapositions of privation and opulence. This has served to erode the spatial and ideological dominance of an aging 'white' status quo and its 'suburban ideal' (Purcell 2001, 182–83). The resultant drastic shift in the balance of cultural influence is complicated by the fact that no other group has yet emerged with a sufficient preponderance of members and/or resources to establish itself as the new majority. Lacking such a majority, no one group is empowered to determine new behavioral standards and, thus, there is no single standard.

With the decay of previously-established cultural standards and the absence of widely accepted new ones, a wealth of differing ways of life have surfaced, each with its own rules governing spatial use and interpersonal contact. The result is a fluid postmodernized urban matrix in which likely outcomes of encounters are unpredictable, territorial clues are misread or ignored, and persons and groups continuously encroach upon one another. In response to the uncertainties of this fragmented and dynamic urban milieu, social groups form into "defended neighborhoods" in order to insulate themselves from "danger, insult and the impairment of status claims" (Suttles 1972). Such defended neighborhoods are characterized by a homogeneous social group exerting dominance within its boundaries, a reaction to perceived threats of territorial violation by outsiders. Street gangs use spray paint, homeowners associations neighborhood watch signs. But both are informal militias, albeit some better funded and legitimized than others.

Interdiction, then, is not an answer to crime, but an expression of xenophobia. And its proliferation raises much larger questions about our evolving relationship with the urban, and the hard cities we create. Are we attracted to cities because they are exciting places? Or are we attracted to cities, despite the excitement, because they are wealthy places? Interdictory space suggests that it is both wealth and excitement that are attractive, but only so long as the former can be deployed to both neuter and simulate the latter. In the process the in-beyond is kept "out there" somewhere, and the spatial inequities of this exclusion tastefully legitimized.

The Othered City: In the Metapolis, You Are What You Pay For

Interdictory space is not just space that operates neutrally to intercept and filter would-be users. It does not cut all ways equally. It is commonly designed, built and administered by those affluent enough to do so, and with the wants and sensibilities of the similarly affluent consumer in mind. By corollary, interdictory space functions to systematically exclude those adjudged unsuitable and even threatening, people whose class and cultural positions diverge from the builders and their target markets. As a result, the majority of L.A.'s diverse community landscape is redefined as an imminently excludable other. Which is not to say, however, that the others making up the bulk of the city are forever banned from interdicted precincts. They are, in fact, often welcomed in. But only so long as they behave appropriately. And what constitutes appropriate behavior in interdicted spaces is rigidly defined and strenuously enforced by management. In short, difference is fine, so long as it is surrendered at the gate.

The paranoia now pervading Los Angeles is fueled in large part by fears of complex social change that is increasingly nonlocal in its formation and dislocalizing in its effect. In and of itself this is nothing unique—rather, it has been the case throughout American history when official morality is threatened. Consider, for example, the antiimmigrant movements of the mid-to late 1800s and into the 1900s, or the Red Scare of the early to mid-1900s (see Walker 1980). What is unique in the context of the metapolis and its Angeleno dislocale is how this threat is exacerbated by the proliferation of alternative moralities, multiple worldviews, and by the immorality and instability of accreting asymmetries in resource distribution. The concomitant "war on crime" is thus a means of forcibly maintaining, or at least salvaging, a challenged and collapsing social consensus. And not surprisingly, this consensus-salvaging operation includes simultaneously protecting the perquisites of that consensus' established beneficiaries. Spatial segmentation, and its enactment via paranoid typologies comprised of interdictory spaces, are the critical means to this end. The ultimate form of the new world bipolar disorder, then, is woven of interdictory space. Such a perspective in turn provides new ways to interpret interdictory spaces themselves.

The luxury laager may thus be seen as the territory of social groups possessing the considerable resources required to assert their spatial claims with walls and mercenaries. Luxury laagers are therefore intended to exclude not merely crime, but a wide range of behavior deviating from the community norms. This overriding concern with conformance to behavioral standards is demonstrated by the fact of residents' voluntary subjection to covenants, conditions and restrictions (CCRs). CCRs serve first and foremost to forbid behavioral difference, especially devalued differences like painting one's home a color objectionable to the Architectural Committee, working on one's vehicle outside of one's garage, use of overstuffed or other indoor furniture on patios or front lawns, or putting one's garbage pails out early (Monterey Country Club Association, n.d.).

The blockhome may be interpreted as an attempt by those unwilling to submit to the conformity of the laagers, but unable to afford large lots of their own, to similarly substitute blank walls for wide lawns as a means of establishing a comfortable distance from difference. Walls need not even be high for the symbolic exertion of spatial dominance to the owner's satisfaction; many blockhomes' perimeter fences are five feet tall or less, topped with blunt spikes, and even held upright by easily climbed support columns.

It is the unenviable task of the strongpoint of sale, if it is to survive, to draw prospective tenant merchants and customers into a setting that, by virtue of accessibility to a variety of social groups, precludes the ability of tenants or customers to enforce their own social norms. To resolve this contradiction, the strongpoint of sale acts to reassure visitors against the likelihood of unpredictable encounters by itself becoming the arbiter of behavioral standards even more conservative than those of the luxury laager.

Like luxury laagers, the plazas of citidels are configured more for the symbolic defense of status than for the physical protection of occupants. This status, however, is not held by the people within, but must be attained through exhibition to very particular publics: specifically, other businesses, and select subsets of consuming investors. The plaza is thus a front yard reflecting upon the tenant corporation's aesthetic sensibility and management competence. Therefore, management and tenants view a plaza's white-collar user mix adulterated by vagrants or a janitor's family on a picnic as a loss of prestige before the "business community," and a resulting loss of clientele.

The confluent agendas of these new urban forms makes it clear they are more than just scattershot attempts to salvage a status quo. Rather, they are commudities that embody an ideology of hostile privatism (McKenzie 1994, 19), common-interest privatopias that give rise to an antiparticipatory incivil society. Far from being an inconsequential trend, such privatopian commudities define a new norm for the mass-production of built landscapes to accommodate the "secession of the successful" (as coined by Robert Reich), places where citizenship is redefined as satisfying one's obligations to private property (McKenzie 1994, 196). And while the state-of-the-art privatopian commudity may have germinated in L.A., it can now be found throughout the expanding cities of the U.S. Southwest (Frantz 2001), across the American continents, and even in locations as far afield as Karachi and the mountains north of Beirut. True, many of these privatopias emerged as responses to distinctly different local imperatives, e.g. my own private conversations with residents, developers and colleagues have revealed that those in Karachi and Lebanon confer the added benefit of reliably providing electricity and potable water to their residents. But these conversations have also revealed that such privatopias are explicitly modeled after their Southern Californian precedents, and in many instance have been built by Pakistani and Lebanese developers who themselves reside off-and-on in Southern Californian privatopias (see Glaze 2001).

First and foremost, such commudities are intended as high-end marketable commodities, saleable prepackaged landscapes engineered to satisfy the lifestyle preferences of the affluent. This tendency is made clear by Neil Smith's assessment of how urban expansionism is powered by two industries: the real-estate developers who package and define value, and the manufacturers of culture who define taste and consumption preferences (Smith 1992, 75). Whether residential, commercial, or both, privatopian commudities are inhabitable theme parks, places of simulation without end. Carved out by the technics of surveillant control and enabled by the "artificial adjacencies" of virtualizing telematics (Sorkin 1992, xi), the commudity eviscerates the traditional politics of propinquity and simultaneously permits the exclusion of that which is propinquitous.

CityWalk, located in L.A.'s quasi-autonomous hilltop municipality of Universal City, provides the most extreme instance of this phenomenon. Owned by Vivendi, the French transnational corporation responsible for threefold increases in the price of municipal water supplies across Latin America, CityWalk is essentially an open-air mall like many others, but with a difference: its hyperkinetically colorful frontage is encrusted with thin quotations, simulations and simulacra of famous facades to be found around the L.A. area. CityWalk thus strives to be an improved version of L.A. itself, an intent backed up by the facility's founding rhetoric. It is in the visible manifestation of such improvement, however, that CityWalk is most revealing. Being situated atop a hill, charging a parking fee of eight dollars per automobile, and proffering merchandise available less expensively in the city proper, the overall configuration of CityWalk is a multiply slippery one that discourages the presence of L.A.'s less affluent social segments. This strategy of exclusion is reinforced by the mall's relentless jitteriness imparted through a strict code of conduct that is monitored by surveillance cameras prominently numbered into the hundreds, and backed by private security in conjunction with a Los Angeles County Sheriff's substation. The CityWalk code of conduct is an extensive document, proscribing thirteen broadly defined behaviors including the wearing of potentially disturbance-provoking clothing, sitting on surfaces not designated as seating (or on the ground in excess of five minutes), and "in any . . . way creating a disturbance which is disruptive or dangerous to the Complex's patrons or commercial function." This last stipulation is no mere legalistic boilerplate—it has been deployed to interfere with unionization drives and eject union organizers from the property. Further, such proscriptions are thoroughly augmented with the utmost of prickliness throughout the facility, whether by targeted signage prescribing how individual landscape elements may and may not be used, or by large metal spikes ensuring particular landscape elements will not be used.

CityWalk's improvement upon Los Angeles, then, is the wholesale deployment of surveillance and control to extirpate the spontaneous, the unpredictable, free expression, dissidents, alien cultural practices, the rights of labor, and the insufficiently affluent from the built environment. In short, this concretization of an idealized "better" L.A. is a filtered and clamped down upon Anti-L.A., a microcosmic hard world city in which difference itself becomes impossible. Tom Gilmore, CityWalk's leasing director, confirmed this agenda in his comments on Melrose Avenue, an immensely popular public commercial strip in L.A.: "I don't need the excitement of dodging bullets to go there. . . . I don't need to go to a Third World country." Never before has the division of the city into metropolis and megalopolis, commudity and in-beyond, us and the other been so explicitly and vehemently acknowledged, especially by somebody so actively engaged in erecting that division. Lawrence Spungin, president of Universal's parent company at the time, MCA, reinforced this position with his perspective on the public boardwalk of L.A.'s Venice Beach: "There's somebody on every streetcorner with a 'Work for Food' sign. . . . It's not fun anymore" (Wallace 1992, 1).

The Banality of Interdiction

Enter "Commander CityWalk." Commander CityWalk, as introduced in CityWalk's comic-book format "Guest Assistance Guide" (Universal City Studios 1997) is a superhero who fell through a timewarp from 2197 while discharging his duties as the CityWalk "Metropolis of Entertainment" security commander. Upon arrival in the present-day CityWalk strongpoint of sale, he assumed the duty "to protect CityWalk forever" and, with no apparent sense of self-irony, took the title "Guardian of Fun." Not surprisingly, Commander CityWalk's primary duty is the "vigorous" enforcement of the code of conduct, a task he executes with his hypertechnological capacity to "monitor all areas and citizens of this capital of fun." In the guise of Commander CityWalk, exclusionary panoptic control thus becomes something not only reassuring but flamboyantly heroic, keeping a lid on comic-book style villains who would impinge upon the pleasures of commodity consumption.

Being one who *does* aperiodically need to go to "Third World" countries, and who apparently resides within L.A.'s own Third World periphery to boot, I recently put CityWalk's claims about the perils of world-citified L.A. and the necessity for Commander CityWalk to the test. Accompanied by two dozen students, I traveled to Melrose and spent three hours walking the avenue, a commercial strip just south of Hollywood. Centrally located within the L.A. basin and with ample street parking, Melrose is famous for its youth-oriented subcultural specialty shops and attracts an eclectic mix of angelenos to promenade on its absurdly narrow public sidewalks. During our visit, we encountered innumerable people with prominent piercings and tattoos; a fair number of Goths, gangstas, and retropunks; a handful of skate kids asking after spare change; a dredlocked vendor from Cameroon pushing an immense cart stacked with incense and perfume oils; a family of Oaxacaños selling bagfuls of mango slices mixed with lime and chili; and a phalanx of Japanese tourists out on the hunt for bohemia. In short, this was a condensation of the sort of people one would find scattered across L.A., and at the same time, the sort of people who constitute the dense skeins of social linkages between L.A. and the rest of the metapolis. And, as with my innumerable past visits to Melrose, none of us was obliged to dodge a single bullet. To be fair, we then traveled to CityWalk where, similarly, gunfire was not in evidence. But neither were the vendors of chili-coated mangos and incense, the panhandling skaters (or any skaters, for that matter), nor the pierced and tattooed kids so much in evidence on Melrose Avenue. There were plenty of gawking tourists, of course, but not a Goth in sight (with the exception of a few strategically employed at the Hot Topic outlet).

Such experiences further the implication that CityWalk's code of conduct is less about precluding violence (which indeed it has not, as two separate mass melees on the mall have demonstrated; see Curtiss 1994) than about proscribing nonnormative social practices. Equally apparent, however, was that many of my students were largely untroubled by this, and some actively applauded it. A number of these students commented upon how much "nicer" CityWalk was than Melrose Avenue, and how the relative absence of people sporting green hair and extensive tattoos produced a more comfortable shopping experience. In the sentiments of one student, if spatial privatization, omnipresent monitoring, and an all-encompassing code of conduct can produce such nice places, then these control strategies should be promulgated more widely.

And indeed, they have been. CityWalk is neither exceptional nor an exemplar of the gleefully interdicted world city. Rather, it is one of many. The same phenomenon is apparent in the selective population disappearances attendant upon the redevelopment of San Francisco's Yerba Buena Park area, most notably in the vicinity of Sony's Metreon entertainment complex. It can be found in the subcontract constabulary (also known as "the shirts," for their distinctive color-coded polo-style tunics) patrolling the edges of business improvement districts from Hollywood to San Diego's gentrifying waterfront Gaslamp District, the quasi-privatization of Las Vegas' Fremont Street, and in the exclusionarily imagineered resort-casino agglomerate of the Strip (Raento and Flusty, forthcoming). Perhaps most notoriously, it underlies the Disney Company's controversial sterilization of Times Square in Manhattan (accompanied by then mayor Rudolph Guilliani's deployment of the police to thoroughly suppress that city's poorest populations). But it is no less apparent in the infestation of central London's shopping districts by closed-circuit observation cameras, the mallification of downtown Helsinki or, at the extreme, in the police death-squads on the hunt for street kids amid the commercial strips of Rio de Janeiro. It is, in short, the frontline of the metapolis's new world bipolar disorder, and of emergent trends to both dissimulate that disorder and turn a profit off the dissimulation.

This growing prevalence of interdiction is an indicator of the extent to which, under Flexism, world city formation is a zero-sum game played out on a tilted field. In this game, places invariably become nicer for some because others who might (or did) share those places are subordinated. Or worse. In Los Angeles the result is cities within the city where excitement is unmarred by uncertainty and risks are ultimately riskless (Hannigan 1998, 71); which, by extension, necessitates othering and the exclusion of otherness, keeping persons and practices that are different out of mind or, at the very least, well in line (see Bullard, Grigsby, and Lee 1994). The exclusion, in practice, of diversity in practice. Interdictory space, and the new world bipolar disorder it operationalizes and asymmetrically modulates, is thus not just about the production and devaluation of economic difference, but of entire categories of social difference. Seen in this light, the naturalization of interdictory spaces is tantamount to blithely ignoring the enforced disappearance of other ways of being within the city, other ways that in L.A.'s case have come to comprise much of the city itself, constitute the metapolis's cultural milieu and undergird its economy. And to quaintify interdictory space is both to trivialize this disappearance and to celebrate the subordination of those who practice other ways of being.

Throughout her later career, Hannah Arendt investigated the psychology underlying mass *public* complicity in totalitarianism. Her intent was to ascertain how large social collectives could permit, and even support, the emergence of gross systemic injustice. Ultimately, Arendt concluded that such an emergence is nothing inexplicable or even aberrant. Rather, it is the simple outcome of a population choosing en masse to sacrifice some of their number so as to attain peace and order (Arendt 1963).

CityWalk, of course, is not a concentration camp. But the difference between the two does not erase the uncomfortable isomorphisms in their underpinning motivations. In this quartier of the metapolis, the sacrifice of some of our number continues apace. Nor does this sacrifice occur of its own accord: candy-coated video observation cameras and cutely-themed guardhouses, after all, are not crabgrass. They do not pop up on their own. Rather, this sacrifice is *made,* by choice; the choice of consumers who feel most at ease where the overly unfamiliar is understatedly banned, the choice of producers who amass profit by catering to this sensibility, and the choice of administrators who see nothing amiss with the resultant proliferation of highly selective exclusion. It is particular persons, individually and as self-interested collectives, that interdict spaces and assemble them into landscapes of exclusion (Sibley 1995); and not surprisingly, the more such landscapes come to constitute the terrain of the world city the more thoroughly the metapolis's more privileged factions section themselves off from their far more populous other. It is of such stuff as quaintly naturalized interdiction that the new world bipolar disorder is made.

At its broadest, then, the proliferation of interdictory space is critical to the production and maintenance of the new world bi-polar disorder. But at the same time, interdictory space also reveals the probable outcome of such a disorder. The sites in which daily life and face-to-face interaction take place, the streets, parks, bazaars and plazas, are being sacrificed to redundant zones of oversight and proprietary control. This does not only produce a hard city rife with even harder edges and sharp, pointy corners. It also threatens the free exchange of ideas engendering a progressive society. It creates an impediment to the crosscultural communication necessary to knit together the metapolis's increasingly diversifying communities. It is a rejection of people's right to space in which to simply *be.* And it structures the metapolis as electronically linked islands of privilege embedded within an impoverished and brutalized matrix. Interdiction, then, is the most revanchist of techniques by which plutocratic globality is produced in our own backyards, both metaphorically and literally, segregating the metapolis into territories that rigidly reflect and reinforce the global division of labor. Thus, the ultimate outcome of interdiction could well prove to be that of a sugar-coated global caste society.

5
Planet Softeners

The world city is a distinct place, one that through its nonlocal articulation embodies the unique place that is the metapolis. It is a core component in a world system and simultaneously a culturally relativizing global field in which varied landscapes are manifested differently at different locales and for differently situated inhabitants. But such larger order phenomena are themselves a by-product of the ordering of inhabitants within the metapolis, and of authoritative determinations about how different inhabitants "should" be ordered. This latter includes the selective imposition of boundaries, borders and frontiers throughout metapolitan agglomerations like Los Angeles so as to segregate diverse populations, subordinate the different and, in the process, manifest a postmodernism of reaction in the transurban landscape (see Ley and Mills 1993).

Inattention to this reactionary postmodern transurbanism would indicate an absence of social consciousness verging upon the comatose. It is important to bear in mind, though, that the CityWalks of the world are just one piece of the metapolitan fabric, and a piece where very few people actually live. Although such places are prominent presences, focusing exclusively upon them can blind us to the wide range of countervailing places and practices through which other visions of the city and the world are brought into being.

The practice of these other visions entails a different ordering of the metapolis's inhabitants, a self-ordering driven by the positionality and situated knowledges (Haraway 1991) of the inhabitants themselves. No matter how unequal their relations, diverse persons are necessarily interdependent within the world city. Therefore, assuming world cities are to function at all, their commonplace social relations must—sooner or later, in one way or another—cross the boundaries that authoritatively inscribe a partitioned metapolitan order. In the process, experiences, perspectives, and ways of knowing previously held apart elide interdiction to cross paths. They influence one another in highly unpredictable ways, and in so doing tacitly disregard imposed conceptions of what the world city is to be. Thus, as interdictory space's disciplining logic is circumstantially transgressed over and over again, othered versions of the city propagate, intermix, and become concrete within the world city, producing more-or-less temporary autonomous zones (or TAZs; see Bey 1991)—postmodernisms of resistance in the transurban landscape wherein the impugned, the impermissible, and the supposedly impossible become the actual.

Further, such multifarious resistances are not necessarily intended as resistances at all. In pursuing our everyday lives, after all, we are each of us much more than either resistors or reactors. While our everyday TAZs may not remain entirely autonomous, neither do they necessarily cry out to be crushed. Rather, they are well suited to persist, propagate, and even bring about sanctioned coexistence, thus initiating effects with ever widening repercussions. In so doing they soften our conceptions of the world city and the world, illuminating how a multiplicity of unofficial, coterminous worlds embed themselves within the flesh of the world city, become that flesh, and in the process revector the formative trajectories of transurbanism itself. Seen in relation to a plutocratic globality made up of tightly nested interdictory spaces, the unofficial worlds of these soft planets entail other ways of being that remake portions of the city, stake a claim in the world, and tacitly refuse to disappear beneath the imperatives of spatial regulation and its select target markets.

So despite the pervasive and starkly asymmetric application of quaintly banal interdiction, and despite the scope, scale and depth of the new world bipolar disorder, the little actions of everyday life, whether overtly resistant or nonconfrontationally nonconformative, do not necessarily average out of the big picture. Rather, they can have deeply formative effects in the arenas of both discourse and the concrete at multiple scales, those of the self and the globe as well as the world city.

Worm's-eye Views of the World

Transgressions of the metapolis's official order are more often than not unnoticed events, patently unheroic accidents that revolve about the most commonplace of stuff. By way of example, a couple standout instances of my own transgressions have involved the most ordinary things, one a shirt and the other a name. And it was only after much subsequent work that I understood how these artifacts, and their corollary social relations, revealed that the global is not the monolithic structure we are lead to believe. In their transit, these two ephemeral objects had to breach not just interdictory space but the new world bipolar disorder at large, and along the way they deconstructed globalization to reveal it as an aggregate of underlying relations between identifiable people and objects in identifiable locales. Such people and things, in turn, showed themselves to be participants in sustained relationships with one another that extend across the planet and transform it. Thus, the metapolis takes on the form of innumerable connections that are subject to redirection, disruption, and collapse. It was here that globalization viscerally ceased to be, for me, some faceless force of nature, and became instead the product of particular relationships within and between places, and eminently susceptible to intervention. Seen in this light, scale itself is not so much jumped as it is both elided and redefined by means of everyday practice. Thus, global formation becomes more than just the emplaced concrete practices that impinge upon and reorder everyday life, it is no less the planetary hyperextension of the personal and collective practices of everyday life. And space thus becomes a terrain that is continually contested and reforged at multiple scales, the largest no less than the immediate and the personal, by even the most intimate of everyday activities.

That is a great deal of responsibility to pin to one shirt or a single name. But these two bits of quotidiana are simultaneously barium traces through the globe's bodies politic, mappings of narrative material culture that do more than just clothe and identify particular persons. They form global geographies of people and things together, explicate the underpinnings of alternate globalities, and collapse the global into everyday life.

As Seen by a Shirt

The shirt in question is a *barong tagalog*, or *barong* for short. It is a Filipino men's dress tunic with collar, cuffs, and a side vent at either hip. It is similar to the Caribbean-cum-Yucatecan *guayabera* "wedding" shirt, and to other formal-dress garments diffused from Madrid to Manila via Mexico City by the preeminent globally formative institution of the mid-second millennium, the Spanish Empire. The barong is traditionally made of jussi pineapple fiber, the pineapple also having been introduced from South America almost five centuries ago by the same empire. Organza is now often substituted for jussi, both being light, transparent fabrics well suited to the heat and humidity of the Philippines. Barongs are worn on special occasions by street vendors and the president alike, untucked and long, usually over a crew- or V-necked white cotton undershirt.

The significance of the barong here, however, is less a matter of what it is, than of how I ended up getting one. I had wanted a barong ever since I had first seen one during a brief visit to Hawaii in the 1970s, but only succeeded in obtaining one in 1997. And in a bow to the urban culture of my own point of entry, Los Angeles, this particular barong's travels and ultimate acquisition were inadvertently initiated by my automobile.

My car is a 1987 Nissan pickup, a "Japanese" truck assembled in Smyrna, Tennessee, of parts originating in more than half a dozen countries, few of them Japan. Ever since I purchased the truck, I have taken it for service at Imperial Automotive, largely because Imperial is only a few blocks from my home. For as long as Imperial has existed, it has been owned by Rob. Rob is a member of the Armenian diaspora. His family was deported to Syria in 1915, when the Armenians on the Ottoman Empire's northern frontier were othered as alien elements detrimental to the "Young Turk's" nation-building project. The outcomes of Turkey's inauguration into the modern world system of nation-states included the execution of somewhere from 600,000 to 1,100,000 of Rob's people (Chaliland and Rageau 1997, 85). But other, less dramatic outcomes remain visible to this day in the commonplace urban landscape. As outsiders in Syria, Rob's family was denied all forms of higher education. Thus, they pursued a trade and (like many Armenian refugees in the Middle East) became automobile mechanics. Many of his family members carried that trade with them to the United States, ultimately comprising the present ownership and staff of Imperial, and ultimately reconstituting Rob as a Syrian Armenian American.

During one visit for a tune-up and oil change, I expressed interest in the dance music being played in the garage. Rob filled me in on the performer, a Los Angeles based Irani Armenian known as Avak. Avak is something of the Michael Jackson of Persian pop, famous for performing such Persian popular music hits as Gloria Gaynor's "I Will Survive." Such music having been banned from Iran's Islamic republic, Avak and his band shuttle through particular neighborhoods of Los Angeles, Manhattan, London, Milan, Frankfurt, Paris, Stockholm, and Dubai. With the collapse of the Pahlavi Dynasty in the late 1970s, these cities have became home to an affluent, urbanized class of Persian professionals. In the process, these cities comprise a circuit in which Avak and similar musicians stage concerts.

This concert circuit includes the Assyrian Hall, some eight miles from my house, where I attended one of Avak's performances at Rob's recommendation. There, I reencountered an acquaintance of many years previous: Sheryl. Sheryl is a second-and-a-half-generation Japanese American, and had recently become Avak's bassist. She was hired for her musical talents and retained for the rapidity with which she learned to rap in Farsi. We became close friends. On one occasion not long after, as we sat idly channel surfing, we paused on one of L.A.'s "international" stations. At any given moment such channels may screen anything from grainy video reruns of 1970s Soviet variety hours to locally produced Chinese music-video shows. Lately, the latter have been hosted by a woman clad in hip-hop-cum-raver baggies who interviews the latest rap acts from Taiwan in a mixture of Mandarin and Ebonics. But on this occasion, the broadcast was a newscast from the Philippines, anchored by a newsreader dressed in a barong. I commented upon how I had long wanted such a shirt, and we proceeded on to other topics of conversation, and to other channels.

At this juncture of my barong's journey, its continuing adventures hinge upon a more complete description of Sheryl herself. In addition to all her previously mentioned attributes, Sheryl is, in her own words, a "dyke." One result of this has been Sheryl's predilection for a coffeehouse called Little Frida's, named for the Mexican Hungarian Jewish artist Frida Kahlo. Little Frida's was some twenty miles from my house in the city of West Hollywood, an independent city embedded within Los Angeles. West Hollywood is noteworthy as a mecca for gay men, but includes a small collection of women's bars and lesbian-owned businesses, of which Frida's was one of the most prominent. It was at Frida's that Sheryl befriended Moira, a self-described "Filipina lesbian feminist." Moira was also an employee of telecommunications corporation AT&T, selling discounted phone access accounts designed primarily to accommodate Asian expatriots in the United States seeking affordable transpacific telephone contact with family and friends "back home." As a favor to Sheryl, Moira used her own AT&T account to contact a sibling visiting family in Manila, roughly seven thousand miles from my house. This sibling returned with a barong, and handed it over to Moira. Moira passed the barong along to Sheryl. And Sheryl gave the shirt to me.

Now, in this globally expanding nonlocal network of day-to-day relations, the barong is just one of a plethora of possible protagonists. As an alternative track, the tale could branch off with Avak's music, and discuss how his sense of "Armenian-ness" has led him to approve the circulation of pirated cassette tapes among cash-strapped fans in Yerevan. Or I could follow an edgy subset of Little Frida's habitués a few blocks east to the Pleasure Chest, an "adult novelties" emporium that has responded to neighborhood demographic change by installing signs reading "Parking for Customers Only" in Russian.

All of these parallel stories reinforce the quotidian processes of global formation exemplified by my barong's adventures, processes real enough to put the very shirt on my back. Broadly, it could be said that I got the shirt on account of globalization. But this shirt came to me not *just* on account of an internationalized division of labor, or a relativizing intercultural flow of symbolic forms, or a collision of discursive realms problematizing construction of the other. I acquired the shirt on account of specific people who, in the course of negotiating their daily lives, happened to find themselves coming together in particular places.

None of this is to suggest that these emplaced people are not materially, symbolically, and discursively constituted. But central to my shirt's travels are these people's daily lives, and how those lives are spatially situated. My conspirators in this tale are each members of hyperextended collective social formations, whether technical affiliations (or, as I term them, *technicities*) like musicians, ethnic affiliations like Armenians, or affiliations predicated upon a shared condition of marginalization like lesbians. These various social collectives are both globally dispersed and technologically interconnected. Simultaneously, they are clustered together in the space of a single world city. Thus they inform neighborhood overlappings of dislocalized transurban communities, and create distinct networks of materiality (Law and Hetherington 2000): worldwide channels for the dissemination of symbols and material goods.

Enmeshed in these vectors are intimate experiential dimensions that highlight the much overtaxed term *difference*. The story I have sketched consists of differences that do not just exist, but that actively occur. Such differences occur by reason of their relational coming together in particular places. In this coming together we witness the proliferation of a special kind of concrete place where differences are produced and must be actively translated into some mutually approximate language if commonplace social interactions are to occur. Such places are "third spaces" in brick and mortar, built places of translation that materialize at multiple sites. Sites as (quasi-)public as a garage where the owner of a "Japanese" vehicle is exposed to Persian pop music, or a coffeehouse where the same vehicle owner becomes a social unit with a Japanese American dyke bassist and a Filipina lesbian feminist telecommunications worker. As such, these places are literal manifestations of "thirdspace," loci of critical exchange and extraordinary openness (Soja 1996b). In holography, this kind of synchronized coincidence of vectors is called "constructive interference," and generates the illumined points constituting the holographic image. Likewise, it is the synchronized coincidence of nonlocal fields that constructively interfere to illumine the holographic composite that is the metapolis.

Places of translation materialize at multiple sites, but also at multiple scales. These include places as intimately private as the very person of a Filipina lesbian feminist employed by a multinational telecommunications corporation. Such people constitute identities of translation (Rushdie 1991), thirdspace made flesh. This points to the fact that the everyday "comings together" that generate the global occur at both interpersonal and intrapersonal levels. It is significant that the conspirators in acquiring my barong are members of propinquitous, hyperextended social collectives. But it is

The Pleasure Chest
CUSTOMER
PARKING ONLY!
UNAUTHORIZED VEHICLES WILL BE
TOWED AT OWNER'S EXPENSE

В ИНОМ СЛУЧАЕ АВТОМОБИЛЬ БУДЕТ
УДАЛЁН ЗА СЧЁТ ВЛАДЕЛЬЦА
C.V.C. 22658A   (213) 913-404G

Bilingual signage at adult novelties emporium, West Hollywood.

equally significant that each of these conspirators is simultaneously a member of more than one such collective. Each person in my story possesses multiple identities. Thus, each acts as a point of contact between imagined worlds. Each is a bodily site where pluralities of soft planets overlap to facilitate an interpenetration of social formations. And such bodily points of contact underpin not just the intrapersonal dimensions of the everyday processes of global formation, but their interpersonal dimensions as well. In the absence of this intrapersonal dimension, there would be no connections among the numerous social terrains separating me from the Philippines, and my barong's journey would have been impossible from the start. Thus the formation of nonlocal fields and their attendant dislocalities is itself reliant upon carriers, carriers who so become the very practitioners of everyday global formation. My second artifact will make this even clearer.

As Seen by a Name

Tokunboh is not strictly an item of material culture. It is a set of phonemes, arranged in a sequence unique to the Yoruba language. But together, these phonemes comprise an "attributed unconventional object" (Hoskins 1998, 162), a male proper name that translates roughly as "he who comes from outside/abroad." While this name was once relatively unusual among the

Yoruba people, it has become increasingly common throughout the twentieth century. Tokunboh's growing popularity is to some extent a product of this people's location within the Nigerian nation-state. The colonial and postcolonial establishment of Nigeria placed the Yoruba within the same political territory as the Ibo, the Hausa, and more than 250 other peoples. Of these groups, the Yoruba exert a particularly strong cultural influence, exemplified by their founding of the country's former capital and still-primate city, Lagos. Further, solidarity among peoples like the commonly christianized Yoruba, Ibo, and Ishan has been intensified by their intermittent opposition, in both the British colonial and contemporary eras, to rule by the predominantly Muslim Hausa people. All these factors have resulted in intensifying cross-transfers of Yoruban culture, most notably in language, music, and naming practices.

But it is events in Nigeria throughout the 1980s and 1990s that have popularized the name Tokunboh globally. The end of the oil boom and the corollary introduction of International Monetary Fund structural adjustment programs (or SAPs) deeply disrupted the petroleum-dependent Nigerian economy. Faced with sudden prosperity that gave way to equally sudden economic collapse, there has emerged a sense that hopes for improved material living standards are futile, and that Nigeria's internal condition can only continue to deteriorate. This hopelessness has been exacerbated by a succession of military dictatorships notorious for rampant corruption, and for physical coercion, no small amount of which is in support of transnational petroleum firms (Kretzmann and Rolfes 1998). One Nigerian journalist, in self-imposed exile but nonetheless requesting anonymity for fear of state-sponsored repercussions against family left behind, has been quite clear to me about this last point. Referring to the 1993 handover of power from the Babangida to Abacha regimes, she characterizes the succession as a change from a president "who'd smile while he'd kill you" to one "who won't even bother to smile." Economic and political realities in Nigeria have thus engendered massive waves of emigration. Many of these émigrés believe their prospects in Nigeria are so irreparably bad that there is no reason to ever return for more than prolonged visits. Such immigrants comprise what is proving to be a permanent Nigerian diaspora. Thus, growing numbers of Nigerians have indeed come from overseas, rendering Tokunboh an especially popular and apropos name.

As with the barong, however, the significance of the name Tokunboh in this story is that, among certain social circles, it has become my name. I am not Nigerian, let alone Yoruba. And in relation to West Africa, I have yet to cross the sea. In fact, to receive the name I traveled no further than one hundred feet, from my front door to the house across the street.

While London remains perhaps the locale of choice for Nigerian immigrants, many proceed on to the metropolitan centers of the United States. Of these U.S. metropolitan centers, Los Angeles is gaining prominence. According to the 2000 census there were almost seven thousand Nigerians resident in L.A., a number that community members insist quintuples once circular migrants, unauthorized immigrants, U.S.-born children, and Nigerians who prefer to dissimulate their place of origin are taken into account.

The Ogbidis are among these expatriates. Their multigenerational extended family is spread between Lagos and the West Coast of the United States. Roughly a score of them now reside in Los Angeles. In early 1997, a subset of these moved into the house across the street from mine, and this house has become a site of regular visitation for the remainder. Similarly, it had become a site of regular visitation for me. On one of these visits, on Christmas Eve of 1997, I stumbled into a boisterous conversation conducted simultaneously in Yoruba, Ishan, Pidgin, and English. The topic of the conversation, insofar as I could follow it, was something about the appropriateness of one name versus another. Only when the conversation came to some sort of resolution, and I was presented with my Christmas gift, did I understand what had transpired. Because I was "learning to be Nigerian," as the Ogbidis put it, I was given the name Tokunboh. The name caused particular amusement, because it inverted the Ogbidis' geographical mobility relative to my own.

Although the name was a gift, there was the tacit implication in its mode of presentation that it was also something I had earned, however inadvertently. The gift name was thus an acknowledgment of something I had not fully realized: over the course of my continual visits to the Ogbidi home, and subsequent outings around the city, I had gradually acculturated to what the Ogbidis considered intrinsically Nigerian everyday practices. Gradually, I have learned that a party will start some two to five hours later than its announced time, and have adjusted my own sense of punctuality accordingly. I know that when the family matriarch calls and requests transportation to one of the local big-box retail outlets, it is incumbent upon me to accede. I ceased to see anything unusual in using my bare hands to eat stews with fufu, a sticky pounded yam dough. I became familiar with the musical differences between Femi Kuti and his father, the late Fela Kuti, and I picked up how to dance to either. I can tell stories about the Shrine, a club founded in Lagos by Fela himself, despite never having visited the place. I find myself understanding a fair amount of conversational Pidgin. I have developed a visceral sense of the human-rights abuses committed by multinational petrochemical companies prospecting for oil in Ogoniland. And I have participated in the boisterous cynicism when we gathered to watch the 1999 inaugural address of President Olusegun Obasanjo.

None of these things makes me either Yoruba or Nigerian any more than donning a barong makes me a Filipino. Nor, in entering into dialogue with the Ogbidis, have I lost anything that I was prior to that dialogue, much as I lose nothing in encountering Avak's music. Rather, I have been augmented and, in some ways, reconfigured by new perspectives and new ways of being. I remain *me*, but what constitutes me has subtly skewed. In a sense, my ongoing dialogical engagement with the Ogbidis has simultaneously displaced and replaced me, turning me into a point of contact between multiple worlds. In the instance of this book, for instance, I have become an identity of translation between diasporic Nigerians, academicians, and you, the reader of this text. And I expect that you have in times past been likewise pressed into service as a translator between social collectives.

Such diversification of our selves enables us to act as adapters through which seemingly disparate social and geographical realms do not merely overlap, but plug into one another and constructively interoperate. In the process, soft planets are both born and collectively negotiated. Thus the "global" is formed in the everyday by practices that play along (and across) the physical and psychic boundaries of both widespread social collectives and their particular members. This contradicts the hypothesis that focusing on identity and difference must necessarily yield hostile divisiveness and a balkanized social terrain. Rather, the amity and invention inherent in the commonplace practices of global formation, at both intrapersonal and interpersonal levels, provide ample cause not just for investigation, but also for optimism (see Martin 1997 for a contrasting view from just outside London).

The (Dis)Location of Everyday Life

None of this is to deny that globalization is in flows of capital and waves of migration, in satellite broadcasts and in transoceanic air routes. But the global is no less in the heads, and in the commonplace interactions, of those whose daily lives underpin these larger-order phenomena. After all, if the flapping of a butterfly's wings in L.A. today can hypothetically transform storm systems in Manila next month (Thuan 2001, 68; Bauman 1992), how much turbulence must be induced by hundreds of millions of flapping butterfly wings? Given the critical significance of global formation's interpersonal and intrapersonal dynamics, my heading that characterizes them as a "worm's-eye view'" may thus seem belittling. Indeed, I had contemplated revising that heading to read "an insider's view." But as both my adventurous barong and my new name demonstrate, to do so would have been to commit a redundancy. We are all insiders, no matter how cosmopolitan or local we may appear. This is not to imply that we are all equal in the efficacy of our global reach. But can we say with certainty that the ultimate impact of a dislocalized itinerant musician or a dissident émigré is any less real, and their soft planet any less valid, than that of a transnational corporation?

All views of the global are views from the inside. *We* are the inscribers of globalization, *we* are the participants in complex webs of emerging relationships that are simultaneously spatially extensive and psychically intensive. Thus, we enact globalities in various ways, as part and parcel of our everyday practices. Through these practices, we formulate our soft planets, and in their image we strive, whether consciously or no, to reforge the hard planet. Thus, global formation *is* nonsovereign. It is constituted by *and* it constitutes human and nonhuman actors. It is molded by *and* remolds the concrete spaces these actors stand on, sit in and move through. And it is enacted by *and* conditions the enactment of those actors' everyday lives: their production and consumption, their transporting and their meaning making.

Such actors seem to be puny things when contemplated from a distance sufficient to encompass multinational markets, world systems, global fields, and a riot of chaotic global landscapes. By finding global formation in the circulation of a shirt or the granting of a name, however, it becomes apparent that human and nonhuman actors make the world. Without these actors there can be no global flows to speak of, and thus no processes of global formation. And because of these actors, our comprehension of the "global" must necessarily remain insufficient until we approach 'the global' from its most intimate basis in localized everyday existence. But, in so doing, we must also remain cognizant that we, the practitioners of global formation in the everyday, are not autonomous of the processes we inform. To the contrary, they reforge us as much as we them. The miscegenative processes of global formation undermine our self-certainties and our certainties about our selves. And in so reordering us, such processes lead us to assemble our soft planets and the planet at large in their image.

6
Miscege-Nation

My own limited integration with Nigerian-ness and Yoruban-ness illumi-nates the intrapersonal dimensions within which soft planets are produced and reconfigured in the everyday. But it is also predicated upon underlying assumptions that are not so unproblematic as their labels suggest. The terms *Nigerian* and *Yoruban* conceal as much as they reveal, and neither is nec-essarily any more unequivocal than my own kluged-together self. Rather, such signifiers of identity are themselves quite complex, and in need of problematizing. This is not a new condition, given that the very invention of Nigeria entailed the sublimation of numerous tribal identities. But the ways these identities have subsequently hyperextended across global space, and attenuated into newly diffuse forms as a result of their hyperextension, significantly heightens the problematic.

The problematics of identity point to the extent to which the articulation of many axes of identity we take for granted are contingent assemblages presently in radical flux. As we have seen, changes in global interconnectiv-ity have densely interwoven cities across the planet with one another. This permits an unprecedentedly broad and rapid diffusion of peoples, artifacts, and information, compressing both space and time. And again as we have seen, insofar as these diffusions converge in large urban agglomerations, urban centers become condensers of people, networks, and commodities, but most significantly of a growing plethora of worldviews and experiences. The sudden juxtaposition of differing soft planets within urban space ne-cessitates, in turn, that these differences be acknowledged, negotiated, and recombined, giving rise in the process not just to new soft cities but to new soft planets as well.

This diversifying confluence of flexist capital, heterogenization, and soft planets within each cityfull of soft cities is not a unidirectional phenomena. At the same time as the world in general, and indeed multiple worlds, materialize in the city, the city links itself ever more tightly to others around the world. Disparate and distant places embody themselves within one another as cities continually swap pieces of themselves. In the process cities become not only world cities and components of the metapolis, but a global accretion of dislocalities—communities predicated less upon proximity than upon common interests shared over vast distances, diffuse neighborhoods bound together with landsat phone calls, air travel, transcontinental bus trips, and wired remittances.

The metapolis, then, holds a widening array of fluctuating languages, pictures, beliefs, foods, songs, stories, and other cultural materiel, and it is from such materiel that we "weave" ourselves (Dennett 1991). Or, more specifically, our identities are ultimately formed by how we mobilize such cultural materiel to represent ourselves to, and to be represented by, others (Taylor 1994). But our latitude for self-representation is not unlimited: "We do make choices, but we do not determine the options among which we choose" (Appiah in Taylor 1994, 155). The narratives defining self become legible to others only in the context of larger narratives of group identity. Group identities serve as "lifescripts," imparting meaning to narratives of self in accordance with the extent to which the self adheres to, or deviates from, that lifescript. In this way, lifescripts serve as templates that, at the level of the "individual," can both impart much needed meaning and enforce oppressive standards. The lifescript may function to constitute a collective in opposition to others, providing an ideal type that can be creatively played against, and that frequently establishes collective solidarity against hostile social contexts.

This description of lifescripts contradicts our common understanding of the axes of identity we tend to consider most fundamental to ourselves: race, ethnicity, and nationality. Such axes, however, are very slippery to begin with. Ethnicity, for example, is currently understood as a heritage or cultural descent that inheres in each and every individual, an "autonomous, endogamous and self-sufficient formation" (Naumkin 1993, 17; see also J. Friedman, 1994a). Yet in different times and places, ethnicity has been cobbled together from an ever shifting menu of linguistic, religious and mythico-historic signifiers (see Richards in Welchman 1996, 77). So despite their naturalization and seeming timelessness, ethnicities are "collective fictions that are continually reinvented" (Sollors 1989, xi–xiv). Race, the ascription of categorical identity to persons based upon their supposed biological bloodlines, is no less fluid. Population genetics has demonstrated that depending upon the genetic traits tested for, it is common to find greater variation between members of one supposed racial group than between members of two supposedly distinct groups. Race is thus revealed as folkloric groupings of persons based upon the most superficial phenotypic similarities (Cavalli-Sforza, Menozzi, and Piazza 1994), groupings utilized to devalorize other populations as inherently inferior, even accursed, and thus deserving subordination (see, e.g., Auerbach 1994; Lalloo 1998; but see also Pulido 1996 and 1998, for "race" as a position from which to collectively resist racialization). And nationality, in turn, pieces together widely varying assortments of ethnicized and racialized human attributes into "a people" with entitlement to state and territorial sovereignty (see, e.g., Jackson and Penrose 1993). The implication is that the state is an organic excrescence of the people, but in practice it has commonly been the state that stitches "[t]he scraps, patches and rags of daily life ... into the signs of a coherent national culture" (Bhabha 1994, 145) so as to nationalize its subjects and thereby secure its prerogatives.

No particular lifescript, then, can be seen as personally inherent, geographically consistent or historically stable. They merge and decohere depending upon the specificities of practice, the materiel of which they are comprised, and the different configurations into which that material is assembled. And how much more complex, unstable and open-ended must lifescripts become when written within and across dislocalities, when the options from which we may choose to assemble ourselves (and be assembled) proliferate and undergo increasing flux? Given that bodies are spatialized entities, and that spaces and bodies reciprocally (re)produce one another, then transurban spaces must certainly embody new kinds of selves, and entail collective, dialogical and ongoing renegotiation of the construction of identity, whether in the invention of the self or the production of broadly shared lifescripts. So it is not just the boundaries imposed within and between world cities that are here crossed, but those constituting and categorizing the self as well. Such new or, more appropriately, hybrid selves and collectives comprise the rhizomatic grassroots of globalities.

If we are made of such subsets of cultural materiel as happen to fall within our experiential reach, then global reach insures that the materiel has become quite varied indeed. And it is relentlessly increasing. With so extensive a menu of possible ingredients, how do we choose what to include in our selves? How do we combine the selected ingredients into constellations that can be personally fulfilling and collectively coherent? And what becomes of lifescripts like race, ethnicity, and nationality, written as though carved in stone, when they are renegotiated globally? Certainly, it is deeply disordering the more collective identification is produced within tangled skeins of hyperextended social relations. It is these relations that accelerate the motion of the kaleidoscope that is collective experience, turning fixities to fragments by shattering the grids superimposing categorical order upon identity (Nederveen Pieterse 1995). This absence of clarity in representing identity, however, does not necessarily entail chaos on the ground. It can entail bloody fratricidal strife, but it can also become merely part of the background noise of daily life, some of the messiness negotiated along with the rest of messy reality. This renegotiation of collective identity, however, points toward new potentialities. Potentials for anxiety and friction, but also for pleasure and for empowerment. It threatens old collectives with disintegration, but also holds open possibilities for their reformation and for the creation of new ones. Such potentials become actualities as the processes of self and collective formation increasingly play out upon nonlocal fields. And it is across these fields that the constitutive boundaries of identity and locality are conjointly decomposed, transgressed, and eccentrically reconstituted in the hyperextended practices of everyday life.

Recombinant Worlds

This continuing diversification of the self and the world together by means of recombinative everyday practices may more simply be termed *hybridization,* and its outcomes *hybrids.* And insofar as hybridizaton refers to things mixing together that were previously held apart, hybridity constitutes a counterdynamic to how interdiction keeps the metapolis authoritatively ordered by keeping worlds separate.

Some of my recent observations, made at a New Year's festival put on by a local religious order, will concretize this rather abstruse definition. The festival attracted a cross-section of the neighborhood: young couples, nuclear families, grannies in long silk skirts, and middle-aged veterans in light green uniforms carrying small-caliber side arms to serve as informal event security. This latter contingent frequently had their attention riveted on two groups of teenagers eyeing each other warily across a plaza.

The males of both groups were dressed in black pants so baggy as to be within moments of falling to their knees, exposing the tops of boxer shorts between hip and navel. Over this they wore huge, boxy jackets, with telltale bulges suggesting the presence of firearms beneath. Some completed their ensembles with bandannas and baseball caps worn front-to-back, and the colors of these finishing touches clearly communicated the nature of the tension between both groups and the de facto security force. One group of youths was ornamented exclusively in blue, the other in red. The females in the two groups were less elaborately distinct in their garb, but compensated for this with long hair structured into elaborate flourishes around their faces, highlighting a uniform motif in their choices of cosmetics. Their eyebrows were minimized or entirely absent, and across their eyes and cheeks they wore the frosted white "warpaint" of *cholas*-chicana homegirls.

What most attracted my attention was not the two groups' clothing, though, but their speech. It was studded with English, Ebonics, and Spanglish, serving as punctuation to a primary language, Thai. This entire linguistic stew was served up in tonal Southeast Asian pronunciation.

The festival in question was in honor of the Thai lunar-aquatic New Year, Songkran, held by the Theravadan monks of the Wat Thai Temple and cultural center in North Hollywood. The temple was completed in 1972 and, in the following decade and a half, attracted a residential population of over a thousand Thai immigrants into what had previously been a majority working-class Chicano area (Allen and Turner 1997, esp. 160). Clearly, various cultural facets of these two groups had somehow come together, embodying a new kind of young Thai. This hybrid becomes even more complex when one considers that while the chola look does have a long-standing visibility in the neighborhood, neither the sagging-baggies-and-bandanna style nor the use of Ebonics are common to the area.

What is occurring in the vicinity of the Wat Thai is a clear-cut strategy of cultural hybridity (Grossberg 1993). This points in turn to the growing presence of the hybrid as an empirical presence in daily life. But then again, to what extent is Thai itself a hybrid? The hybrid, and its representation as process, object, or both, is not unproblematic. It may be modeled in numerous ways, and some observers deny its very existence while questioning the motives of those who would assert otherwise.

Generally, *hybridity* refers to the coalescence of new personal and collective identities from novel combinations of previously disparate cultural attributes, practices, and influences. This definition of the hybrid is commonly seen to have emerged from conditions of being cut off from one's roots and left without a place of one's own, themes central to the writings of such postcolonial authors as Frantz Fanon (see, e.g., Bhabha 1994). Identification of this sense of displacement through processes of forced estrangement, however, is best described in the less cited anticolonial work of Albert Memmi.

In *The Colonizer and the Colonized,* Memmi analyzes colonialism as a psychologically pathogenic structure that thoroughly deforms colonized peoples and their colonizers. For the colonizer, this deformation results from a life of relative ease and privilege, instrumentalized by the subjugation of entire peoples to support that privilege. To legitimize this injustice, colonizers must construct both the subjugated and their culture as inherently inferior. Simultaneously, the colonizers valorize their own self-image and idealize their own homeland to such an extent that this reimagined motherland ceases to bear any resemblance to the reality back home. Thus, colonialism renders colonizers pampered and brutalizing, self-righteous megalomaniacs, contemptuous of both the colonized society and the reality of their home society (Memmi 1991).

More central to the question of hybridization, according to Memmi colonialism deforms the colonized by rendering them servants in their own home while forcibly arresting further development of their precolonized culture. This leaves the colonized caught between the choice of assimilating to the alien lifeways of a conquering society that will not have them, or clinging to a culture that, robbed of past history and dynamism, becomes a reactionary complex of debilitating forms purged of living meaning. Trapped in such a lose-lose scenario, the colonized can not go home again, as they have been deprived of a home to begin with. They are, at root, rendered rootless. They are unhomed, and so subject to the reciprocal transculturating dynamics of deterritorialization and reterritorialization (Deleuze and Guattari 1987).

The condition of "unhomeliness" (Bhabha 1994, 172) is particularly acute for the colonized who travel between the colony and the colonizer's motherland. Such people become partially acculturated to the forms of both, while simultaneously remaining alien to the latter and becoming alienated from the former. In such cases, the fragmenting effects of political boundaries are inscribed onto the body, producing similarly fragmented identities. Unhomeliness is thus a condition of living unsettled *in* multiple places at once while being *of* none of them (Memmi 1991, 107; see also Trinh in Welchman 1996). Corollary to this, a life of unhomeliness entails an ever-shifting self in which what you are, what you know and what things mean must be continually reinterpreted in light of whichever spatiocultural context you inhabit at any given moment.

Unhomeliness is in no way confined to the excolonial traveler. Recall that colonization renders the colonized foreigners in their own home, and their indigenous contexts unhomely. Nor is this condition restricted to the subjects of formal colonialism, as Memmi suggests in dedicating his book to "the American Negro, also colonized" (see also Spivak 1987). Thus, owing to the pervasive, culturally-restructuring presence of alien hegemons (Carpenter 1972), fragmenting borders also become inscribed upon the bodies and minds of the sedentary colonized. Therefore, borders form and must be negotiated not just between places but within them as well. Negotiating these internal divisions takes the form of uneasy accommodations of established cultural meanings to newly introduced influences (see, e.g., Watts 1997 on the mutation of human-eating animal spirits into human-mangling automobile spirits in the cautionary tales of rural Nigeria).

In these ways, subaltern categories of people are produced at home and abroad. They are assigned devalorized lifescripts, rendered liminal, and banished beyond the discursive pale of settlement. The problematic of fragmentation is thus redefined as one of resisting spatial and discursive situatedness in a silenced, disappeared nonposition of disinclusion from two or more essentializing hegemonies. Such resistance is accomplished by incorporatively reinterpreting bits of each hegemonic discourse so as to assert an alternative that refuses the assigned nonpositionality of one's position. This reclamation of a subject position, a place in the world for those at the margins, identifies an interstitial zone of inhabitation (see Soja and Hooper 1993). The existence of such a habitable zone explicitly problematizes the social norms that hierarchically structure such interdependent terrains as colonizer and colonized, masculine and feminine, heterosexual and homosexual. Thus, the divisive sharp-edged borderline is reterritorialized into an expansive borderland, a dwelling place that abides within and cuts across geopolitical and categorical boundaries. In the process, what was displaced and deterritorialized is reterritorialized, bringing resolution (however contingent it may be) to the conflicted disorientation inherent in occupying multiple "psychical and cultural realms."

Borderlands are places where two or more worlds come together to define a habitable margin. They take deeply metaphorical forms, like thirdspace, and intensely personal ones, like identities of translation. But they can also be literal topographies, terrains like the *interworld cities*—cities located at the interstice of highly divergent cultural, political, and economic demesnes. Tijuana, Mexico is an excellent example of such a place, as is Tallinn, Estonia. But what is most telling about such places is not how they are sited geographically, but their social isomorphisms. Tijuana is on the opposite side of the planet from Tallinn, and both emerge from very different cultural and political circumstances. Yet both evince marked similarities as urban societies and fulfill similar functions with respect to their surrounding regions. Both cities are commanding points of passage for significant diasporas, preeminent shopping destinations for hyperconsumptive bargain hunters, and investment beachheads for dominant abutting ecumenes. They are also both "wild" and potentially lethal frontiers in the popular imaginary, an imaginary not entirely without tangible roots in such shadow realities as *narcotraficantes* and post-Soviet *mafiyas*. Further, the relationship of both cities to their adjacent milieus gives rise to markedly similar experiences. The intense ambivalency with which Nords and Russians are perceived in Tallinn is indistinguishable from that with which *gringos* are commonly regarded in Tijuana, while the experiences of a Mexicana street-vendor in Southern California are comparable in many ways (although certainly not all!) to those of an Estonian sex worker in Scandinavia's urbanized south.

Most significant, however, is how culture is assembled in these places. Tijuanenso culture in no mere arithmetical formula that adds the United States into Mexico, nor is Tallinn some Baltic portmanteau of the Nordic and the Soviet. Rather, cultural materiel appropriated within these borderlands is thoroughly broken up, dismantled, and uniquely reassembled according to long-standing local operating procedures to create something entirely new (Fusco 1995)—not a hybridization *of* distinct cultures but hybridity *as* a culture, a *culturas hibridas* (García Canclini 1995; see also Gómez-Peña, Chagoya, and Rice 2000; McGuire and Scrymgeour 1998; and Theroux 1994, for interpretations of L.A. as just such a borderland). And once assembled, of course, culturas hibridas need not stay in place, confined to the precincts of the interworld cities. Rather, they travel, carried by migrant persons and export products even into the hegemonic hearts of Europe and the United States (Mattelart 1994, chap. 11).

Hybrid to Whom?

Culturas hibridas, however, are not to everyone's taste, and some are dubious of their very existence. Such critics interpret hybridity as the miscegenation of previously separate and pure originary cultures (see, e.g., J. Friedman, 1994a, and in Werbner and Modood 1997), an impossibility given that all cultures are hybrids of other culture's influences and always have been. Thus, hybridity is neither new nor distinct, but an omnipresent underpinning of cultural formation. Therefore, hybridity means both everything and nothing. And those who assert otherwise are an elite of opportunistic, academic cosmopolitans, concerned primarily with making a name for themselves at the expense of the place-bound and parochialized locals.

For his part, Jonathan Friedman places this counterargument in a larger Spenglerian perspective to argue that preoccupations with hybridity are principally an indicator that a hegemonic commercial civilization is on the verge of overextension and collapse, weakened by luxury and penetrated by migrants in search of those same luxuries. Owing to these factors, precollapse decadence sets in, symptomatized by cosmopolites flirtations with exoticism and a loss of clear civilizational borders. Thus, hybridity becomes a frivolous piebald owl of Minerva, winging its way through the dusky *Götterdämmerung* of the Enlightenment West, with a cabal of self-promoting cultural elites astride its back. Meanwhile, the reality implied is one of affluent cosmopolitans sight-seeing through the windows of a stretch limousine as it drives through "a rundown, crowded planet of skinhead Cossacks and *juju* warriors, influenced by the worst refuse of Western pop culture and ancient tribal hatreds" (Kaplan 1996, 62).

This apocalyptically dismissive representation of hybridity is deeply problematic for a number of reasons. First, the equation of cosmopolitanism with placeless privilege is far too reminiscent of late eighteenth and early-nineteenth-century anti-Semitic discourses positing Jews as footloose financiers with no ties or loyalties to place. *Kosmopolit* was a disparaging euphemism for Jew in late Imperial Russia, and a justification for their often bloody exclusion from national society (Naumkin 1993). Further, hybridity's detractors take a position that is itself not innocent of strategic maneuvering. Assigning determinations of cosmopolitanism and localism serves to arrogate to the assignor the power to essentialize both, while doing most violence to those assigned to the latter category by imprisoning them in a description of benighted lumpen native-ness (J. Clifford 1992).

In line with the problematic of presuming the authority to essentialize, the reduction of hybridity into an artifact of the polar opposites "cosmopolitan" and "local" is no less objectionable. This position equates the cosmopolitan with a combination of affluence, travel, and indoctrination to the modern, and the local with relative impoverishment, immobility, and hewing to particularisms verging on parochialism. And as touched upon previously, this cosmopolitan/local division comes apart on closer scrutiny.

Further, arguments against the hybrid as a synthesis of two previously pure things misinterpret hybridity itself. Rather, per Mendel's work on heredity, a hybrid is something that combines particular traits that had not existed in combination before, and is not concerned with any categorical "purity" of those traits' sources. Thinking in terms of hybrids thus yields a useful way of marking where, when, and how a given set of differences first came together in a single entity, whether in plant breeding or pop culture (Cavalli-Sforza and Feldman 1981; see also Benzinberg Stein and Moxley 1992, for an interpretation of vegetal transplantation and cross-pollination *as* cultural hybridization). And finally, the novel combination of Thai American gangstas with which this discussion began must have currency beyond certain privileged academic circles, given that these gangstas' parents and monks found the phenomenon no less novel than I, and considerably more disturbing! Thus, there is certainly cultural hybridity of the sort represented by the Thai American gangstas. They are not the contamination of some prior essential "Thainess" by something else, but they are certainly a new combination of previously disparate cultural forms that calls our attention to the excentric (J. Clifford 1992) and to the expanding reach afforded our projects of cultural assemblage.

It must be remembered, of course, that the hybrid is itself a discursive/material formation, and a huge and abstract one at that. It is the product of the union of increasingly widespread ways of thinking and of doing, of dislocalized practices that intersect in local spaces. Spaces as near to hand as the house across the street.

Things Fall Together

In mid-March of 1997, just across the street, Andrew Eromosele Ogbidi died suddenly of congestive heart failure. He was a prince, not just figuratively but literally as well: son of a king of the Ishan people and one of his wives. So

Mr. Ogbidi's body was returned to Nigeria for burial in his old room in the family compound. Upon returning to the U.S. from the funeral, Andrew's second son (and owner of the house across the street), Osagie, presented me with three masks he, his brother Kevin, and their childhood friend Oluyemi (Yemi for short) had taken great pains to select for me. Each mask represented one of the three majority ethnicities of Nigeria. One mask, blockier in shape and with a grid of "tribal marks" on each cheek, physically concretized the Yoruba. The second, wearing a hat knotted over in the front, signified the Ibo of the southeast. The third, with a complex high head-wrap and what Osagie termed "refined facial features, especially notice the lips," represented the Hausa, the Muslimized people of the north. It is these Hausa who the now departed British administrators had established as the intervening elite and who, through maintaining that colonial-era advantage, have long controlled the Nigerian state's military apparatuses.

This clear tripartite division carved in ebony, however, began to disintegrate when I asked Osagie with which of the three groups he most identified. He responded that while he is Ishan, a people from the Edo and Delta states of Nigeria, he had grown up in a city around Ibos. Thus, in many ways, both his first language and culture was Ibo, although he was also heavily exposed to and influenced by Yorubas. On top of which, he has resided in the United States for the past twenty years (since his early twenties) and, during much of this time, he had little contact with any Nigerians. Finally, he made reference to his technicity, adding his professional classification as an attorney.

This provoked further conversation, with Kevin and Oluyemi, that underscored the difficulties of distinguishing these ethnic boundaries. Yemi, whose father is Nigerian and mother from Hamburg by way of the German-Polish border, sees himself as "Nigerian first, other things second." The primary second thing he identifies as is Yoruba, which led me to inquire what makes a Yoruba a Yoruba. Yemi responded that the Yoruba are totally different, speak a different language, eat different foods, and have a different culture, which Yemi exemplified as the wearing of long shirts and, until fairly recently, the facial scarifications of tribal marks. Kevin, however, argued that such cultural signifiers were not necessarily unique to the Yoruba, for instance by suggesting that Yoruba cuisine was not all that distinctive, leading to an elaborated discussion of differences in Nigerian society.

Yemi: The Ibo are more anarchistic, every man for himself. The Yoruba have a hierarchy with the elders as the leaders.

Kevin: No, that's the Ibo.

Yemi: No, the Ibo follow the top man, the one who is the strongest. Not physically strongest, not anymore, but richest or smartest, that's what makes Ibo better capitalists.

> Kevin: But the Yoruba don't follow all elders, just the richest or smartest ones, and the richest, smartest Ibo are older.
> Yemi: Yes, but the Yoruba are more hierarchical.
> Kevin: No, that's the Hausa. They have the one king.
> Yemi: More an ayatollah, like in Iran.

To clarify, I asked whether the Hausa are distinctively Muslim, and thus clearly marked as different from the largely christianized Yoruba and Ibo.

> Yemi: At least half the Hausa are Christian now, too, especially towards the south. But the Muslim Hausa run the military and Nigeria [taking the oil from the southern regions].
> Kevin: If you are driving and the police stop you, unless you have a name like Yusuf Ali Muhammed whatever, they will beat you.

The conversation then turned to descriptions of "Hausaness," revealing that while neither Kevin nor Yemi could definitively agree on what it is to be Yoruba or Ibo, they were united in describing themselves as *not* Hausa. Amongst the Hausa characteristics they enumerated were smoking too much, eating dog meat (a practice I myself am not innocent of), and a propensity among their poor to huff shoemaker's glue.

Despite these difficulties in conclusively bounding Nigerian identities, Osagie has indicated that these conceptions delivered from outside Nigeria are clearer than those perceived from within Nigeria, in that "In Nigeria, all the ethnic groups seem alike, you're just so busy living your life but, once you're outside, you really notice the differences." This consciousness of difference was demonstrated at one of the Ogbidi's parties, where Kevin estimated the attendance as 80 percent Ishan, with only one Hausa present (who was introduced to me, with jocular good spirit, as "our Hausa overlord.")

Dayo, a former editor for a major Lagos newspaper and in-law to both Osagie and Kevin, has indicated that this constitution of Nigerian identities from the outside is gaining in prominence. She noted that a torrent of emigration was unleashed as the Nigerian government became increasingly repressive, a torrent that continues despite the recent change from a military dictatorship to an elected presidency. For Dayo as a news editor, such a political climate is particularly threatening, raising the omnipresent risk of being "clapped in detention" and spurring her move to Los Angeles.

Exacerbating the political tensions is the belief that, with the end of the oil boom, the outside imposition of nationally impoverishing International Monetary Fund structural adjustment programs, and the resultant nose dive of the Nigerian economy, Nigeria will go on falling apart and driving its citizens overseas. Hence, the Nigerian diaspora. Kevin sees an additional problematic in the sudden prosperity and equally sudden collapse of the oil boom: an increase in the expectations of Nigerians for affluence. When

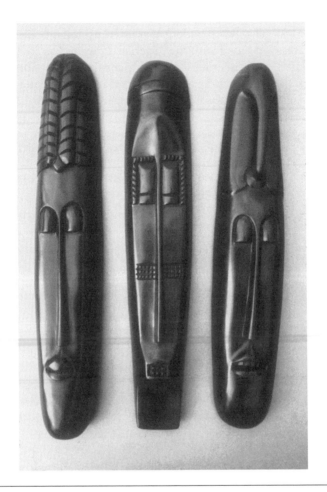

Decorative wooden masks from Nigeria.

not met by the reality of a collapsing economy, these radically disappointed expectations have generated not only emigration but also a class of "419ers," young confidence artists named for Nigerian government edict Number 419 criminalizing "advance fee fraud." Such fraud is a highly sophisticated operation wherein wealthy businesspeople from outside Nigeria, eager to make a fast buck from business within Nigeria, are lured into paying lucrative advance fees in exchange for the promise of exorbitant profits to follow. On occasions, confidence may be elaborately reinforced by holding meetings in high government or banking offices, commonly when the office's legitimate occupant is out to lunch. Such profits, of course, never materialize, nor do those who made the promise and took the advance fee. In a sense, this is a radical capital repatriation tactic, whereby financially savvy operators engage in extralegal sting operations that invert exploitative neocolonialist trade practices. But along with the Nigerian diaspora has come the diasporization of 419, engendering some highly creative transnational criminal organizations (TCOs) that have appropriated prodigious sums of capital from banks across the United States and Europe and, as of 2002, successfully infiltrated the three principle U.S. credit reporting agencies.

This presence of 419 TCOs among the Nigerian diaspora results in an international prejudice against Nigerians, as Kevin says: "We do not have a good reputation in the world, we are ambitious and sometimes will do fast 'business' to get what we want." This prejudice has been felt viscerally by Nigerians outside Nigeria like the Ogbidis. Osagie, for instance, has been subjected to interrogations by U.S. customs, badgering him with questions like "a U.S. passport? How'd you get that?" and Yemi has encountered similar treatment in Germany. At times, some of the younger Ogbidis themselves have accepted this outsiders' popular conception of Nigeria, choosing not to associate with Nigerians in the United States.

Owing in part to such disassociation, Kevin believes that he and his brothers "were becoming 'individuals,' neglectful of family and suspicious of other Nigerians." Kevin sees this as an extension of a deterritorialization process no less at work in Nigeria itself where, due to influences like the CNN television network, most residents of Lagos "know more about what's happening in Los Angeles than in their own backyards." Other factors, however, have exacerbated this sense of being de-Nigerianized into isolated individuation. Upon arrival, Kevin assumed that, given his self-conception and outward ascription as 'black,' he would find friends amongst Arican-Americans. He rapidly concluded, however, that the differences between culture, outlook, and historical conception were too great:

> I tried to befriend some [African-Americans] but one said he hated me, that it was my ancestors who sold his into slavery. Why are they always so angry about history? I am black and from Nigeria, it is much tougher to make it there, yet here I will be an attorney.

Of course, the relative ease with which Kevin can "make it here" suggests the extent to which the history and contemporary practice of racial discrimination is as much, if not more, predicated upon differential ethnicization as it is upon the scientist construction of race. This is, of course, an academic issue from the perspective of Kevin's lived experience. But the more immediately experiential slipperiness of "race," its application, its euphemization and, most significantly, its devalorization are not. One long-term resident of the Ogbidis' new neighborhood initially responded to their presence with trepidation, describing them as "big, shave-headed African Americans" who would prevent him from "enjoying the home and property values" for which he had "worked so hard." (I remain uncertain whether the term *African American* was here used in presuming Americans of distant African descent, or as an automatically invoked euphemism for *black*. Further, given that most of the Ogbidis have been naturalized as U.S. citizens, the term African American is technically not incorrect.) Less ominous, but no less telling, was a statement by Osagie's then significant other. At the conclusion of our first introduction, she told me I'd have no difficulty recalling her: "I'm easy to remember, I'm the white one." Finally, residing somewhere between these two responses on a scale of malignancy was that of a self-described "generic white guy" at one of the Ogbidi's gatherings. He declined to join in moving to Femi Kuti's music on the grounds that "it's genetic... my people just don't have the same ability for dance." Thus, the Ogbidis have been located by outsiders upon an axis of identity that Kevin himself felt rebuffed from consciously inhabiting.

This question of contextualized race plays out even more complexly for Yemi, who finds himself categorized "black" in the United States, but "half-caste" (in Kevin's words) in Nigeria. Further, Yemi asserts that he finds himself thinking of Germany when he's in the United States and Nigeria, but of life in Lagos whenever he's in Germany. But more generally, Yemi, Kevin and his (and Osagie's) mother, Victoria, are continually nonplussed by what they see as an American obsession with ancestral identity. In numerous conversations, they have laughed bemusedly at the way "Americans" are continually asking one another "where are you from?" as a veiled request for information on ancestral origin. Conversely, for the Ogbidis and many others in the Nigerian diaspora, concerns over difference, boundedness, and separation focus on much more immediate issues of locational proxemics. The Ogbidi's scattering throughout Los Angeles' sprawl leads both Victoria and Dayo to observe how dull and lonely it can be to sit and look out the window. Very few people ever walk by like "back home," and fewer still comprise a local network of associates who'll stop in and socialize with any frequency. At the same time, the diasporization of Nigerian sociospatial networks has not so much severed as attenuated them. By way of example, the practice of grandmothers assisting in the upbringing of new children remains, only now augmented by jet travel and lengthy overseas stays, giving rise to a transatlantic circuit of itinerant Nigerian grandmas.

Also countering these perceptions of collective disintegration has been a more recent reterritorialization in the form of a re-Nigerianization, one that in the Ogbidi's case Kevin pegs to the arrival of his parents from Nigeria in the mid-1990s. As Kevin related, "We didn't really deal much with Nigerians here, they have such a bad reputation, till my father [Andrew] came to live here." Upon arrival, Andrew repeatedly cajoled his children for having abandoned their culture and for failing to associate with others of that culture. This ultimately constituted a predominantly Ishan network of Nigerian social contacts that continues to the present, as with the aforesaid parties that, according to Kevin, wouldn't have occurred prior to his parent's arrival. Other signifiers of this process include Osagie's decision to use the name Osagie, his middle name, in lieu of his previously preferred first name, Lawrence. On a larger scale, there has also been the rapid formation of coalitions of Nigerian professionals working to redress negative popular conceptions of Nigerians. Central to much of this is the emphasis on a "Nigerian," as opposed to more specific ethnic, identity. This testifies to the formation of a pan-Nigerian consciousness both among the growing diaspora and in Nigeria itself, where numerous ethnic divisions are being crossed to form coalitions of resistance. Some of these coalitions are deadly serious, opposing the previous dictatorships through activities like disrupting infrastructure and sabotaging petroleum extraction. In Kevin's words, "All tribes are coming together to fight the dictator in the night, there is becoming for the first time only Nigerians." In this context, then, Nigerian-ness becomes a new, nonlocally articulated identity, one formed through personal engagement with communal and national politics that occur in multiple dis-localities simultaneously.

Despite this (re-)Nigerianization, however, it is difficult to say with certainty that the younger generation of Ogbidis' daily lives were indeed "deculturated" prior to the arrival of their parents. For instance, when I asked Osagie whether he found it spatially constricting to have his parents, brother, sister-in-law, and a rotating series of visitors sharing a house with him, he flatly stated: "No problem. We're African, we're used to it." (Of course, in so saying, he mobilized continentality as yet another axis for the ascription of identity!) Similarly, I now number among my valuables a photo badge, a plastic drinking cup, and a ballpoint pen all bearing the legend, "In loving memory of PRINCE ANDREW EROMOSELE OGBIDI, 1919–1997." While most residents of the neighborhood would likely consider this an unusual method of commemorating the dead, the Ogbidis simply took it for granted. As Dayo explained, among Nigerians, "So long as you can afford it, it is important to remember those you love, who were a part of your life, in the things you use every day." This explanation, I might add, struck me with such force that, when the time comes for me to acknowledge the loss of loved ones, I will likely adopt a similar method. But conversely, all signs point to the likelihood that the most recent generation of L.A.-born Ogbidis will be far less prone than myself to follow suit.

I have intentionally not redacted these stories of the Ogbidis (and of Yemi) as an integrated narrative, and I do not intend these stories to be somehow representative of a statistical average or the qualitatively typical. As a group, and as particular human beings, these stories are complex blends of diverse influences, synthesized uniquely by each person involved and, further, I have intersected with these lives in limited ways and times as another person formed by his own influences. Nor am I suggesting that viewpoints like Kevin's and Yemi's be taken as authoritative statements about identity in Nigeria, let alone West Africa as a whole. Indeed, there is much inconsistency among members of the family about such basics as whether their affiliation should properly be termed Edo or Ishan. Some have tacitly used Edo as the tribe and Ishan as the language, others have pointedly stated that Edo is the state and Ishan both the language and people, yet others have specified that the Ishan are a distinct subgroup of the Edo. At a larger level, while Osagie believes that tribal difference is magnified the further away one is, other Ogbidis have expressed the contrary: that the further away one is, the more differences fade in the face of seeking others from home in an alien setting.

But it is precisely these contradictions, their fluidity, irregularity, and nonauthoritativeness that point toward the manifold ways identities are forged, and reforged as they are attenuated through their spatial hyper-extension. And simultaneously, it is these practiced renegotiations of collective identity that generate and maintain dislocalized collectives, and so bring transurbanism and soft planets into being. Thus, polysemous selves are not merely symptoms of complex societies and their nonlocal social relations in some top-down way. Rather, polysemousness is a more-or-less unselfconscious strategy for navigating the complexities inherent in the hyperextended articulation of the social and, in the process, for yielding soft planets as tacit maps of the world so navigated. In the process, such identity categorizations as race, ethnicity, and nationality are remolded into new permutations as their "carriers" travel into and constitute new contexts within and across space. At the extreme they can even give rise to entirely new identity formations, literally out of the air.

Wanna-be Warriors

The quotations opening this section come from a new "translation" of Shakespeare's *Hamlet*, the first edition of which sits upon my bookshelf. It is published in Harvard folio format, with English to the right and the language of translation at the left. While Shakespeare's work has been repeatedly translated into many languages, this particular version is unique in that the language of translation is tlHingan Hol, known more commonly as Klingon. Further, this book claims not to be a translation into a new language, but a restoration of the work into its original tongue. To emphasize the point, the frontispiece of this book features a traditional woodcut of the author, but with his high forehead augmented by the pronounced ridges and furrows of Klingon cranial physiognomy. My copy of the book was a gift from a friend who, in addition to considering herself a woman, a software coder, and an African American (in the commonly understood U.S. sense), also identifies as a Klingon. Thus, she has adopted an identity that now constitutes a "shared reality" that until relatively recently existed only in an electronically mass-mediated science-fiction universe. Equally significant is the fact that this book is not a rough-edged piece of photo-copied fan literature. It is hardbound with a sewn spine, printed on archival acid free paper, and can also be had leatherbound with gilt edges. Neither is this book an authorized piece of *Star Trek* related merchandising produced under the auspices of Viacom Entertainment. Rather it is the product of a highly organized fictive community made flesh.

Klingons originated in Los Angeles, created in the mid-1960s by Gene Roddenberry as a narrative analog for the Soviets in his "wagon train to the stars" space opera *Star Trek*. Throughout the multifold incarnations of *Star Trek*, Klingons have also been produced and developed in Los Angeles at Paramount Studios, at the eastern edge of Hollywood on Melrose Avenue. Initially, their concretization is the result of the labor of numerous screen-writers, actors, makeup artists, costumers, and associated film crews. But as a landmark in a globally disseminating mediascape, *Star Trek* has dis-seminated globally as a science-fictionized mythos of liberal-humanistic globalism. In the process, "Klingonness" has been radically co-opted in its reception, and mutated into something entirely unexpected.

There now exists widely distributed networks of people who self-identify as, among other things, Klingons. These people generally acknowledge Klingonness to be a roughly thirty-year-old invention by way of Paramount Studios (later a Viacom subsidiary). None I've encountered literally iden-tifies as an extraterrestrial interloper nor spends the bulk of their waking hours clad in black leather armor and cranial ridges. (The exception is a few hardcore enthusiasts who, employed at the Las Vegas Hilton Hotel's *Star Trek: The Experience* simulator attraction, look, dress, speak and act Klingon full-time as wage labor.) Thus, it would not necessarily be unfair to view Klingonness as a lifestyle, a leisure identity. Nonetheless, this confabulated axis of identity is being actively invented by its practitioners not as a fan club, but as a global collective that blurs the boundaries between fandom and ethnicity. They meet as small groups in private, in hordes at conventions and retreats, and most prolifically across the Internet. In the process, they have evolved a complex and more-or-less uniformly applied social struc-ture. Within this structure social and regional affinities are redefined as clan affiliations or, in many instances, "house lines." Such house lines are main-tained by a "house proctor," and local affiliations are commonly constituted as "imperial Klingon vessels" answerable to commanding *epetais*. Positions like house proctor and *epitai* constitute "fleet positions," attained through involvement in organizing the community. Initiation as a Klingon entails the taking of a Klingon name which, in current practice, lengthens as one attains "honors" for community engagement.

Such communities are reinforced by a variety of means. Most immediately, there are daily interactions, both face-to-face and across the Internet. Further, the communal watching of series episodes and attendance at new movie releases constitute ceremonial "diasporic rituals" (a term originally applied to the Jewish seder by Daniel Dayan and Elihu Katz in Curran 1987) through which separated people and households define a community by reason of simultaneous performance. While such diasporic rituals underlay the initial production of a Klingon community, other more visceral and elaborate rituals have become equally central. Such performances, often informed by Star Trek's television and cinematic corpus, can include martial arts training and specialized forms of physical combat, "rites of ascension" (a coming-of-age practice centered upon withstanding pain) and "curse warfare" (a kind of jocular drunken name calling). Curse warfare (along with many other interactions) is conducted in Klingon, and thus some knowledge of the language is de rigueur for one who would emerge victorious and 'authentically' claim a Klingon identity.

Here, language is a vital axis along which Klingon self-identity is symbolically and performatively assembled. The language, based upon the Native American dialect of Mutsun, extinct since 1930 (Gaslin 2001, 12), was originally a handful of phrases developed by linguist Marc Okrand for the earliest installments in the *Star Trek* movie series (see Okrand 1995). Under the intensive development of the Klingon Language Institute (KLI), however, Klingon has become a full-fledged invented tongue, disseminated by means of instructional tapes, CD-ROMs and printed manuals (250,000 copies of which are presently in circulation). The KLI itself has tallied approximately 1,600 members (although the percentage of those fluent in the language is an open question, likely far fewer), many of whom are actively involved with other Klingon social organizations internationally. Indeed, some of the KLI linguists themselves perform to varying degrees as Klingon, Internet home pages showing them with the elaborately furrowed Klingon forehead. Such linkages have been vital to one of the KLI's showpiece projects, the semi-tongue-in-cheek "restoration of Shakespeare's works back into their original Klingon" that yielded my own copy of the Klingonized *Hamlet*. In addition to the translation itself, this volume includes extensive endnotes in the spirit of the Shakespeare Harvard folio editions serving to place the play within its Klingon cultural context. Thus, organizations like the KLI are collectively engaged in confabulating not just a common language, but

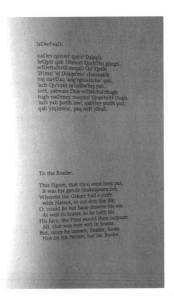

Frontispiece to the Klingon language *Hamlet, Prince of Denmark.*

also a shared history, a codified culture, ritual performances—in short, the list of attributes that Vithly Naumkin (1993) claims constitute an ethnicity.

Who becomes a Klingon, and why? In answering this question, I will avoid excess speculation and stick to what I've seen, and what I've been told by those who so identify. Most could be classified as self-reflexively cosmopolitan, commonly (though not exclusively) white, relatively affluent technical professionals and students of both sexes. Klingons, then, are in many ways (and senses) a distinctly virtual collective. Many of them express feelings that, in the words of one I've corresponded with at length, outside of their Klingonness they "don't have a culture." At its most basic, Klingonness constitutes a romantically savage cultural identity formation. This strongly counters adherents' perceptions of culturelessness, and simultaneously provides an alternative to the more mundane lived realities of adherents' sedate technicity. But reading deeper, the sense of being without a culture resonates with themes of Klingon struggles against assimilation presented repeatedly in episodes of the television series *Star Trek: The Next Generation, Deep Space Nine,* and *Voyager.* In these series, Klingon culture is indeed strongly stated and savage, but also newly liminalized within the galactic order and subject to "a colonialist narrative of enculturation" (Vande Berg 1996, 66) within a pacifistic, bureaucratic, and human dominated galactic political order. Members of the "proud Klingon warrior race" (ibid) are thus compelled to continually grapple with what it means to be Klingon, how Klingon heritage should be preserved and exercised, and whether that which distinguishes Klingons as a people can survive assimilation.

It could, of course, be argued that this response to perceived culturelessness is inherently inauthentic, engendering a self-consciously synthesized identity lacking any inner essence or lived history. I would certainly argue that ascription/inscription as a Klingon is a choice. It does not entail a lived history of cultural struggle and even suppression, and a corollary tradition of resistance. Nobody, to my knowledge, has ever died for their Klingonness. But insofar as all collective identities are constructed, authenticity is not so self-evident as we may believe and, therefore, dismissing out of hand those who would claim a Klingon identity becomes deeply problematic. Identifying as a Klingon entails giving bodily and practical form to personal anxieties and aspirations. Further, these anxieties and aspirations, and the response of Klingonization, is now inherently collective. Klingons form networks of social interaction based upon the invented identity that members find pleasurable and personally empowering, and this identity requires investment in a formalized social structure, shared rituals, the fabrication of a history and a common language. It also entails considerable investment in costuming and cosmetics. While few may spend the bulk of their waking hours looking like Klingons, all acknowledge that being Klingon entails periodically donning the armor and ridged craniums so as to bodily present as Klingon (see Joseph-Witham 1996, esp. 22–29). Thus, Klingons constitute both a materially distinct (self-) ethnicized social formation, and one that is sharply differentiated from other social formations. And in so being, practices of suppression, resistance and struggle do indeed come into play.

This sense of collective devalorization is apparent in the initial hesitancy with which those I spoke to addressed their identification, providing responses that sometimes suggested feelings verging on personal shame. When made visible to others, the adoption of Klingonness commonly can render one a social pariah. It entails inscription as a physically unattractive, ill-socialized geek, and as a passive consumer of media product who needs to "get a life" (Jenkins 1992, 10–11). Klingonness can also entail more serious consequences, in some instances colliding head on with the state. As an individual example, in Sedgwick County, Kansas, four children were removed from their home by police and placed in court-ordered foster care. The primary rationale was unsanitary conditions in their residence. Matters were significantly exacerbated, however, by the fact that the children's father spoke Klingon in the home and that the children proved to be bilingual, fluent in both Klingon and English (*Wichita Eagle* 1999). More systemically, Klingon associations in Europe have been misconstrued as illegal breeding grounds for militarism and neo-Nazism. Most seriously, in the mid-1990s German Klingons' use of banners, uniforms and pseudomilitary organizational hierarchies derived from the *Star Trek* corpus left them subject to lengthy investigations and censure by the national prosecutor's office (*Renegade* 1995).

But conversely, Klingonness has also provided a position of collective organization and resistance. During 1997–1998, Viacom attempted to proscribe unauthorized use of their copyrights on the Internet, including the posting of images and other intellectual property pertaining to *Star Trek*. Beyond copyright protection, the apparent intent was to herd *Star Trek* fans (known as "Trekkers") to the sole sanctioned *Star Trek* website, newly opened and operated in conjunction with Microsoft. But for Klingons, this was a direct assault upon their web presence and a fundamental threat to their identities: after all, what Viacom regarded as intellectual property was precisely the materiel the Klingons had poached, elaborated upon and developed as their own selves. In short, Viacom was threatening to render Klingonness virtually unperformable. Further, many felt their elaborations had, in turn, been repoached by Viacom and incorporated into the movies and television series (or, in Viacom's parlance, "the Franchise"). Thus, couched in slogans trumpeting "join the glorious battle" and "resistance is not futile," Klingons joined with free speech on the web campaigns to launch boycotts, protests, and less conventional forms of harassment against both Viacom and Microsoft. By late 1998 Viacom surrendered, tacitly but unconditionally. As might be expected of imagined warriors fighting on virtual turf, the Klingons had won.

Klingonness constitutes a distinctly hybridic collective identity, one that fictively mobilizes elements of ethnicity and nationality and couches them within a benignly racialized (or, perhaps more appropriately, species-ized) framework. Of course, in the absence of all but an irremediably fictive (although intensely elaborated) homeland, language and collective history, Klingonness is strictly performative, its attributes are open to highly creative reinvention, and its boundaries in constant flux. One *is* Klingon by how one chooses to identify, speak, dress, and associate. But unless we are prepared to accept notions of group-specific collective memory that is somehow present in each person from birth on or, more radically, a supposition of biologically inherent cultural traits that verges on racism, then the difference between Klingons and other identity collectives is more one of degree than of essence. Whether Klingon or other, we become what we are through what we receive into our bodies, what we put out through them, and the modalities we have adopted for how this should be done (Gurnah 1997). Thus, while performing bodily as Klingon affords tremendous latitude for adoption and collective reinvention, performative adoption, reinvention, and actively negotiated hybridization are critical dynamics of any nonlocally articulated and articulating social collective. This is true even for collectives we take to be the most inherently and inviolably "pure." And it becomes all the more so as the relations that make us what we are hyperextend across ever wider spaces, and simultaneously attenuate our identities—stretch out and deform our selves and our self-certainties. Hence the growing latitude for, and imperative to, performatively renegotiate collective identity. In the process, the practices of such collective reinvention produce effects that re-invent the global itself.

Out on a Limen

Clearly Nigerianness and Klingonness are very different identity formulations. (They are not necessarily mutually exclusive, though, despite the fact that I have yet to encounter a Klingon Nigerian; for a discussion of the construction of Klingonness in relation to broader questions of devalorized blackness and subalterity see Vande Berg, 1996.) In the case of Nigerians, we are confronted with some harsh realities that have impelled bodies across space and, in the process, motivated a re-imagining of self- and collective identity and a rearticulation of the axes along which that identity is formed. In the case of Klingons, we deal instead with self- and collective identities built around formative axes that elaborate an entirely imaginary world. Yet both identities are particularly vivid instances of the in-process constitution of "imagined communities" (Anderson 1983) at a global scale. Both entail the assembly and intersection of soft planets, and both are thus agents of hybridization within the world city and across Metapolis. So diasporic Nigerians and Klingons are world-imaginers and points of contact between imagined worlds, they birth new soft planets through commonplace practices of hybridization. All of which entails that soft planets don't just happen. They are socially practiced by particular persons, concerted and de facto coordinated.

Such persons and practices, no matter how locally concurrent, are diverse and kaleidoscopic, predicated upon divergent assumptions and active at different scales. In part this is a statement of the obvious, given that all the persons and practices I have discussed thus far are copresent and interwoven in the terrain of their observation, Los Angeles. But in being so interwoven, and so observed, they (and many more like them) describe explicit intersections and nested scalar relations with one another. Such relations reveal a transurban field constituted and inhabited by populations that are socially and culturally heterogeneous but politically and economically polarized, subject to multiple layers of interdictory networks but also adept at eliding those networks. Select minorities of these inhabitants ensconce themselves within commudities. The growing ranks of the remainder are consigned to the in-beyond. Yet all repeatedly cross paths locally and nonlocally on a daily basis in variform ways. The built environment conditions and expresses this field, a crazy quilt of affluence and privation but also of personal thirdspaces and dislocal neighborhoods.

From out this relational field there emerges a constellation of intersecting phenomena that describe the metapolis. As with any constellation, my own description of the metapolis is not the only configuration possible. There is always more than one way to connect the dots. So my description has inevitably been partial and incomplete. But the proxemic, scalar and experiential relationships of L.A.'s emergent transurbanisms do catalyze into a vision of a postmodern world city that reaches across scale, inwards towards the body and outwards across the planet. This vision of Los Angeles in transurbanity is not intended as a newly hegemonic vision of the world. To advance it as such would be to directly violate the ontology of my own project. Rather, the Angeleno transurbanism I have explicated is fragmented, partial, positional, and begging for further dialogical engagement.

Noting this positional partiality is not a qualification or a rhetorical proviso. Rather, it is an insight into the metapolis itself. It suggests that the metapolis is holographic. Its totality is manifest in every constituent world city. But as per the holographic trope, each world city constitutes a different facet of, and a different perspective on, all that is the metapolis. Each address within the metapolis is a different angle of view affording differing triangulations of similar elements, a locally distinct configuration of all the metapolis' dynamic phenomena. In short, each connects much the same dots, but connects them a bit differently. Thus, my description of the world city of/as L.A. is both quite close to, and very removed from, seeing L.A. as Jorge Luis Borges's Aleph (Soja 1989, 222–23). Like that Aleph, L.A. is indeed a "place on earth where all places are. . . ." But unlike the Aleph, it is not a place where all those places can be "seen from every angle, each standing clear, without any confusion of blending" (Borges, cited in Soja 1989, 222). L.A. is, rather, a piece of Aleph, a piece of a place that contains all places at every point within it.

This is a necessary start, and an extension of current thinking about transurbanity. It describes an urbanism that is a consequence of how nonlocal skeins of human and nonhuman actors knot into dislocalities. These dislocalities accrue asymmetrically and tangle with one another across the earth's surface, giving rise to soft planets that, through our everyday practices, run up against one another, recombine, crystallize and propagate as globalities in their own right. Thus does the planet go soft along with the city, making the global itself a discursive/material formation in which "the amplification and diversification of 'sources of the self'" (Nederveen Pieterse

1995) challenges official pronouncements and authoritative enactments of globalization.

And so "the concrete, localized practices through which globalization exists" (Sassen 1999, 101) are produced and articulated through the conscious imposition *and* the performed elision of boundaries, borders and frontiers not just within the world city, but across the metapolis and the world at large.

Macrointerdiction

Given the metapolis's global holographicity, neither the bodily disciplining imposed by interdictory space nor the practices of its de facto dissidents are phenomena localized to a given city. The material practices that asymmetrically modulate, (re)produce and contest the new world bipolar disorder and othering-through-exclusion are no less transnational in scale. Thus, the forms and dysfunctions of interdiction presenced within world cities manifest similarly (although by no means identically) between them.

This is apparent just two and a half hours south of Los Angeles, at the line that bifurcates the interworld city-region of San Diego/Tijuana and simultaneously demarcates the United States of America from the United States of Mexico. Here interdictory space takes on pharaonic proportions, and border transgression is much more than a metaphor. The border dividing these places, from the beach to Otay Mesa fourteen miles due east, is a hyperthyroidic hybrid of crusty, jittery, and prickly spaces. Fences welded of solid steel plate, previously used as portable runway by the U.S. military, span much of this distance. In some locations they are arrayed in double and triple layers. Behind this is another, intermittent fence. In some places, it is a fifteen-foot-high steel wall curving outward at the top toward Mexico. In others, it is fourteen-foot-high concrete "bollard" columns set roughly six inches apart and topped with canted steel mesh. Similarly spaced ten-foot-high pilings extend approximately 340 feet into the ocean, driven some twenty feet into the sea floor to discourage swimmers from side-stepping the fortifications. In the no-man's-land behind and between these fences the ground is lined with twelve-foot steel sheets to prevent tunneling, sprouts high-intensity stadium-style lighting, and is liberally sprinkled with seismic monitors to detect footfalls. In addition, the area is regularly patrolled by agents of the U.S. Bureau of Customs and Border Protection, equipped with off-road vehicles and such "mil-spec" equipment as night-vision scopes.

Of course, this border is the territorial definer, container, and "external organ" of the state. Its inviolability reflects back upon the state's viability as expressed through its territorial sovereignty, and serves to shore up such state-mandated prohibitions as those against the importation of contraband (or, at least, its import by those lacking state sponsorship). But in the context of plutocratic globality's hegemony, this same boundary takes on a new primary function: to mass produce and write large the divide of the new world bipolar disorder. This is baldly expressed in a parody of the placard on the Statue of Liberty, spontaneously composed for me one evening by a Tijuanenso poet who's had his own less-than-amicable encounters with border interdiction: "Keep your poor, your tired, your huddled masses, but send us your capital and your consumer goods, affordably assembled in the maquilas of your EPZs [export production zones]" (Flusty 2000, February). Those here othered, however, are not so easily dissuaded. Thousands attempt to transgress this boundary every day. Many of those who succeed will go on to provide indispensable labor, both commercial and domestic, for the world city of Los Angeles. In so doing, most will also invert this border's logic by modestly reversing the directional flow of capital, sending remittances back home in what amounts to a mundane yet radical tactic of capital repatriation. Seven billion dollars per year's worth, constituting "Mexico's third largest source of legal income after oil and tourism" (Jones 2000).

In this instance, the border reconstitutes the simple act of moving from here to there as one of transgression. This collision, however, attracts additional acts to and across the national border, practices that are more explicitly confrontational in both overt and subtle ways. As a particularly visible instance of this, nativists in the U.S. have executed "Light Up the Border" campaigns, in which they turn their automobile headlights on unauthorized border crossers. In response to this politics of reaction, opponents have carried large mirrors to the frontier to light up the nativists in the glare of their own reflected headlights. Or there is the beach of Playas, butt up against the border fortifications' western terminus and the Border Fields State Park on the U.S. side. Here the wall for a time was turned into a memorial akin to that for Vietnam War veterans in Washington D.C. The steel plate of the border fence was affixed with the names of 455 would-be border crossers who died in the attempt, pushed east into more treacherous terrain by the ever-intensifying fortifications at Tijuana's northern edge. On the hill just above this beach is a small plaza spanning the frontier, in the middle of which stands an obelisk proclaiming the eternal friendship of the U.S. and Mexican peoples. Both the plaza, and the obelisk itself, are neatly bifurcated by the fence, but in deference to the monument's intended symbolism the fence is made of see-through steel mesh. It is not uncommon to see members of Mexican families divided by the border picnicking with one another through this fence, occasionally tossing goodies back and forth over its top. Masses are occasionally conducted here, both to permit divided families to worship together and as a form of church-based protest. And on other occasions, adolescents on the Playas side make sport of bad-mouthing and catcalling *gringos* peering through from the other.

These dynamics have reshaped political engagement and the state on both sides of the border. During Mexico's 2000 presidential campaign

Internationally crusty space—the border fence dividing Playas de Tijuana, Mexico from Border Fields State Park, San Diego, U.S.A.

the dominant political parties, the PRI, Institutional Revolution Party (Partido Revolucionario Institucional); the PAN, National Action Party (Partido Acción Nacional); and the PRD, Party of the Democratic Revolution (Partido Dela Revolución Democrática) established offices in Los Angeles. Both PAN's Vicente Fox and PRD's Cuahtemoc Cardenas campaigned in L.A. for the votes of Mexican expatriates, promising Mexican nationals in Los Angeles and Chicago three at-large seats in Mexico's Congress should they win enough votes in congressional elections (Jones 2000). Upon winning this campaign, Mexican President-Elect Vicente Fox established a high-level state apparatus for the administration of Mexicans living abroad, and immediately made a state visit to the United States. He brought with him a proposal for U.S. president George W. Bush that the border be opened to permit the free movement of people, a proposal to which, not surprisingly, Bush was not particularly receptive.

The transnational (and indeed, here they are very much trans*national*) orderings and disorderings along the border render it a place of both exclusionary violence and of merry promiscuous mixing, which points to a broader question. We have seen how the world city is no unitary object, and will not become one no matter the authoritarian disciplines applied to its streets. Simultaneously, this pluralistic world city is a world city by reason of its nonlocal integration with others of its kind. Can the globe, then, be any more a singular place, and globalization any more an authoritarian imposition? Admittedly, the lion's share of hyperextending everyday practices are neither so interdicted against, nor so willfully resistant, as those at the far western edge of the U.S./Mexico border. But this does not entail that they are any less globally formative. They may even be more so, given that their accidental and seemingly innocuous nature lets them slip through interdiction's cordon sanitaire. Such practices do, however, tend both to disappoint our romance with resistance, and to fly below our theoretical radar screens. But this neither stops such practices from existing nor precludes their real impacts, and we ignore them to our detriment. It is, after all, these practices that render soft cities simultaneously soft planets, and that enact them as globalities.

So soft cities and soft planets are very similar, closely related animals. Like soft cities, each soft planet has its own formative underpinning experiences, its own internal logics and agendas, and its own validity. And as with soft cities, some soft planets are more equal than others. There are multiple versions of the world at play on the global field, and there are inarguably winners that claim the lion's share of the spoils. But which soft planets predominate is neither a foregone nor stable conclusion. All remain engaged in continuous, polyvalent, and dislocated struggles for control over both symbolic and literal terrains, all work to be concretized as globalities with the power to influence (or refuse) the order of the world. Thus, the global may well gel, and it may do so as the dominant demand, but it never fully hardens. It remains instead a persistently viscous planet, an arena where all manner of institutions and other hybrid social collectives advance incommensurable globalities, plutocratic and otherwise, of their own devising.

PART III

The Clash of Globalizations

From near to far, from here to there, funny things are everywhere.
—Dr. Seuss, *One Fish, Two Fish, Red Fish, Blue Fish*

The notion of accidental resistance is not merely an academic abstraction. I just committed it myself, while caught in the throes of completing this book. And, at least in part, my barong is to blame—or, more specifically, its shortcomings. As much as I enjoy getting away with attending professional gatherings shirt untucked and sans tie, there are times when a barong attracts the evil eye from colleagues, and climes where it can invite frostbite. So, regretfully, I set about finding myself a proper suit. Fortunately, I stumbled across catalog photos of one that I would not regret donning at all, a three-piece modeled after the sort of suit worn in Anatolia circa 1900. I ordered it, and received a quick e-mail reply from one of the clothing company's managers that the suit would be produced for me and shipped immediately . . . from Damascus, Syria! My interest piqued, I began peppering this manager with endless queries about the history, philosophy, and production relations of his company, and he in turn provided prompt and thoughtful responses.

The company handles its production in house at a small factory in Damascus, and is headquartered elsewhere in the Middle East. Although coordinated between headquarters and Damascus, the company's product distribution reaches across Europe and North America. Management is comprised of personnel drawn from literally around the world, some of Middle Eastern descent and others not. Three things bring this far-flung assortment of people and places together as a single entity. Most obviously, there is the Internet—communication between the company's various divisions is conducted via email. Additionally, nearly all of the company's managers have long experience with the high-end clothes trade as manufacturers, designers, marketers or even models. But, most important, all the company's managers are devout Sunni Muslims, with half of them having converted to Islam from the middle 1990s onward. The company itself is run according to the tenets of Hanafi (Malik 2003), one of the oldest and most liberal rites of the Sunni confessional. Further, it is this devotional aspect of the company that brought Damascus into the mix. Damascus is not just a major craft center in the Middle East, but also a broadly inclusive center of Islamic learning. It is in many ways the contemporary equivalent of ninth century Baghdad—a magnet for serious students of Islam the world over—and it is one of the locales in which the company's principles crossed paths while conducting their own studies.

So my suit is the product of a unique miniature nonlocal field unto itself, a collection of everyday practices technologically articulated along a dual axis of faith and fashion. Additionally, it is a nonlocal field which now, in some small way, incorporates me as a customer and correspondent. I, in turn, have found the persons within this field attentive, helpful, and unfailingly gracious with my prolonged pestering. And upon receipt of the suit, I also found the company's personnel to be top-notch couturiers.

Of course, there is nothing inherently resistant about ordering a suit from overseas. Between the time I ordered the suit and the time I received it, however, larger circumstances had changed in such a way as to render my order an act of dissent, and perhaps even treason. In those few intervening weeks, the duly appointed executive branch of my government had begun wrapping up a military adventure into Iraq, and was turning its sights upon Iraq's westerly neighbor. This was not an entirely unexpected development. For the past couple of years, statements have issued from Washington, D.C., to accuse Syria of roguish tendencies and even nominate it as a suitable candidate for preemptive nuclear strikes (NPR 2001). But over the same period as my exchanges with the company, official rhetoric about Syria had begun heating to fever pitch, characterizing the country as a rogue state and terrorist haven, a barbaric and dictatorial adjunct to the "axis of evil," riddled with so-called weapons of mass destruction and irrational hatred of "the West."

Such declarations from the state, by corollary, entail that I have provided material support and sympathy to an up and coming enemy. And even more damning, I will continue to do so in future. This is because despite the official campaign to demonize Syria, the hyperextension of my own everyday relations has provided me firsthand experience that the people of world city Damascus are neither rogues, barbarians, enemies nor even necessarily anti-Western—in fact, no small number of Damascus's residents are from "the West." And unsurprisingly, the suit I received in return for inadvertently reaching out to Damascus arrived impeccably styled, carefully crafted, and without the slightest whiff of either biochemical agents or evil about it. All of which has, in a sense, indeed rendered me a sympathizer—the prospect that my new suit could become an epitaph for its Damascene makers fills me with a combination of sorrow, frustration, and—of greatest significance—a deepening certainty that my government's geostrategic pronouncements are highly suspect.

My growing unease with the state's truths illustrates how the dislocalization of our own everyday experiences can not only elide interdiction but also delegitimize the authorities and authoritative narratives that do the interdicting. With the hyperextension of our commonplace social interactions, we breach the boundaries of the body politic to become tangled hybrids of multiaxial collective identities, practiced at and across numerous scales. In the process, our loyalties are challenged repeatedly. Of course, this challenge doesn't make either interdiction or authority simply disappear. But behind interdiction and authority lie institutional collectives like the state, transnational corporations (TNCs), and transnational criminal organizations (TCOs). And behind such institutions are large numbers of people, people who are also hybridizing selves no less engaged in dislocalized practices. So in conjunction with our own dislocalization, our institutions are dismantled, dispersed, remolded, replaced, recombined and set against one another, until they resemble nothing so much as Fernand Leger's murals of the Gordian Knot affixed prophetically to the walls of the U.N. General Assembly Hall. In this tangle is institutional hybridity, produced in the everyday, and a corollary end to geopolitics as we knew them.

The Flexist Triad

Throughout the twentieth century geopolitics was the game of the nation-state, and for much of that century the nation-state was securely propped up by the three legs of the Fordist triad—big government, big business, and big labor. This long-standing formulation of the body politic, however, is fast coming undone. Consider, for instance, border crossers like those at Tijuana's northern edge or, conversely, the industrial plants migrating in the opposite direction—the nonlocal coordination of social relations, their networks of fast transportation and instantaneous communication, has given rise to waves of migration and fluid capital. These waves render the defining boundaries of the nation-state persistently porous. Simultaneously, the growing suspicion of metanarratives (and the vested interests they conceal) increasingly delegitimizes the underlying axioms of the state. This may be seen at both the national and international levels.

Nationally, global formation has amplified the contestation of hegemonic (and often oppressive) regimes, increasing the audibility and influence of previously marginalized others. The drive toward social polyvocality has in turn engendered a backlash, producing a conflicted domestic political landscape of miniworlds and micronations. For example, in the twentieth century's closing decades, the United States saw the emergence of an Afrocentric panracial hip-hop Universal Zulu Nation, a Queer Nation of gay citizen-activists, and a white supremacist Aryan Nation that would like nothing better than the disappearance of the previous two and the federal government along with them.

Diasporization has both heightened and rewoven this fragmentation of the body politic. Such migration is prodigious, abrupt and diverse. And unlike in times previous when departures necessarily curtailed regular contact with the homeland (however conceived), rapid and relatively cheap transport and communications technologies now permit the sustenance of active links with both the homeland and other widespread outposts of the diaspora. Thus dislocalities are strung between world cities, abruptly bringing together "right here" a plethora of the different worlds "out there" and so reforging the streetscapes of world cities into neighborhood intersections of nonlocal fields. As a result, the contents of the territorial nation-state are increasingly denationalized and resistant to unitary renationalization (Appadurai 1996, 189).

Internationally, global formation has entailed the accelerated dislocations of "quicksilver capital." With this has come a chronic transgression of the boundaries of the national economy, one taken advantage of by transnational commercial enterprises both legally sanctioned and otherwise. This foregrounds Gilles Deleuze and Félix Guattari's (1983) claims about capitalism's tendency to "schizophrenize," to wrest all things free from fixed discursive and spatial coordinates. As capital undergoes extraction (and progressively higher degrees of abstraction) from its ecological sources and their transformation through human labor, it is traded less in the form of material such as land or machines and more as a fungibly unitized symbolic thing in itself. Thus capital is ever more readily translated from an emplaced asset into displaced flows. In the process, extracted capital becomes deterritorializable and, in its capacity to flow more freely across territories and their administrative borders, deterritorializing. The territorial state's administrative organs are increasingly elided, dictated to, fused with and, in many instances, purchased outright by the primary players in the international financial markets: the TNC and its shadowy twin, the TCO. Nor are these two institutional categories so exclusive of each other as might be assumed. For example, TNCs and TCOs pass capital back and forth through often circuitous routes. They are also intimately bound up with immigration, and hence contribute heavily to the proliferation of soft planets. Many TNCs, for instance, draw specialized personnel from certain globally mobile ethnonational groups (i.e. Filipino medical personnel, or electrical engineers from India's northeast), and many TCOs, too, are rooted in particular ethnonational formations.

The institutionally hybrid criss-crossing of administrative levels and categories by overlapping memberships in more and less formal "functional networks" (Nederveen Pieterse 1995) is particularly critical when viewed in light of geopolitical futures. It erodes the already permeable walls dividing transnational business enterprises, "legitimate" or otherwise, from the state itself. The revolving door between state apparatuses and TNCs commonly enables legislators, bureaucrats, board members and chief executive officers to swap places at will among ever more diffuse and widespread institutions (see Burkeman and Borger 2001). And a similar access way is yawning wide between the state and TCOs, as exemplified by the speculative links between members of Mexico's former ruling party and narcotics barons, or by the participation of former members of the KGB in the new Russian *mafiya*. Further, the state often welcomes such hybridization in the form of increasingly common "public/private partnerships." Consider, for example, the hybrid of the prison industrial complex (Schlosser 1998). This new cutting edge of absolutist spatial interdiction is a distinct institutional hybrid of the TNC and the state, whether in the form of inmates assembling consumer goods in the People's Republic of China or inmates taking telephone orders for such consumer goods in the for-profit incarceration centers of the United States.

None of this is to claim that institutional hybridity and its new geopolitics entails the death of the nation-state. To the contrary, faced with such punctures and compound fractures of the body politic, nation-states have transformed to adopt an arsenal of tactics bolstering their own bodily integrity. Some have advocated multiculturalism, the idea that a modern nation-state must encompass many nationalities and regulate their interactions. Others have partnered with TNCs to simultaneously institute neomercantilist protections and to champion the ideology of economic neoliberalism, the notion that deregulated international trade enriches all while minimizing the possibility of war (except, apparently, war against those nation-states resistant to neoliberalism). Others have sought to shore up their dominant social order and economic autarchy by cracking down on minority dissent, militarizing their borders against migrants and contraband goods, and tightly delimiting who is entitled to citizenship and trade privileges. Often the same state has deployed these seemingly contradictory strategies simultaneously, as when the passage of the NAFTA is accompanied by the installation of that multilayered interdictory space between San Diego and Tijuana.

Despite efforts to restabilize the territorial state and its constitutive boundaries, the survival of the nation-state as we've known it remains debatable. Perhaps the most extreme example of this is (or, more correctly, was) Yugoslavia, where pressures brought to bear by external financial institutions and Western intelligence operations combined with friction among internal nationalities to provoke the country's violent collapse. More stable nations like the United States, however, are no less immune as citizen militias take up arms in the heartland while affluent urbanites take flight to their privatopian commudities. Despite this, the state shows little sign of withering away. It is, however, not what it used to be. Restructured, replaced onto the scale of the supranational and spliced onto the TNC, the state is now just one of a number of collective players that comprise the apparatuses of globalism—the managerial administration of global formation. And given that corruption refers to the condition wherein state and private administrative apparatuses with extremely varied degrees of legitimacy commingle, in this new geopolitics of postmodernity corruption is not the exception but the norm. The Fordist triad, then, has not so much died as it has drastically transformed into a flexist mutant: ginormous business fused with retrenchant government and infested with metastasized crime.

This hybrid geopolitics and its commingling institutions are not merely suggestive metaphors. They can be explicated in the concrete and by recourse to material artifacts. I have selected three, each a markedly divergent instance of this phenomena. The first, and most briefly told, is a nationality retooled as a globality. The second is a corporate globality transformed and devalorized through its reception in the everyday. And the last is a local resistance plucked from its home to rally opposition to plutocratic globality itself. But behind these heroic scales of analysis, they all begin with us: ourselves, our bodies, and, in the first instance, our taste buds.

Recipe for a Global People

Food is implicit in the construction and reconstitution of identity, personally and collectively. To be Klingon is to eat *gach,* a delicacy indistinguishable from (and often consisting of) a bowl of writhing worms. Hamburgers and a Coke have a long-standing association with being (or wishing to be) "American." Similarly, Ethiopians will often refer to Ndoro Wat, a spicy chicken stew, as their "national dish." And such associations are pregnant with meaning for their consumers. Can one afford a hamburger instead of Ndoro Wat? Does one prefer Ndoro Wat to a hamburger? Does one make a point of proclaiming this preference? These questions take on practical importance for the reconceptualization of self and collective identity, and for their hyperextended enactment as full-blown globalities.

Meiji's Chelsea brand Yogurt Scotch Toffee.

My own discovery of how mastication serves as a means of collective reenactment came upon me as a happy accident, when I happened upon a specific food: the Meiji confectionery company's Chelsea brand toffees, available in flavors including "Yogurt Scotch" and "Sherpa Tea." (For reference, sherpas are native Himalayan guides, and sherpa tea is a hot buttered and churned tea-leaf infusion drunk throughout the highlands of South Asia). There was nothing startling about the toffees themselves. They were commonplace rectangular pieces of hard candy, available ten to a box. The box was emblazoned with the brand name Chelsea, the manufacturer's name, Meiji, the product's flavor designation, and the slogan, "the taste of old Scotland."

All printed in English. On second thought, then, there was indeed something peculiar about this combination of old Scottish tastes with Himalayan beverages and semifermented dairy product.

In calling this combination peculiar, however, I do not mean to say it is somehow senseless or bizarre. Each element of the fusion that is these Meiji toffees carries meanings peculiar to how Japan has negotiated a place in the world throughout the twentieth century. By recovering these meanings (or "lost signifieds"; see Gottdiener 1995), the toffees prove to be a tool for grappling with the emergence of the global within the specific social contexts of Japan. The candy is a symptom of, an active participant in, and a lens on Japanese efforts to reenvision a national identity as "global people" both presently and retroactively into the past. Such efforts are central to claiming a place in the world by countering long-standing historical narratives of isolationism and valorizations of population homogeneity. Thus, unpacking these toffees also reveals how emplaced peculiarities persist, drive the institutional enactment of globalities in very peculiar ways, and so thoroughly imbue the global with distinct eccentricities.

From a long historical perspective, Japan hardly seems the most likely hearth of an alternate globality. The island chain's geographic peripherality, coupled with a succession of isolationist social policies, fostered extreme limitations to off-island contact. Japan was a *sakoku,* a closed country, cut-off under the auspices of the Tokugawa Shogunate's increasingly draconian seclusion decrees of 1634, 1635, and 1636. At least this has long been the official and popularly accepted discourse, going back to the invention of the term *sakoku.* Said invention, however, was not until so late as 1850 (Jansen 2000, 91–92). Under the seclusion decrees, the Shogunate did indeed strictly regulate outside contact, and periodically forbade under pain of death the return of those who had left the islands. Through this, established political and social institutions were preserved from external destabilization. Indigenous unifying discourses were also reinforced by means of these strictures, most significantly the belief that the Japanese can trace their roots to the legendary warrior-deity Ninigi, grandson of the sun-goddess Amaterasu Ōmikami, and the lesser deities who escorted his descent to earth (Philippi 1977). Japan was not, however, isolated. Intense exchanges were maintained with China and intermittently with Korea, and the quasi-annual trade visits of the Dutch "black ships" maintained contact with the opposite end of Eurasia. Japan was, however, pointedly closed to the advances of the missionizing Christian states of Europe, and it was these states that would become imperial powers over the run of Japan's selective seclusion.

How then to reconcile the appearance and persistence of English toffees within Japanese commodity landscapes, let alone toffees infused with the "taste of old Scotland"? An instance of mere exoticism, perhaps? But no exoticism is ever "mere"; there are indeed reasons the Anglo-exotic (or, in this instance, Scotto-exotic) found special favor.

With the appearance of Admiral Matthew Perry's expeditionary force in Edo harbor in 1853, Japanese political elites were motivated at gunpoint to engage the burgeoning world system, which at that time took the form of imperial spheres of influence. Beginning with the populations of major port cities like Edo, Japanese were suddenly forced to consider themselves in relation to those societies they had previously been enjoined to ignore. In essence, reflexiveness went from being willfully immaterial to instrumental in the construction of a national identity. This collective identity crisis was exacerbated by the ease with which Amaterasu's people had been forced into this position by previously inconsequential outsiders, the so-called western barbarians (Paske-Smith 1930). New conceptions of individual and collective selfhood were thus required to overcome the sudden redefinition of being apart-and-above as being parochial, and a corollary recognition that the outcome of such parochialism was collective vulnerability to subjugation.

Such self-reinvention began in earnest with the collapse of the Shogunate and the restoration of the Meiji emperor in 1868. The restoration included the elaboration of the doctrine of *Kokutai* atop the collective originary myth of Amaterasu, claiming that all Japanese were a pyramidal familial hierarchy with the divinely-descended imperial family at the top (Jansen 2000, 601). This nationalizing discourse of valorized particularity, however, was conjoined with a tacit valorization of outsiders' techne. Throughout the Meiji era, the radically restructured apparatuses of the Japanese state pursued the acquisition of foreign expertise with a vengeance, particularly that of the then-leading maritime and industrial powers. Nationally, this entailed reorganizing the Japanese aristocracy after the model of the British royal system (but the governance and policing structure in the Prussian mold), and modeling Japanese industry after that to be found in places like Manchester. At a more immediately personal level, English peppered the speech of young urbanites, kimonos were supplemented with Victorian corsets and bonnets, and English-style confections were consumed in lieu of more familiar sweets like *manju* cakes (for contemporaneous graphic documentation of these transformations, see Yonemura 1990). Thus, faced with an inescapable world system, many Japanese responded by adapting their selves through what they did with, put on, and took into their bodies. Further, it was in this context that Tokyo Kaisha was founded in 1916 to produce caramels and English-style biscuits, the company being renamed Meiji Seika (Meiji Candy) Kaisha in 1924. (*Kaisha* translates as "imperially licensed," itself a post-Shogunate Japanicization of the European mercantilist practice of royally patenting business enterprises). And thus we have Japanese English toffees imbued with Scottish flavor, named for the first post-Shogunate emperor and a well-known district of Central London. Nor is this Anglo-Japanese linkage merely an historical curiosity. It remains active and has taken form beyond the symbolic, as evinced by Meiji's 1973 joint venture with McVities (a subsidiary of the United Kingdom's United Biscuits, which itself became a property of the transnational Finalrealm consortium as of May 2000).

Still, this doesn't explain how Meiji's old Scottish taste comes to foreground yogurt and, more unequivocally incongruous, sherpa tea. The answer to this question lies in a more contemporaneous sense of Japanese social milieus.

Despite the growing assertiveness of both a long-term Korean population and more recent immigrant groups, strong echoes of the Kokutai doctrine persist in Japanese discourses of nationality. Most prominently, it takes the form of *Nihonjinron,* a belief in the inherent superiority of an indivisible and exceptional Japanese people. Nihonjinron is embodied most dramatically in the practices of ultraright activists who, wrapped in *fundoshi* loincloths and brandishing *tanto* daggers, issue calls for the purification of Japan from atop loudspeaker-equipped black vans emblazoned with archaic slogans like "Tenno Heiko Banzai" (roughly translatable as "Vigorously honor the emperor"). Such instances, however, are merely the most extreme expressions of the doctrine. In the mid-1980s, for example, Japanese Government spokesmen repeatedly attributed their country's relative economic success to the supposed racial homogeneity of Japan's labor-force. Most notorious was then prime minister Yasuhiro Nakasone's expansion of this doctrine into a kind of occidentalism (Morley and Robins 1992, 149–50), projected onto the geopolitical stage in his public pronouncement that "America's intellectual level is lower than Japan's because American society has too many blacks, Mexicans, and Puerto Ricans."

Such nativistic racism from a nation-state's principle representative does not serve to endear a national society to others within a system of national societies. It is also an unacceptable liability for a national economy dependent upon amicable export-trade relations, as evinced by U.S. protests against Nakasone's statement and subsequent apologies and amends made by the Japanese state and businesses. Thus, Nihonjinron has been counterbalanced by the practical imperative to protect access to international trade. But equally important, Nihonjinron has been counterbalanced by an escalating consciousness of the pleasures and respect to be reaped by adapting one's mindset to accommodate and experience outside societies. Thus, the "global person" arose as a counterposition to the advocacy of Nihonjinron. "Global person" is a Japanese descriptor for those who jettison their parochial worldviews so as to make the most of worldwide cultural and business opportunities. Since the late 1970s, Japanese aspirations to global personhood have run high, especially among two influential classes: lifelong corporate employees called *sararimen* (a Japanicization of "salary man"), and the *shinjinrui* (literally, "new people") born into a Japan that had already become a world industrial and financial power. (It is interesting to note the isomorphism between the idea of attaining the status of "global person" by means of self-conscious adaptation to a larger society of cultures, and the Confucian idea of elevating oneself to the status of a "sage/cultured person/superior person" through the equipoise absorption of elite urban norms.)

By the late 1980s the global people became sufficiently influential to impel a reconceptualization of Nihonjinron and also a conjoined reconstruction of Japan's history. In the new history, Japan's long-standing depiction as a willfully isolated periphery was replaced by depictions of Japan as the eastern trading terminus of the ancient Silk Road, and a fully participating partner in the development and dissemination of everything from noodles to Buddhism. While evidentially debatable both pro and con, this Silk Road association was rendered factual by means of a barrage of popular and material culture. Japan Home Broadcasting funded extensive documentaries on Central Asia, as with 1990's multiple-part (and multimillion-yen) travelogue across the breadth of the Silk Road. Beers were advertised in the context of young Japanese safariing through the Gobi desert on camelback. And most prominently, food was infused with flavors from South Asia, the Himalayas, and the Middle East. Curries became a fixture of Japanese fast food, giving rise to products like Tohato Seika Company's Kararit brand curry puffs (featuring "much hotter ethnic taste"). But owing to the Japanese culinary tradition's disinclination toward spicy heat, flavors like yogurt and masala tea proved particularly popular. Hence Meiji's Chelsea brand Yogurt Scotch toffees, introduced among a deluge of yogurt flavored products throughout the 1980s, and Sherpa Tea toffees, introduced roughly a decade later. They are both candy and flavor novelties, accommodating national tastes for what one Japanese confectionery developer described to me as "ethnically inauthentic shifty food." But through their consumption, they are simultaneously a means by which to viscerally cultivate one's self as global, consciously positioned both presently and in the ancestral past within a larger community of societies.

But the contextual problematics of location throw a further twist into this story. My own initial exposure to Meiji Yogurt Scotch toffees did not occur in Japan. Rather, I encountered them at the downtown L.A. branch of the nations-wide (in Japan and the United States) Yaohan supermarket (now Mitsuwa Marketplace). As I have noted elsewhere in this work, global formation does indeed include capital flows and internationally dispersed offices, in this instance those of Japanese TNCs with an overseas presence in L.A. And such flows and offices are reliant upon the presence of specific sorts of persons. In this instance the persons in question are sararimen posted to Los Angeles, and the families that accompany them. Their concentration in L.A.'s Little Tokyo (or "J-Town," to locals) in turn invigorated existent Japanese schools, cultural institutions, innumerable curry restaurants, and department stores, and accelerated the creation of new ones. Yaohan was one such store and on its shelves, amongst the sheets of seaweed, green tea powder, and dried cuttlefish, Yogurt Scotch and Sherpa Tea toffees were a constant presence. And seemingly a relatively popular one: I periodically indented tiny inconspicuous *xs* into the cellophane wrapping on the bottoms of these boxes and found they had disappeared in two to three weeks.

There is no certainty, of course, that the candies were purchased by Japanese. According to staffers (augmented by my own observations), clientele at any given moment ranged from one tenth to one third non-Japanese. Thus, L.A.'s Yaohan cum Mitsuwa has become a particularly dense space of translation, where it is not uncommon to see Japanese shoppers describing to their non-Japanese compatriots how certain foods are 'correctly' prepared and consumed. But this polyvalence only heightens the complexity of the candies in question. In Japan, they are elements in an emergent commodity landscape that historicizes the hyperextension of Japanese identity, sensually associating it with mythic locales distant in time and space. For the Japanese expatriate in L.A.'s Mitsuwa, the candies are elements in a dislocalized commodity landscape that reminds the expats of their distinctiveness and sensually reconnects them with home. And for the non-Japanese customer, the candies are components in a transplanted commodity landscape that affords vicarious experiences of an exotic Japanese other.

Thus this confection plays a role in redefining and helps to express a globally constituted identity when consumed in Japan, yet becomes a constituent element of "Japaneseness" elsewhere. In the process, Meiji's toffees point towards the emergence of a hyperextendedly attenuated Japanese identity that complexly articulates Nihonjinron with global personhood. This identity reimagines Japaneseness not in terms of isolate purity or global assimilation but as a uniquely valuable collective actor in the globally formative exchanges of both the present and the early-to-middle second millennium. And the contribution of this valuable collective actor has been globally formative indeed: the set of (post)industrial practices now known as "just in time" were originally known by a number of names: *haijinka, jidoka, kanban, muda, muri, nagara, seiketsa, seiso,* and *seiton* (Skorstad 1991, 1077). All are Japanese words describing a form of industrial organization wherein the rapid transfer of small batches of goods is coordinated by means of trust-based face-to-face relations between solitary craftspeople and small businesses. Thus particular everyday practices embedded in Japanese social relations have hyperextended and been adapted worldwide to become one of the largest-order dynamics of global formation: Flexism.

But this hyperextension of Japaneseness is more than just a constellation of practices that has happened to inform the global. It is also an assemblage of policy practices that self-reflexively strives to shape the global. This is made clear by the fact that, following in the footsteps of Japanese taste buds, tourism, culture workers, and capital, in 1999 the Silk Road was traversed by a functionary of the Japanese state. In this crossing, an established apparatus of supranational governance has been transformed. Following intense lobbying by Japanese state ministries (most notably the Cultural Affairs Department of the Foreign Ministry) and allied cultural organizations, Japan's former ambassador to France, Koichiro Matsuura, was chosen to head the United Nations Educational, Scientific, and Cultural Organization (UNESCO). The larger intent of this selection was to counter Japanese assertions of UNESCO's Eurocentric bias, to restore some degree of universality by injecting an Asian intellectual influence, and to reform the organization's notoriously inefficient and cronyistic bureaucracy (Millett 1999).

More concretely, the effect of Matsuura's selection has been a redirection of UNESCO's attention and funding toward such relatively new Central Asian nation-states as Kazakhstan, Uzbekistan, and Kirghizia. In this reformulation of UNESCO's priorities, increased attention was paid to the identification, preservation and restoration of Buddhist sites and artifacts, and hence to preserving a legacy newly redefined as evidence of Japan's historical hyperextension throughout the region. At the level of geopolitical discourse, this in turn raised the specter of Huntington's clash of "Japanese" and "Western" civilizations. In fact, the frequency with which critics equated Matsuura's appointment with nascent anti-Westernism led Yasukuni Enoki, director-general of the Cultural Affairs Department, to issue public statements hotly denying that civilizational clash had anything to do with the matter (Millett 1999).

But the real outcomes of how this Silk Road–centric globality has been institutionally actualized are not to be found in any supposed fissure between Japan and its occidental other. Rather, such outcomes have emerged as unintended consequences on the ground, where the global people have stumbled over an assortment of other would-be globalities rising and falling along the Silk Road's itinerary. In the formerly Soviet Central Asian republics, at least according to UNESCO staff members, Matsuura's supranationally bureaucratic enactment of reinvented Japaneseness has run across capital-starved ex-commissars torn between reimagining themselves as khans, caliphs, or some combination of the two. Here, investments in cultural preservation have had a great deal to do with following through on promises made by midlevel diplomats over a fifth round of vodka toasts, and have frequently ended up redirected towards disinterring epic histories of nomadic tribal groups from out of the contents of Soviet-era museum vaults.

In other settings, though, the diversity of opinion over just whose globality the Silk Road's evidentiary artifacts and heritage sites should serve has been more explosive. This proved especially true in 2001, when the explosions became literal. In late February of that year, the Taliban regime governing much of Afghanistan announced that, in keeping with their idiosyncratically literal interpretation of Qur'anic proscriptions against idolatrous imagery, two gigantic Buddha sculptures in Bamian would be demolished (AP 2001a, 4 March, 5 March, 6 March). This provoked a crash effort, spearheaded by UNESCO's Matsuura, to either preserve or relocate the sculptures. UNESCO's campaign in turn produced such effects as protests by numerous presidents, prime ministers and high priests, and an offer by the New York Metropolitan Museum to transport the 120- and 175-foot-tall stone statues to Manhattan. By March 12, however, the sculptures had instead been blasted to oblivion. All that remained were two empty twenty-story-tall nooks in the cliffs where the statues had sheltered since the early part of the first millennium (AP 2001a, 27 March). In response, Matsuura declared an "Afghan cultural heritage crisis" and decried the Taliban's act as the "cold and calculated destruction of cultural properties which were the heritage of the Afghan people, and, indeed, of the whole of humanity." Further, Matsuura instructed his special envoy, Pierre Lafrance, to "explore all avenues that may allow for the safeguarding of the other treasures of Afghanistan's pre-Islamic heritage" from a repetition of this "true cultural crime" (UNESCO Press, 2001). Thus, the geopolitical discourse was again tacitly cast in the mold of civilizational clash: a tug of war for the Silk Road between Japanese Buddhism and resurgent Islam, couched in the political rhetorics of Western humanism and fought through the very material practice of the conservation and demolition of signifying artifacts.

But once again, circumstances on the ground evince far more tangled webs across which globalities are enacted. The Taliban's focus at the time was not outward toward Japan or the world at large, but inwards towards consolidating control of Afghanistan's territory. Critical to completing this task was the conquest of Bamian's contested terrain. Long inhabited by ethnic Hazara practitioners of Shiite Islam, Bamian had been less than receptive to the Taliban's militant hybrid of Pashtun nationalism and intensely puritanized Sunnism (Santos 2001). Further, many Pashtuns saw themselves as deserving retribution against the Hazaras who, as members of the United

Front that ruled Afghanistan immediately after the Soviet withdrawal, were implicated in widespread abuses of power. And in turn, many Hazara remained embittered over how, under Afghanistan's ancien regime, they were regarded as a servant class. (But despite these frictions, all the Pashtuns and Hazaras I have spoken with have been unanimous in their insistence that the destruction of the Bamian sculptures was un-Qur'anic and that, were this not the case, Egypt's Valley of the Kings would be just a rubble pit today.)

Caught in the midst of all this historical, ideological, and territorial tension were the two megalithic sculptures. Regarded locally not as Buddhas at all but as Solsol (Year after Year) and Shahmamma (King Mother) (AP 2001a, 27 March), the twinned personifications of time and space, the sculptures were both longstanding signifiers of Hazara identity and a source of tourist income. Thus, as a proclamation of territorial dominance and for the price of a few artillery shells, the war machine of the Taliban demolished the Bamian Hazaras' most beloved and enduring landmarks, and legitimized the act by mobilizing a questionably Qur'anic discourse. In erasing these towering sculptural elements from the landscape, the Taliban therefore accomplished three ends. First, they eradicated the prodigious spatiomaterial anchors of an intensely localized and restive collective, stripping the Hazara's space of its uniquely (and literally) anthropomorphized "placeness." Second, they expunged the Hazara's terrain as a point-of-interest from the maps of world travelers for the long term. Finally, the cavernous nooks in the cliff face are now left haunted by the seething ghostly presence (see Gordon 1997) of Solsol's and Shahmamma's palpable absence, a lacuna that will serve for perhaps centuries to come as a reminder of a violently authorial redefinition of place.

Knotted about the voided cliff face at Bamian, then, is a scale-crossing tangle of institutionally embodied identities. Bamian has become a site where one collective's self-reinvention and hyperextension through the mechanisms of international bureaucracy collided with another collective's struggle for territory in which to nationalize a neotraditionalist theology. Out of kindness for you, the reader, I will refrain from further complicating this tale with a full discussion of the Taliban's rootedness in Saudi Arabia's dominant religious doxa, its contentious prior relations with the U.N., or of its active linkages to the intelligence and aid agencies of the U.S. and Pakistani states (see, e.g., *Times of India* 2001) and their intersection with such highly dubious and now defunct transnational financial institutions as the Bank Commerce Credit International (Truell 1992; Labvier 2000). Suffice it to say that such complication is both present and precisely the point. It is such cross-connections between administrative sectors, spatial scales and highly varied degrees of legitimacy that constitute alternate globalities, their manifold intersections, and their hybridic participants.

Toward a Viscous Planet

The marked disorderliness produced at the crossroads of these would-be world reorderings reveals how institutional hybridization, and such concomitant dynamics as social fragmentation, cultural dislocation, economic integration and administrative interoperation, do not occur of their own accord. They find common cause in the hyperextension of the messiness of everyday life. And at the same time, these larger dynamics intersect to form chains of hyperextended processes by means of which the reconstitution of personal and collective identity may jump scale to remold and cross-connect institutions while projecting them erratically into the global arena. In so doing, it becomes apparent that every institution, from business enterprises to legislative apparatuses and criminal syndicates, is being reforged and spliced together from the inside and the everyday outwards, out as far as planetary supranationality.

The administrative mechanisms of global formation, then, are characterized by the proliferation and magnification of distinct and persistent eccentricities. These overarching mechanisms are practiced and produced in the everyday, constructed and repeatedly reconstructed differently across different scales at different locales. Thus, our aggregated everyday practices of global formation recombinatively form us and, through us, hybridize our collectives and institutions. Nor is there any reason that the institutions created to regulate, abet and valorize global capital flow should be any different. So the distinct, the eccentric, difference and the everyday must therefore be part and parcel of institutional hybridity's currently hegemonic structural outcomes: supranational state apparatuses, globally enforced macroeconomic logic, and the corollary spread of commodity culture.

7
The Limits of Coca-Colonization

At their broadest, supranational state apparatuses enact collective claims about how the world is and should be, claims to empowerment and claims about rights. Insofar as formal pursuance of such claims is globally enacted through membership in collective bodies, the administration of global formation is thus a corporatist endeavor. To leave it at this, however, would be woefully imprecise. After all, corporatism as a form of social organization can include both Benito Mussolini's Italy and the now fraying social welfare states of Fennoscandia. Further, leaving it at this would be hopelessly naïve: some claims are heard more loudly and enacted more unreservedly than others. At present, the claims carrying the loudest voice and greatest weight are those made upon "national states to guarantee the domestic and global rights of capital" (Sassen 1999, 108–9). It is these claims, underpinned by appeals to a technical rationality of economic expertise, that are engendering the preeminent international regulatory institutions and, through them, the hegemony of plutocratic globality.

The dominance of such claims upon the state renders it equally apparent that the claimant must be a well-organized collective with broad reach, deep pockets, and a corollary reliance upon capital's "quicksilverization": the transnational corporation (TNC). Thus the TNC becomes a principal actor in the institutionally hybrid formation of the supranational state, producing through globalist administration an operating environment best suited to the practices and worldview of the TNC. Such an environment is one of a liberalized unitary world market, a readily utilizable world labor pool, and accessible global consumersheds. In the process we see the emergence of an

149

economistically (or, perhaps more correctly, economystically) legitimized plutocratic corporatism on a planetary scale (see Hardt and Negri 2000, which refers to this emergent world order simply as "empire"). This constitutes a significant shift in the determination of which claims will be heard and accommodated—away from the long-valorized ideal of one person/one vote and toward that of one dollar (or euro, or yen)/one vote. In this shift lies the privatopian shadow state (Wolch 1990) on a grand scale, from whence those aforesaid claims to the domestic and international rights of capital are privileged. Nor is such privileging merely discursive. It takes concrete form in adjudicative decisions rendered from behind a thinning relict veneer of liberal democracy. Unmitigated, the end result of this process is a global latifundium: an ecocidal planetary plantation in which all things from animals, vegetables and minerals to human desires are monocultured for ready harvest.

The degree to which such a global latifundium is already a material given is illustrated by how much more equal some collectives have become than others. While every collective has its own geographical distribution and discourses that enable it to wrest influence, there are inarguable asymmetries in the scope and scale of these influences. Akin to ethnicities, dislocalized nationalities, technicities and the like, institutions like Citibank or Vivendi are axes of identity and dislocalized collectives. What distinguishes a Citibank or a Vivendi, however, is the fact that unlike other collectives, they are first and foremost teleological (Churchman 1971). They have an explicit codified purpose with formally identified subgoals, and clearly delineated organizational hierarchies for the accomplishment of that purpose. This purposiveness is what defines the collectivity of the TNC, and it is toward the accomplishment of its purpose that the TNC's members are carefully selected, their practices explicitly defined, and their relationships consciously coordinated and concerted. In so doing, the TNC is uniquely effective in achieving its purpose through reconfiguring the material world into shapes of its own choosing (see Orwell 1949, 270).

This is not to say that all TNCs are alike. Each has its own strategies, practices, and culture (Schoenberger 1997), varying degrees of local embeddedness (e.g., Yeung and Li 2000), and each is made up of persons with their own complexly articulated identities (were this not the case, I would have been deprived the insights of the former Nike employees so critical to the discussion to follow). But the raison d'être common to all TNCs, as defined by shareholders and directors alike, is profit optimization over a given period of time. Subgoals (or means) are determined by a nested hierarchy of autocracies, beginning with chief executive and operating officers who delegate varying degrees of decision making autonomy to corporate divisions and geographically distinct branches. Delegation is the key to the TNC in other senses as well. In their discussion of how "knowledge, global networks and flows, or sociality" are *materially produced* in specific and local circumstances," John Law and Kevin Hetherington (2000; italics in original) point to the TNC as a space-spanning hybrid actor-network of humans and nonhumans together. Such a "net of materially heterogeneous elements" creates the possibility of action and knowledge at a distance (or perhaps more accurately, intervention and surveillance, respectively). This possibility embodies as "capitalized" territorial and bodily "knowing locations," principle sites at which data is gathered, analyzed, and acted upon. Knowing locations therefore are uniquely empowered to function as "obligatory points of passage," junctions from whence all roads emanate, and as a result enjoy concentrated "discretion" to make decisions and issue determinations. In turn, the competitive advantages of such knowing locations are established, sustained and expanded by two processes. The first is the production of "immutable mobiles," a hybridic agent-like "network of elements that holds its shape as it moves" through space to arrive and act at some distant locale. And the second is delegation in a very specific sense, the knowing location's power to tell immutable mobiles what they will do once they have arrived at their intended destinations. Through this system, the significance of directly controlling the *means* of production is deemphasized in favor of the command of production and distribution in general. Thus, an executive is able to sit at a desk in an office, see global fluctuations in coffee prices, and initiate actions that may concentrate a TNC's wealth while simultaneously impoverishing multiple agrarian communities in Kenya or Columbia.

This actor-network perspective casts a new light on the two different bodies of thought explicating the *T* in TNC. Market power theory views corporate transnationalization as a result of firms attempting to increase their market share and control of labor by expanding beyond mature and stagnating nationally bounded consumersheds and labor pools (Hymers 1976). Internalization theory stresses the transaction costs of doing business over broad distances, and proposes the TNC as the result of firms' cutting out the "middleman" and related costs by absorbing oversees operations (Coase 1937). But in so doing, the enactments and performances comprising the networked heterogeneous relations of the TNC position it between and above the administrative collectives of territorial nation-states, and undermine the teleological collectivitization of more place-bound technicities like labor unions. Therefore neither Stephen Hymer's nor Ronald Coase's view necessarily excludes the other's (Pitelis and Sugden, 1991), recasting the TNC as a not at all invisible hand in a velvet-lined iron glove. It is this hand that is most active in sculpting, and lies heaviest upon, both the globally deregulated marketplace and the supranationalizing state apparatuses responsible for its (de)regulation.

The TNC's concentration of capital, influence and discretion renders it central to the globally deregulated market, and the TNC's personnel central to the enactment of global administration and supranational state apparatuses. But it also renders the TNC the primary player in determining what and how materiel flows through the global marketplace, and thus in the formation of a relentlessly influential commodity culture. Or more completely, in the formation of a planetary ecumene characterized by waged labor, the mass production and distribution of commodities, and the broad dissemination via mass communications of meanings ascribed to these artifacts. At its extreme the reach of TNCs (particularly those of the United States, Europe and Japan) takes the form of coca-colonization, a seeming force of neocolonial nature by which Western consumer culture is globally disseminated to supplant all other cultural forms. Such a force gives the appearance of stark inevitability. This was exemplified during a 1998 action against the construction of a McDonald's in Pecs, Hungary, just across the central square from the city's Dom Ter cathedral. According to Hungarian colleagues, protesters who had occupied the square chanted "Ez a mi wesztunk," Magyar for "This is *our* west!" In Magyar, however, there is no *w*. It is used exclusively for foreign "borrow-words", and not readily pronounced by Hungarians. As a result the chant often came out, with willfully ironic intent on the part of the chanters, as "Ez a mi vestunk"—"This is our destiny" (Krinski 2000). Thus, the enactment of hegemony (Gramsci 1971) by and in the collective body of the TNC appears as a foregone conclusion. But is this indeed our destiny? Or, as with the world city and the metapolis at large, are there other persons and practices at serious play as well?

Polyvalent Commodity Cultures

An old friend and mentor of mine has one answer to these questions, an answer that mixes hope and despair to impel a personal practice of hyperextended activism. Following a bout with cancer some years ago, this friend retired to indulge his love of mountaineering and took to spending much of the year in Nepal. He did not, however, concentrate his attentions on the country's legendary peaks, but upon the southern flatland of the Terai and its villagers, the Tharu.

For centuries, the Tharu have lived in courtyard houses formed and covered by the women of the house in seamless layers of local white clay. Once a year, during the festival of Tihar (know as Divali in much of South Asia), these same women paint the white walls with elaborate murals inviting good fortune by welcoming in the goddess Lakshmi.

My mentor's focus has become photodocumenting the paintings and one-of-a-kind column forms on these sculpted clay houses. He regards this mission with no small urgency because, as expressed by Croneille Jest, "If you want to see more of this culture, you'd better act fast, for it is rapidly disappearing under the impact of the newly completed highway and the influx of other peoples from the mountains and India" (cited in Meyer and Deuel 1993). Or, in the succinct words of one Tharu, "Yes, we used to paint our houses, but not anymore" (Meyer and Deuel 1994).

It is not just the paintings on the houses that are vanishing, but the houses themselves. As the East-West Highway brings tourism and trade between India and Katmandu, income disparities within Tharu villages have increased sharply. Corollary to this, the new elites "improve" their residences first by reconstructing them in more durable (but less plastic) concrete masonry units, and ultimately by replacing the house forms with entirely new ones. The designs of these new houses are commonly imported from India, but they ultimately originate with such Southern Californian suburban tract development companies as Kaufman and Broad. And while the painted houses may be fewer and farther between, the paintings are not. Increasingly, they are produced on portable substrates like paper or bark by village collaboratives comprised of both women and men, generating a mass of Tharu tourist art for export.

Central to the design of the East-West Highway is its layout and dimensioning, intended to accommodate tractor-trailer traffic carrying forty-foot-long intermodal cargo containers. These prosaic steel containers have quietly become the totem of our age, standardized and perpetually circulating units that may carry anything from automobile components to stowaway refugees or Taliban prisoners of war across land and sea. States throughout the world, otherwise subjected to strict austerity measures, are indebting themselves with spending on highway rationalization to obviate the common sight of overturned intermodal cargo containers alongside dirt roads. But are these containers cornucopias brimming with surreal gardens of global delights, Pandora's boxes concealing a blitzkrieg of consumerism, or something else entirely?

At first glance, the proliferation of commodities and associated advertising suggests the ascendance of a TNC puppet master employing the air-, sea- and roadways as strings firmly affixed to the bodies of consumers across the globe. Near Tiananmen and Red Squares, queues form around McDonald's franchises. Kellogg's builds a plant in central India with the expectation of eventually shifting regional breakfast tastes from chapatis to Corn Flakes. Both the Czech president and Druze militiamen cover their butts with Levis jeans. The precise incrementalization of time, essential to operation of a 'round-the-clock capital market, has become nearly as omnipresent as Mickey Mouse and Michael Jackson. Or consider the growing global utilization of logo T-shirts as outerwear. The garment is increasingly incidental to the imprinted symbol, with body width corporate logos indicating "the status and income of the wearer, loyalty or trust in the trademark" and "an identity of sorts: I am a person (are you?) who drinks this sort of beer, or soft drink, and wears this brand of sunglasses" (Cullum-Swan and Manning in Riggins 1994, 416).

Such a story of coca-colonization triumphant, however, would imply the emergence of a world well-ordered (or perhaps "new ordered") from the top down. Or, more apropos, from the West outward. But such a place seems to have no real world correlate. Consider, for instance, how that West is regularly nettled and the TNC periodically under siege across North Africa and South Asia (sometimes literally, as with the Indian state's forced closure of McDonalds or the destruction of Cargill RSA Proprietary Limited facilities by Karnatic farmers), or the (spottily obeyed, admittedly) edicts of Iran's Revolutionary Council banning the use of satellite reception dishes.

But a tale of supranational Western advance and non-Western resistance drastically oversimplifies. The same broadcast signals exiled by the mullahs are excoriated on the floor of the U.S. Congress. Cultural critics in Taiwan decry the penetration of subtitled American entertainment while spokespersons for the People's Republic of China decry that of Taiwan, and the Tibetan government in exile that of the PRC. Exxon and Amnesty International may both insist on globally applicable standards, but are the standards of these two Western institutions in accord, or even commensurable? Is the Confucianist corporatism of the Singaporean citistate Westernized or resistant? How to situate the fact that, following the 1991 attack on Ayodhya's Babri Masjid mosque in northern India, toy stores catering to Hindu nationalist clientele began selling (and selling out of) Lord Rama action figures mass-produced under the auspices of small U.S.-based import/export firms? Where do we situate the "West" and the "non-West" in transactions where Afghani kilims, woven in Pakistan's refugee camps with depictions of the Kalashnikovs and Hind E's of the Soviet intervention, are sold on L.A.'s Melrose Avenue to twenty-somethings tattooed with archaic Maori spirals?

Even where the outright disappearance of locally distinct cultural forms is occurring, it is not necessarily an indicator of underlying coca-colonization but of more complex and polyvalent articulations. Consider, for instance, the Ndebele of South Africa. Like the Tharu, the Ndebele are noted for their painted houses, decorated with bold polychromed geometric designs. Often, these designs are rich with such "Westernisms" (Vogel 1991; see also Jules-Rosette 1990) as celebratory geometric stylizations of airplanes, electric street lights, and assorted other commodities denied the Ndebele under apartheid. But the relationship of the ruling regime to the Ndebele was not a simple one of hegemon to disappeared other. During the apartheid era the ruling National Party celebrated tribal differences. This served to represent South Africa as a nation of separate ethnic states, maintaining white minority rule by geographically and culturally dividing 'black Africans' into separate, and hence disarticulated, tribal formations (Christopher 1994). Part of this practice took the form of state support for the display and marketing of tribally distinct material culture, as with the Department of Tourism's Ndebele KwaMsiza "tourist village." In response, South African blacks sought to detribalize themselves in order to unite against white rule, resulting in "a somewhat ironical situation, with interest groups associated with the white government of the past enthusiastically promoting African tradition, and the inheritors of that tradition rejecting it." As a result, "the only people who appear to be immune to that charm [of Ndebele painted motifs] are the urban Ndebele; one is far more likely to see Ndebele designs in the suburbs of traditionally white cities than in the traditionally black townships. (Powell 1995, 138).

Further, the motifs can now be found in Washington, D.C., as a mural commissioned by Bavarian Motor Works of North America for the Museum of Women's Art, and machine-printed on the textiles of Kar Hing brand blouses from the PRC. Thus, while the Tharu house-forms may fall victim to Tharu inclusion *in* a global commodity culture, the Ndebele equivalent has been undermined by Ndebele resistance to forced isolation *from* global commodity culture, and the motifs now largely survive through their assimilation into that same culture.

So in answer to the question that began this discussion, coca-colonization need not be our destiny. It is the case that the TNC's flexibly delegated autocracy has enabled it, as a teleological collective, to assert hegemony within the global market. But control of markets does not necessarily correlate with control of people's consciousness, which maintain variable degrees of autonomy (Althusser 1997), and of their subsequent practices. Thus, coca-colonization is not a fait accompli. A global commodity culture is necessarily polyvalent and indeterminate. Certainly, it is to some extent formed deterministically within the vertical circuits of global formation; the productive, administrative and distributive organs of supranational institutions. But the product of these organs must eventually tangle in the lateral circuits of global formation; the nonlocal webs within which located persons negotiate the courses and meanings of their everyday lives. Owing to this articulation of plutocratic globality with hyperextended everyday life "a world economy under the control of multinational corporations and institutions . . . the dismantling of social welfare structures in the metropolis and the externalization of class tensions onto unprotected workers and consumers at the periphery . . . [and] the relentlessness of capital in seeking new areas for investment has also led to unexpected emergences and convergences in the field of culture" (Lipsitz 1994, 32). Further, such unexpected convergences themselves extend outward to inform globalities. This underscores the imperative to confront the specificities of how the TNC and its output are received, refashioned, and resisted in the everyday, while simultaneously engaging the ongoing everyday (re)formation of the TNC itself. I do so by explicating these problematics through an exploration of an iconically global commodity as it drifts from its globally diffuse production processes and, in turn, gradually comes loose from its brand image. In my own narration of this artifact, I will drift among the object, its production, and its image to delineate the specificities and significances of intersections between the TNC, nation-states, territorial markets, and identities both local and otherwise.

Nike: The Fallen Icon

Some years ago, twenty-one intermodal cargo containers fell overboard off the container ship Hansa Carrier during a severe storm. At least four of those containers broke open on the floor of the north Pacific Ocean, leaving their contents of roughly 60,000 Nike sneakers at the mercy of deep-water currents. This accident proved to be a happy one, however, as researchers descended upon the event to read oceanic turbulence from the subsequent spatial disposition of the shoes (Ebbesmeyer and Ingraham 1992). Thus, Nike athletic shoes can be as useful for gauging turbulent flows as for covering feet.

To be precise, though, the shoes themselves are not actually the product of Nike. Nike is expert at marketing and design, but doesn't "know the first thing about manufacturing" (Korzeniewicz 1994, 251), so the company is an obligatory point of passage for the production of athletic wear, and one exceedingly rich in discretionary decision-making power. But in the diverse unauthorized ways the Nike brand has been popularly received, refashioned, and retransmitted, it has suffered extreme degrees of detournement, subversion, and contradiction. In the process, the turbulence of global formation's everyday practice has transformed the company from a celebrated point of passage into a demonized locus of opposition to the TNC and to plutocratic globality in general.

Nike was founded by Phil Knight, a University of Oregon business student and avid runner. He entered the shoe industry in 1964, selling running shoes manufactured by the Japanese firm Onitsuka Tiger. In 1968, Knight and his former coach formed Nike (originally Blue Ribbon Sports) and began production of shoes to their own specifications, initially through Onitsuka and, following a break with the Japanese firm over distribution rights, through a number of subcontractors. Competing against then leaders in the field, German firms Adidas and Puma, Nike concentrated on technological innovation. They invented the rubber waffle sole in 1975, followed in 1978 by the "Air Nike," a shoe cushioned by a balloon-like air-filled insole (Korzeniewicz 1994).

Selling initially to track-and-field athletes and joggers during the running boom of the 1970s, Nike responded to the collapse of the jogging fad by shifting focus onto other sports, most notably basketball (Strasser and Becklund 1991). This shift, coupled with aggressive marketing (forty million dollars in advertising for 1988) and diversification into full lines of sportswear and athlete promotion, earned Nike 37 percent of the U.S. sportswear market. In 1989, Nike topped Reebok to become the highest grossing sportswear manufacturer globally, and according to the Hoover Company Database currently sells merchandise in about 140 countries (and online). The Nike logo is prominently displayed on numerous nation-states' Olympic teams, uniforms of the National Football League, various collegiate athletic associations, and the bodies of innumerable top-ranked athletes (many of whom are themselves incorporated).

Flexist production processes dependent on new communications technologies are largely responsible for Nike's structural organization, and for its success. Nike's headquarter "World Campus," a three-billion-dollar complex built around an artificial lake in Beaverton, Oregon, houses the company's chief administrators, marketers, and product designers. These core employees collaborate to generate designs for the roughly one hundred new shoes added to Nike's product range each year. These designs are then sent via satellite to computer assisted design and manufacturing contractors in Taiwan and South Korea for the production of prototypes and higher-end models, and faxed to production contractors who will be responsible for taking the prototypes of lower-end models into mass production.

Ninety-nine percent of Nike's shoes are physically produced in Asia and, increasingly, Mexico and Central America. Product assembly consists of sewing together pieces of the leather uppers, gluing rolled and pressed outsoles together with insoles, adhering the upper to completed soles and trimming the product prior to labeling and packaging. While this work is commonly conducted under the auspices of South Korean and Taiwanese contractors, the majority of the work is performed in the Peoples' Republic of China, Vietnam, Thailand, the Philippines, and Indonesia. By working through subcontractors, Nike from its earliest inception has been able to externalize the burden of relocating production, a significant expense given that "Nike is forever on the lookout for cheap production sites. If costs in a particular factory move too far out of line, productivity will have to rise to compensate, or Nike will take its business elsewhere. The firm uses about

40 factories; 20 have closed in the past five years or so and another 35 have opened" (M. Clifford 1992, 56). This "ruthlessness with which Nike pares its costs," conferring the additional benefit of rapid response to changing consumer tastes, earned Nike a net profit of $325 million at the time, up over 300 percent from five years earlier.

Flexist production arrangements also provided Nike an early layer of plausible deniability against charges of labor exploitation, as demonstrated by Nike's then general manager in Jakarta: "They are our subcontractors, it's not within our scope to investigate [alleged labor violations]" (Schwarz 1991, 16). In that year, six Indonesian factories with a total indigenous work-force of 24,000 exported more than $200 million worth of Nikes. Selling for as much as $130, these shoes cost roughly twelve dollars a pair to produce and, of that, labor costs comprised twelve cents (based on a wage of just under fourteen cents hourly and under an hour production time per pair of shoes; Schwarz 1991; Ballinger 1992). The typical assembly employee of a Nike subcontractor in Indonesia at the time was, and a decade later still is, a woman in her late teens or early twenties, commonly an immigrant from outlying agricultural areas (Ballinger 1992). She had likely been selected for the job because, as a young migrant female, she would have better eyesight, smaller and more nimble hands, and would be less likely to object to work-ing conditions. She earned approximately $1.03 per day in 1992 and up to $2.26 by 1996, well below the Indonesian Government's definition of $4.00 as 'minimum physical need' (Global Exchange 1996). She likely rented, and still rents, a shanty without electricity or running water on the outskirts of Jakarta. Among these workers, malnutrition remains common, as well as intestinal parasites and iron deficiencies. These conditions are exacerbated in the factory by poor seating, intense heat, poor air circulation, excessive dust and noise levels, poor lighting, unsatisfactory sanitation facilities, toxin exposure, and work schedules of more than sixty hours per week (White 1991; Global Exchange 1996; for the sunsequent reproduction of these con-ditions in Vietnam see CounterPunch 1999). Finally, overtime often goes uncompensated, and complaints about working conditions or failures to meet quotas may result in verbal abuse or docked wages.

While such working conditions are forbidden under Indonesian labor law, a shortage of inspectors keeps enforcement lax. Attempts to unionize outside the meek, state-controlled All Indonesia Workers Union are met with intimidation and physical violence and, although "the right to hold a strike is protected by the constitution . . . exercise of that right is still not tolerated in Indonesia because it is harmful to both sides" (Manpower Minister Batubara, quoted in Schwarz 1991, 14). The situation is little different in Vietnam, one of Nike's newest production sites. Here workers receive less than $2.00 per day—$1.00 short of "adequate living standards" (Cushman 1998, 1), safety protections are spottily provided at best (CounterPunch 1999), and workers have regularly experienced abuse. Most notorious of the latter, in 1997, fifty-six female employees were forced to run twice around the 1.2-mile perimeter of the Pouchen factory in Dong Nai as punishment for wearing nonregulation workshoes. Ironically, this occurred on March 8, marked in Vietnam as International Women's Day (CLR 1997).

Production conditions contrast dramatically with conditions amongst core employees back at the Beaverton World Campus, who receive annual incomes in the five-to-six figure range augmented by the "LifeTrek" flexible benefits plan. Michael Jordan, signed in 1984 as a guard for the Chicago Bulls, offers an even greater contrast. Nike structured its entrance into the field of basketball around the Air Jordan, a red and black air-insoled athletic shoe tied to the specifications and person of Michael Jordan himself. In return, Jordan's agency, ProServ, secured him a three-million-dollar, five-year contract before he played his first game of professional ball. Michael Jordan has gone on to become the highest-earning athlete to date, making $3.9 million on the court and $40 million in endorsements during 1995 alone. With the expiration of Jordan's contract in 1989, he re-signed with Nike for a multiyear contract worth $20 million (Strasser and Becklund 1991). In his career to date with Nike, Michael Jordan has earned more than Nike's entire Indonesian workforce earns in two years.

Jordan has since figured centrally in Nike's television and print ads, and the NikeTown chain of stores. Earlier Nike stores presented imagery aggrandizing the customer: changing rooms were made to look like Supermanesque phone booths and elevated floors lit up beneath the footsteps of customers trying on Nike shoes. The NikeTown superstores, opened from 1991 on, aggrandize instead the celebrity endorser. From alcoves, buttresses, and soaring walkways, slightly-larger-than-life sculptures of Jordan and other athletes jump and dive, inviting the consumer to emulate them through consumption.

While the NikeTown statues of Jordan are as plaster white as the interior walls, Nike has always been cognizant of the relation between basketball, Michael Jordan, and blackness. Underlying this connection is the persistence of racism in popular culture, by which "African peoples were defined as having bodies but not minds: in this way the superexploitation of the black body could be justified … sport is a circumscribed zone where blacks are allowed to excel. And we have also seen how black people have entered sports not just for their own individual gain—by using their public status they have articulated a political stance" (Mercer 1994, 138). Athletics thus becomes one of the few realms in the United States where blackness can more readily escape denigration, secure material success, claim a public voice and initiate social change in the face of a tacitly racist society. (Consider, for instance, the now iconic image of medalist Tommie Smith's and John Carlos's downcast heads and upraised black-gloved fists during their victory ceremony at the 1968 Mexico City Olympics or, less pyrrhically, Magic Johnson's projects of community reinvestment and AIDS activism.)

Michael Jordan's rags-to-riches story thus established basketball as a route out of the deindustrializing urban cores for young black men faced with narrowing academic and career prospects throughout the 1980s and 1990s. In the process, U.S. inner cities were positioned as *the* place where basketball shoe styles are made or broken. Nike made careful use of this environment. Spike Lee was employed for the production of Air Jordan commercials. Coach John Thompson was hired as an endorser. And more specifically, the Air Jordan was pushed heavily during a 1986 private dinner showing for "retailers [who] sold shoes in the toughest parts of cities like Oakland, Washington D.C., and Detroit" (Strasser 1991, 623). As a result, the Air Jordan became a hot property in the poorest urban areas, and ultimately sold 2.8 million pair nationwide.

Unfortunately, the shoe also cost $115.50 and, by 1990, numerous incidents had occurred wherein some who couldn't afford the shoes got them by assaulting, and occasionally killing, those who could (Telander 1990). Nike's success in convincing a respect-starved population that a particular pair of shoes was a status symbol worth killing for raised questions about the power of advertising to motivate covetous violence, and the ethics of hyping consumerism to an increasingly divested population. These questions spurred a boycott of Nike products to protest the company's contradictory reliance upon black consumers and dearth of black core employees (Wilkerson 1990). Despite the boycott, Air Jordans and other Nike products (including a shoe festooned with Afrocentric kente cloth designs) continued to permeate the black youth market in major urban centers.

This omnipresence of Nikes among black kids in divested urban cores was synchronous with two other developments: the influx of new-immigrant Mexican and Central American populations into formerly majority black neighborhoods throughout the southwestern states of the U.S., and the spread of hip-hop culture.

With the new residential and schoolyard intimacy (and occasional enmity) between black and Latino youth, advertising-inspired valorizations of Nike wear were rapidly adopted by newcomer Latinos. This phenomenon was particularly pronounced among young Latinas anxious to escape subordinate feminine roles, who were receptive both to street-level peer influence and to Nike's "feminist" campaigns conflating athletics, and by association Nike wear, with female empowerment (Cole 1995).

The common appearance of Nike shoes on poor young Latina feet found expression in varied arenas. In public policy, a 1992 peer health program that employed adolescent mothers to educate fellow teens in child care and pregnancy prevention was christened the Nike-Footed Health Worker Project. More surrealistically, a short story entitled "The Storyteller with Nike Airs" related the adventure of a *curandera*'s young apprentice, Lucia, who is called upon to enter the dreams of Josefina, a migrant laborer, and recover her lost soul. Dressed in pink and lavender Nike Airs with fluorescent green laces, Lucia travels through the deserts and dusty towns of Josefina's psyche. Here Lucia encounters the *juveniles de sombra*—the shadow kids— hanging out on the street corners of Josefina's internal landscape. These kids thrust a "sickening green ooze" of "desire-to-have" toward Lucia's feet and, after an exchange of threats, Lucia parts with her Nikes in exchange for directions to Josefina's soul. "Lucia handed over her Nikes and the shadow leader, with this added strength, sucked the other shadow girls in with a smack." By the end of the story, Lucia has retrieved the soul and reenters the world, but with "green, shiny, slimy, goop" all over her Nike Airs (Forte-Escamilla 1994). One would be hard pressed to find a clearer description of the very real power Nikes exercise within certain symbolic landscapes, of their life-or-death exchange value, or of their function as a link between symbolic and material realms of experience.

The association with hip-hop culture, however, carried Nike even farther afield. Hip-hop originated in "various areas of New York City" (Boyd 1996, 137; see also Boyd 1997) as a cultural form that expressed the attitudes and aspirations of young black males subject to marginalization and disappearance (sometimes literally and en masse, through criminalization and wholesale incarceration) by the dominant social order. Hip-hop practitioners communicate their everyday experiences in the lyrics of rap and the visual language of graffiti pieces, and commonly do so through the in-your-face and cost-saving transgressions of sampling others' sounds and spraypainting others' property to make something entirely new.

This culture rapidly spread with stylistic variation throughout the U.S. and, from there, entered into a black Atlantic circuit of exchange connecting the African diaspora in the U.S. with its counterparts in the Caribbean, Europe, and Africa itself (Lipsitz 1994). Beyond the African diaspora, rap diffused to other marginalized and divested minority youth (e.g. Dutch Indonesians, New Zealand Maoris) and to sympathetic or merely rebellious children of more privileged social formations. And given Nike Airs' engineered popularity with the U.S. progenitors of hip-hop, augmented by the shoe's close association with a young black role model in the person of Michael Jordan, Nike traveled alongside. Nikes became international signifiers of hip-hop to such a degree that Senegal-born French rapper MC Solaar disparagingly christened French hip-hop's imitation of U.S. rap forms as "the cult of the sneaker" (Cocks 1992). Many rappers subsequently took to jettisoning the presumptively coca-colonizing oversized athletic wear style in favor of garments like dashikis and batik sarongs, indicating the rappers' ethnic affiliations. But hip-hoppers in the "roughest" scenes continued to stick with Ebonic slang, baggies, and Nikes, with the most serious continental home boys and fly girls being the ones who had access to the latest Nikes available only through U.S. or British connections (Elteren 1994).

In 1995, the depth of the intersection of U.S. hip-hop, its European adaptation, and Nike was fictively revealed in Mathieu Kassovitz's film *Hate* (*La Haine*). Set to a rap score, *Hate* follows a day in the life of three friends, one Central African, one North African, and one Jewish, living in the "Bluebell" cité (public housing estate) on the outskirts of Paris. In the context of a police shooting and antipolice riots, the characters are repeatedly harassed by law enforcement, patronizingly exoticized and spurned by Parisian bourgeoisie, and unconsentingly filmed by a television news crew that treats the cité like a drive-through wild animal park. Confronted with such disrespect, the characters respond with braggadocio and often ill-directed aggression. The Jewish member of the trio is the least visibly other and, therefore, least likely to be harassed. But he compensates for his less apparent otherness by being the angriest. He flies off the handle at slight provocations and practices Robert De Niro's lines from *Taxi Driver* in the mirror. And he spends the entire film clad in Nike Airs and, in numerous scenes, full Nike workout suits.

In its representation of a world city's young, new immigrant poor and their socioeconomic context, *Hate* illustrates the socioeconomic structure of the new world bipolar disorder that sets the global stage for hip-hop culture, how that culture has been deployed against an unsympathetic urban milieu, and the prominence of Nike as a signifier of this resistance. In this, the similarities between the cité and its South Bronx equivalent are striking, both being in-beyonds that served as local cradles of hip-hop. But no less striking is how the Nike "swoosh" flags these similar conditions of urban devalorization and divestment, at the same time as such urban divestment is in no small part a by-product of the down-waged flexist production practices perfected by Nike as a "distributed" TNC. Thus, Nike Airs become more than high-tech (and thus supposedly performance enhancing) athletic footwear. They constitute a profit-generating commodity chain linking social relations in which the shoe transits from hard labor to source of self esteem by way of heroic investiture. Nike is both cognizant and supportive of this adaptive reutilization, having coined the term 'implied performance' in recognition of the fact that 50 percent to 80 percent of total production never sees athletic use. But in the process, the shoes have performed in ways Nike never implied. They transformed into a badge that forged young members of devalorized diasporic collectives into a single dislocalized collective of economically abandoned youth looking to bite the hand they buy from; in short, a nonlocal hip-hop nation.

This contradiction between Nike's making and street-forged meaning came together forcibly around 1996. Simultaneous with the U.S. release of *Hate,* growing publicity around social justice campaigns positioned Nike as the paragon of transnational corporate abuses. Numerous Nike-critical fact-finding missions and publicity barrages (e.g. Global Exchange in 1996, the Fair Trade Center in 1997, Working Assets Long Distance in 1998, the Multinationals Resource Center in 1999) called repeated attention to persistent shortfalls in Nike's oversight and enforcement of East Asian subcontractors' wage structures and working conditions. Such campaigns have included smaller actions as well, like MIT grad student Jonah Peretti's now legendary attempt to have Nike embroider "SWEATSHOP" across a pair of personalizable Nike iD shoes. Nike repeatedly refused, arguing the word was "inappropriate slang," and Peretti widely forwarded the entire e-mail exchange with an appended statement, "This will now go round the world much farther and faster" than any of Nike's advertisements (Mayer 2001).

In its own defense, Nike has deployed extensive public relations testimonials by prominent human rights and economic justice figures (e.g., Andrew Young, and Steve Koenig of Informed Investors; see Nike Incorporated 1998), all the while taking fitfull steps toward materially correcting criticized conditions. The resultant pitched and frequently confused battle continues to the present, with critics periodically switching sides, Nike employees defecting to the opposition, and Nike Incorporated oscillating between giving in and ratcheting up spin control. By way of example, in Indonesia, where Nike now has 110,000 workers in eleven factories, the company has trumpeted wage-raises of some 70 percent over the past few years to 300,000 rupiah per month plus meal and transportation allowances (nikebiz.com 2001). But in real terms and with inflation rampant, this equates with only $1.25 over the government mandated 286,000 rupiah monthly minimum wage, and $4.00 short of minimum physical need. Nor does the wage raise necessarily entail there will be workers to receive it: Nike's flexist contracting arrangements have expedited the layoffs of thousands of Indonesian shoemakers since the U.S. economic slump that began in late 2000 (AP 2001b). Similarly, Nike has initiated Transparency 101, a quasi-independent factory monitoring and reportage program for workers' rights, but immediately thereafter was forced to respond to independent revelations of egregious worker maltreatment at the Kukdong factory in Atlixco, Mexico (Verité 2001). On one occasion, Phil Knight personally pledged to terminate some particularly exploitative workplace practices that his vice president for corporate and social responsibility, Maria Eitel, had denied existed only two weeks earlier (Kieschnick 1998).

Regardless of the battle's ultimate outcome, it has demonstrably done global damage. Nike's now-shaky profits (most notoriously a drop of 50 percent during the Asian slump; see Nike Incorporated, 1998) cannot be attributed exclusively to Nike's vocal discontents. It is no less the case that Nike oversaturated the market, inadvertently demoting itself from icon to staple by reason of its own prodigious success. But the complaints against Nike have now become as mundanely iconic as Nike itself. The extent of the damage became apparent to me in early 2000, during a trip through Stockholm. I was headed toward the neighborhood of Rinkeby in the city's northwest. En route, I encountered a preadolescent Finn with the Nike "swoosh" shaved into both sides of his head, but dressed in Stussy label clothing. Not long after, I encountered another. This one with a full head of hair, but his worn Nikes stood in stark contrast to his thorough cladding in new O'Neil surfwear. Curious, I asked him what he liked about Nike, and in exchange received an earful: "I used to think Nike was cool, and they sponsored my favorite [soccer] team, Arsenal. But Nike's mean to people and beside, surfing's cool. So I like O'Neil" (Flusty 2000, May).

This confluence of social conscience and brand consciousness was reinforced in Rinkeby proper. Rinkeby is Stockholm's own Bluebell cité, a neighborhood of relatively poor immigrants and refugees drawn predominantly from Turkey, Chile, Iran, and the former Yugoslavia. At first glance, the neighborhood looks like much of suburban Stockholm. Closer inspection, however, reveals vital differences. The housing blocks bristle with satellite dishes on every balcony, ensuring reception of broadcasts in residents' native languages. Corner shops feature spices and staple goods common to the Near East. The walls display predominantly Spanish-language graffiti wishing long life to Peru's Maoist Shining Path guerrillas, and Great Cultural Revolution style posters of heroic masses gazing admiringly toward a red sun inscribed with the countenance of Abamael Guzman. And on this weekend, vendor's tables on the sidewalks featured kebabs, Kurdish dance music, and the vocals of Mercedes Sosa. Some of these tables also featured jewelry, necklaces and rings emblazoned with 'NIKE' and the Nike swoosh. Clustered around one such table (despite the vendor's best efforts to shoo them away) was a horde of kids. They were handling the rings and discussing their relative merits, in Spanish peppered with Swedish and English. One snippet of this conversation was particularly instructive:

> "Don't buy that shit, slaves make it"
> "Don't be an idiot. You think this is *real* Nike?!"

Thus, in the everyday life on Rinkeby's sidewalks, the hyperextension of Nike has fused with the hyperextension of its discontents in such a way as to render possession of a counterfeit swoosh far cooler than possession of an authentic one. (This, of course, begs the question of whether those who manufacture the counterfeits are any better treated.)

Cognizant of this popular perception, Nike in turn has attempted to co-opt its discontents as a hip promotional amusement. In early 2001, the company introduced an athletic boot for Australian Rules Football (or footie) into the Oceania market. The ad campaign centered on red billboards proclaiming, in a Russian constructivist typefont, "THE MOST OFFENSIVE BOOTS WE'VE EVER MADE." These billboards were subsequently "defaced" by Nike itself with the tagline "100% SLAVE LABOR," supposedly executed by a protest organization (also fabricated by Nike) called Fans for Fairer Football. Rather than generate sales, however, this jujitsu advertising strategy generated a Ban the Boot resistance mobilization, a weekly Friday night blockade of the Melbourne NikeTown, and subsequent termination of the ad campaign (Lasn 2001; Nike.con 2001).

Just Blew It

Throughout the late 1980s and 1990s, Nike responded to slumping sales of athletic footwear by introducing such nonsneakers as sports sandals and "water socks." One of these new products, a hiking boot, was targeted for a market of adventurers (and wanna-be adventurers) to ruggedly exotic locales. In 1992, a commercial for this boot depicted it hiking through the Kenyan veldt, closing with a shot of local Samburu tribesmen. In close-up, one of the Samburu says something in the native Maa tongue, while the Nike slogan "Just Do It" appears across the screen as a subtitled translation.

In fact, the tribesman said, "I don't want these. Give me big shoes." When the advertisement aired in the U.S., numerous Maa speakers commented on the discrepancy, including one who reported it to Forbes magazine. In turn, Forbes disseminated the story to newspapers and, from thence, onto the Internet. In response to misquoting the Samburu, a Nike spokesperson stated, "We thought nobody in America would know what he said." What Nike failed to recognize is that the same dynamics exporting Nike into new contexts everywhere had also imported the denizens, life ways, and dissonant perspectives of those new contexts, turning everywhere into hotbeds of translation and recontextualization. The global formation of a culture of dislocated and densely interpenetrating cultural contexts therefore undermines the authoritative prescription of meaning. Through this, commodities are rendered polysemic and, quite often, self-defeating. Thus, while the prevalence of hybridization does not entail the end of hegemony, it does confer upon hegemons an incredible shrinking shelf life.

This radically decenters and disperses hegemony as both practice and idea. In its stead are multiple shifting centers of hegemony, wherein French influence in fashion exists parallel to Japanese influences on organizational engineering, Vatican authority over sexual polities, and determinations of right conduct issuing from the Shia center of Qom. Varied dislocalities scattered throughout the metapolis become hegemonic centers for certain purposes, for limited times, and even then only for certain peoples. Further, no center possesses the capacity to conclusively control how its output is interpreted. As the specific forms and meanings of this output are selectively adapted elsewhere they are 'creolized' (Hannerz 1992), transformed sometimes beyond recognition so as to become useful, meaningful and relevant to divergent cultural matrices.

The unpredictability of creolization imparts worldwide significance to Michel de Certeau's (1984) assertion that meaning is made in use. The global cultural economy becomes a collection of menus and submenus rife for poaching. Certainly, some items in the world bricoleurs' toolkits will be more plentiful than others. But expanding and proliferating fields of polyhegemonic influences ensure that coca-colonization must invariably run afoul of the specific creolizations of internally diverse global cultural flows (Elteren 1994). Thus, within the everyday matrices of global formation, the most homogeneous and authoritatively prescribed productions can not escape being reheterogenized. I call this aggregate of reheterogenizing practices and processes "de-coca-colonization," the dynamic by which the repeated dislocalization of things' meanings and enactments causes them to veer ever further from those inscribed and prescribed, thus rendering authoritative practice itself highly impracticable, and even potentially explosive.

Nike Incorporated's own commonplace practices have inspired not just reflexive consumption, but multiplying incidents of stark physical resistance. At its least violent, this has taken the form of culture jamming and the extralegal production of "subvertisements." At its extreme it has taken the form of open warfare, rendering Nike a choice target of direct actions against plutocratic globality. One poster encouraging anarchists to mass on the streets as Black Blocs parodies Nike's "Life is Short, Play Hard" slogan with an image of a brick sailing through a NikeTown store window, accompanied by the phrase "Life is Short, Throw Hard." And indeed the Black Blocing anarchists have been, forcing Nike to board up their shop windows preparatory to May Day parades and supranational summits throughout Europe, Oceania, and the Americas. Similarly, the Earth Liberation Front has called for the destruction of Nike properties "due to the corporation's use of sweatshop labor overseas and it's [sic] role in globalization" (ELF 2001), a call enacted in their April 2001 attempt to burn down a Nike factory outlet store in Albertville, Minnesota.

So Nike has become an unwitting and unwilling participant in the proliferation of resistance to plutocratic globality. Mirroring the copresence of Nike and its discontents, such movements are irrupting with increasing frequency and ferocity in the spaces where the TNC and supranational state apparatuses come together. And like the TNC these movements are transnational affairs. Thus, the practices of the TNC in conjunction with the administrative management of global formation have inadvertently turned globalization against itself.

8
De-Coca-Colonization Classic

The past few years have seen an efflorescence of militant opposition to the hegemony of plutocratic globality, and to its underpinning economic logics. This explosive proliferation of so-called antiglobalization sentiment has manifested as practices of mass bodily confrontation that are relatively new and, to the common knowledge, inexplicable phenomenon. From the standpoint of laissez-faire neoliberal economics such opposition is not just inexplicable, it is at best ill-informed and at worst dangerously obstruction-ist. After all, the freer the market the more wealth created and diffused. This liberates resources for their "highest and best" use, and frees persons to act in their own best interests while providing them the wherewithal to do so. The deregulated global interoperation of markets must therefore necessarily im-prove material living standards globally, producing and distributing wealth planetwide through the competitive transference of goods and know-how (Dunning 1993). Further, the insurance of a global marketplace is simulta-neously insurance of peace and freedom, given that markets depend on both stability and choice to operate. Thus, advocates assert that only by assuring the global rights of capital can we also assure prosperity, meritocratic equity, and amity (see, e.g., Friedman 1992).

Given that the market's invisible hand makes for so enlightened a boss, it is hardly surprising that so many states have adopted the doctrines of neoliberalism. But in so doing, the state has "consented to a regime that allows markets to boss them around" (Paul Krugman in T. L. Friedman 1994, E3). In keeping with this, the supranational attenuation of the state into the alphabet soup of transnationally regulatory agencies has engendered similarly subordinated institutions. Supranational state apparatuses are thus concerned primarily with "assur[ing] an open (although by no means level) playing field for international businesses," placing the state "at the mercy of the . . . transnational corporations" (Barber 1996, 240). In so doing the state has ignored the fact that markets are as prone to self-interested short-sightedness as to enlightenment, and so has willfully forfeited its capacity to counterbalance market forces with the provision of social mediation and environmental sustenance (see, e.g., Greider 2001a).

This transformation constitutes both an unexpectedly systemic manifestation of Schumpeterian "creative destruction" (see Metcalfe 1998), and a mechanism to legitimize the global magnification of creative destruction's deleterious impacts. According to the doctrine of creative destruction, progress in living standards results from economic change through innovation, supplanting old processes and products with new and weeding out "unproductive" sectors. This weeding out, however, extends to the removal of obstacles to creative destruction itself, most visibly such "impediment[s] to a well-functioning creative destruction process" as less economically profitable ways of life, their "politicized institutions" (Caballero and Hammour 2000), and thus established mechanisms of popular political representation. In the absence of such "obstacles," political expression is delimited to the realm of consumer choice—collective social aspirations are conflated with a person's presumptive entitlement to select from a determined range of proffered commodities. In the process, citizenries become consumersheds and public accountability is reduced to accountancy, wherein one is entitled to as much influence as one can purchase. But happily, those with shallower pockets and less economically productive ways of living can rest assured that the creative destruction of their emplaced social relations will, in theory, eventually enrich them sufficiently to claim a voice in this "daily plebiscite of the penny" (Mises in Barber, 1996, 243).

Thus, many experience globalism's creative destruction as widespread and persistent disruption, dislocation and disempowerment. Such experiences recast the deregulated international marketplace's peace and freedom into enforced pacification and hidden constraint. Proceeding from this observation, critics contend that the management of global formation at the intersection of the TNC and the supranational state produces a "unipolar world of the market, [in which] globalization centered on the Total Market is competitive globalization, the globalization of inequalities, the globalization of security and plenty for a few, of the illusion of an eternally happy present for those who can 'consume,' and of oppression, subordination or exclusion for the majority" (Arruda 1996). Under the circumstances, then, there is nothing either inexplicable or inherently novel about opposition to a hegemonic globality (see Walton and Seddon 1994) that, in both theory and practice, is so bluntly plutocratic. To the contrary, such movements are inevitable. They arise from the realization, and call our attention to the fact, that a nonlocal "free market" is not the outcome of immutable natural laws. Whether global or otherwise, markets are socially embedded cultural constructs (Grannovetter 1985). So the world marketplace is a product of articulated social practices, and especially of the commonplace practices by which global formation is managed. Chief among these practices is the assertion of claims to the unrestricted rights of capital, claims that are simultaneously valorizations, naturalizations and mystifications of certain global agendas at the expense of others. Such claims, like any claims, are clearly strategic and must necessarily be advanced by interested claimants who constitute their own nonlocal field, most prominently in collectives like the Transnational Corporation. And insofar as global formation may be characterized as time-space compression (Harvey 1989), if we are to eschew the notion that such compression occurs automagically then two particular collectives, both central to the instrumentalization of space and time, come to the fore. One is an oligopoly of motion (or, with a stylistic nod to Newspeak, *Olimove*), comprised of firms engaged in the production of transportation and its corollary prime movers. Its partner is an oligopoly of memory (or again, more simply newspoken, *Olimem*), firms concerned with the media through which information is stored, synthesized, retrieved and redacted. The claims of such oligopolies are enacted in turn by such supranational regulatory institutions as the World Trade Organization, legitimized through coordinated administrative rubrics like "deregulation" and "privatization" and enacted by means of such acronymic but very unabstract destructive creations as SAPs (structural adjustment programs) and, in particularly recalcitrant cases, multiple-thousand pound GBUs (guided bomb units). It is such claims and corollary enactments in their aggregate that constitute the formative processes of plutocratic globality.

A plutocratic globality is not the outcome of some faceless, irresistible force that roams the heavens and alights upon us. Rather, just like any globality it is emplaced and embodied, albeit in convoluted and intensely nonlocal ways, it acts materially and, most important, it travels. It is a globality engendered by the peregrinations of ideologies and commodities, of direct foreign investors and fiscal policy advisors, of riot policing tactics and, at worst, of rapidly deployed military coalitions and depleted uranium rounds. Such "at worsts" are among the constituent elements of interdiction at a global scale, and reveal the degree to which plutocratic globality relies upon not just the hyperextension of neoliberalism, but of praetorianism as well. Further, this globality has an identifiable commodity chain of its own, originating with its invention at the University of Chicago and running from its brutal beta testing in Augusto Pinochet's Chile, through its fine-tuning by Margaret Thatcher's England, to its wholesale installation back in the United States during the presidency of Ronald Reagan.

Plutocratic globality's material emplacement, enactment and embodiment in transit is precisely what renders it vulnerable to a host of countervailing practices, whether an internationalized boycott or the very localized hurling of a single brick through a chainstore's window. But in describing plutocratic globality's enactment from the perspective of its detractors, there is the risk of falling into the countervailing trap of reifying resistance. Resistance is not some abstract disembodied essence free of time and place. Like the emplaced enactments constituting plutocratic globality, its discontents are similarly the product of hyperextended counterclaims and dissident claimants. Given the multitudes whose lives are subject to being creatively destroyed without their informed consent, such claimants are legion, and this discontent is articulated through precisely the same devices as plutocratic globality itself. The new commodities that drive new prestige economies can also be used to undermine established hierarchies. The mass media that propagandizes consumers can be redeployed to unite strategically divided populations. The increasing (albeit differentially selective) porosity of nation-state borders creates new sociopolitical conditions that disempower, but simultaneously proffer new mobilizing opportunities for the disempowered.

In short, new ways of seeing the world give old things new uses (Lipsitz 1994), and give rise to a host of polyglot battle cries. On the outskirts of Durban, South Africa, township dwellers weave *imbenge* baskets of discarded telephone wire to divert capital from the postindustrial world via mail order and online catalogs (an endeavor so successful that now telephone wire must be imported for the purpose). Across the Maghreb and Anatolia, houses of worship turn to feeding and mobilizing the newly urbanized poor against investor-mandated austerity programs that divide the shortage evenly among the peasants. Thus, while Olimove and Olimem may well condition the terrain of compressed time-space, they neither determine nor fully control it. This indeterminacy opens the potential for hyperextended terrains of resistance that are at once "both metaphoric and literal" (Routledge 1996, 517), terrains that constitute insurgent nonlocal fields while undergirding the social construction of globalities that are not just alternate but overtly oppositional.

This terrain, however, does not lie in thematic abstractions but in specific practices of resistance, their temporal and spatial specificity, and the subsequent circumstances of their dislocalization and adaptation. Following a particular trail of artifacts will prove this point. The trail is marked by a series of dolls, each representing (more or less) the same public figure's body so as to constitute an artifact sequence: the evolutionary genealogy of a family of objects that emerge one from the next in successive iterations. But this trail also marks an intercontinental path that returns us to where this book began: the unrest in Seattle, the person of Subcomandante Insurgente Marcos, and the mountains of southern Mexico. And along this path lies an emergent praxis, iconography, and even material culture of globalizing discontent, an elaborating circuit of traveling dissent that has embodied an alternate globality in the form of a portable carnival of resistance.

Combatting a Disease of the Heart that Only Gold Can Cure

On midnight of January 1, 1994, amid chants of "¡Ya basta!" ("Enough already!"), the Zapatistas appeared. They poured forth, as if out of nowhere, into the central plaza of the centuries-old colonial city of San Cristóbal de las Casas in Chiapas State, Mexico. Clad in black ski masks, fatigues, embroidered smocks, and beribboned hats, some carrying rifles and others sticks carved to look like rifles, they raided the town hall, issued a declaration of principles from the government palace, blanketed the city with broadsheets, and attacked a military base on the way out. This initiated two weeks of skirmishes against the civilian population by local police, the army and the air force. Despite this, the network of Zapatista base communities scattered throughout Chiapas's Lacandón rain forest remained intact and expanded throughout the state and into adjacent regions. Technically, the mobilization of this network constitutes an uprising by the impoverished indigenous peoples of the region, predominantly Western Mayans of the Tzotzil, Tzetal, Tojolabal, and Chol linguistic subgroups. But in the timing of the raid on San Cristóbal, at precisely the moment the North American Free Trade Agreement went into effect, it is also a flip of the proverbial finger at plutocratic globality. It is a flip that has engendered the *coyuntura,* the resistant "'coming together' of distinct social and cultural movements" (Ross in Marcos, 1995, 9) throughout Mexico. And in its visibility in global communications media, it has become the finger flipped around the world.

Of course, the Zapatistas did not come out of nowhere. Southern Mexico in the late seventeenth and early eighteenth centuries was rife with uprisings by agrarian Mayan communities, struggles against the colonial appropriation of agricultural land and the corollary enserfment of indigenous populations. More narrowly, the Zapatistas are a continuation of the Mexican Revolution of 1910, lead in Mexico's South by the Mayan Emiliano Zapata (Aguilar and Meyer 1993). This was a struggle against the predominantly Spanish-descended 1 percent of the population who owned 97 percent of the land, leaving 92 percent of the population indentured. This fight for *tierra,* for land/earth, culminated in the redistribution of land to communes of peasant farmers under the *ejido* system. Under this system, ensconced via Article 27 of the 1917 Mexican Constitution, land is parceled out to persons and families but is nontransferable, held and administered on an institutionalized communal basis (NACEC 2001). The ejido system was not fully implemented until 1934 under then president Lazaro Cardenas, and frequently resulted in marginal parcels of land barely large enough to support a family. Nonetheless, the ejidos constituted a significant increase in autonomy for the everyday lives of rural indigenous populations. But most specifically, the Zapatista uprising is a response to the amendment of Article 27 in 1992, under the administration of then president Carlos Salinas de Gortari. In an effort to expand and stabilize private property rights, realize economies of scale in the rural economy, and so harmonize Mexico with the terms of NAFTA, Salinas sought to decollectivize agrarian land through three significant legislative changes:

- peasants could no longer petition for land, nor could land be expropriated from owners
- title of existing communal lands would be transferred to their individual occupants, made leaseable, and in many instances transferable through sale
- outside investors, and corporations both foreign and domestic, would be allowed to hold land

For the Mayans, this "privatization of the countryside" (Foley 1995) meant nothing less than the reversal of the 1910 revolution. It raised the specter of losing their land to poverty, outside manipulation and competitively advantaged industrial agriculture, and so becoming either hired hands on newly concentrated land holdings or migrants to the cities. And ultimately, it impelled the assault on San Cristóbal.

It has impelled a great deal more as well. Three manifestations of this revived struggle are particularly noteworthy. First is a new way of conducting revolution, and a corollary new political practice. The overwhelming rhetoric of the Zapatista uprising has been that it is a rebellion by long-suffering indigenous peoples. There has even been a popular perception that the Zapatistas are the voice of the indigenous, a perception insulting to the many other indigenous rights organizations that stud Mexico's political landscape. Conversely, critics have claimed that the Zapatistas are a public relations ploy that conceals a Maoist coup d'état by the National Liberation Front (NLF) a "white dominated Marxist guerrilla group" (Oppenheimer 1996, 22; for a similarly deterministic interpretation from a more sympathetic Marxian perspective see Nugent 1995). Yet others have claimed that in the limitedness of its conventional political and territorial claims, this uprising is not a revolution at all (Paz 1994). These characterizations, however, miss the point. The armed wing of the Zapatistas, the EZLN (Ejercito Zapatista Liberacion Nacional, or Zapatista Army of National Liberation), has been explicit that it eschews any and all notion of taking power. Rather, the Zapatistas reject the very notion of power as something to be seized and wielded, believing that in such a taking lay the reproduction of the violences and exclusions they attribute to their enemy. Thus, the Zapatista uprising is not a modernist revolution in the vanguardist Marxist-Leninist mold. Instead it is one that, according to its combatants, "look[s] at power in a different way" so as to "produce a different way of doing politics." This different way does not have "as its premise the objective of power" but instead seeks to construct "space for new political relationships . . . spaces for peace" (Libra 1995), spaces in which people may exercise their own power (cf. "free and democratic 'space'" in Marcos 1995, 233). In keeping with this, such spaces are not by and for a single way of seeing. Again the Zapatistas have been explicit on this point. They repeatedly emphasize that their revolt can and must include the divergent perspectives of all professional (and un-, and antiprofessional) classifications, all sexes and sexual orientations, all age groups, all religions and all intellects so long as they are "rebels, dissidents, inconvenient ones, dreamers" (Marcos 1999). In short, the Zapatistas rhetorically position their uprising as one of the othered against their othering, one in which none are asked to surrender their differences in order to participate. Implicit in this rhetoric of inclusivist spatial metaphors are both a critique and concrete counterproposals—means by which bodies might refuse and resist the arrogated enactment of power through them, and do so proactively by doing differently.

Through the Zapatista's material practices their metaphorical spaces of liberation have produced literal terrain as well, territorial 'plurilocalities' (Rose 1993, 150–51) carved out of Mexico's authoritative place. Spreading from Chiapas into neighboring states, the EZLN's disordering of state-imposed power relations has supported the emergence of somewhere around three thousand base communities, which in turn have organized into forty-three "autonomous municipalities" (Villafuerte 2001, 17). Within this terrain, everyday relations are ordered through local assemblies open to all community members over the age of twelve. Larger decisions are addressed through *consultas,* whereby directly chosen delegates (who may be popularly recalled at any time) carry community decisions to municipal assemblages. Similarly, decisions made at the municipal level are, for all intents and purposes, recommendations that must be carried back for community approval, amendment or rejection. Even the armed force of the EZLN, although hierarchically structured internally, is likewise commanded from below: it takes orders from and issues communiqués by the CCRI (Clandestine Revolutionary

Indigenous Committee), which is itself composed of delegates who may be recalled at any time by their communities (Flood 2001).

This system of self-governance hearkens back to the ejido and earlier Mayan modes of popular community rule, but also equalizes social hierarchies so as to mitigate against tendencies towards patriarchal gerontocracy and readily co-optable *caciques*. This has produced such innovations as the Women's Revolutionary Law mandating gender self-determination and equality in all spheres of everyday life from domestic to military, and youthful mobilizations against such long-standing practices as the payment of marriage dowry. It also has driven negotiators for the Mexican state around the bend, in that any negotiating proposals made by the federal state must be handed down to the Zapatista communities for full discussion and consensus prior to ratification. Thus, the Zapatistas have innovated practices intended to creatively disrupt the embodied networks that act to monopolize the usufruct of power (see Foucault, 1982a; 1982b). In so doing they have opened literal and metaphorical space for self-organization, wherein governance may be popularly reclaimed through an active rearticulation of civil society. It is a proposal and a practice for undermining existing networks of asymmetrical power relations by rejecting centrality entirely. This rejection, in turn, is actualized by carving out spaces that turn their backs upon power centers, and so withdraw from the center without simultaneously establishing the periphery as a new center.

The second noteworthy manifestation of the Zapatista uprising is its spokesman, Subcomandante Marcos. Commonly known as the "Sup," Marcos has become the recognized face (or more precisely, the blue eyes and big nose poking through a ski mask) of the uprising. According to the Mexican state, behind the ski mask is Rafael Sebastián Guillén Vicente, son of a successful Tampico furniture dealer (Golden 2001). While at university in Mexico City, Vicente joined the NLF and went into the mountains of southern Mexico where, in the course of bringing the locals over to his cause, he was no less assimilated into theirs. From this perspective Marcos is a privileged but rurally reeducated white socialist from the Federal District of Mexico, what might be termed an organicized intellectual. Marcos has not denied this identity, but instead has claimed many others, including that of a Mayan and, in response to counterinsurgent psy-op campaigns casting aspersions upon his sexuality, a gay waiter from San Francisco.

Yet in simultaneously concealing the actor in question and heightening his conspicuousness, the mask has come to contain a host of additional meanings in the popular imagination. Mythically, Marcos has become one in a long line of masked Mayan heroes, and a new embodiment of the itinerant prophets of the 1712 and 1868 Mayan revolts (Ross in Marcos, 1995, 8–9). In serving as the youthful voice making the case for the radicalized ejidos, Marcos has become the second coming of Zapata and an irreverent avatar of Ernesto "Che" Guevara (Feinmann 1998) incarnated as the archetypal trickster. Indeed, it is common to see Marcos depicted standing between both. And the mask has in turn become emblematic of the uprising as a whole, with participants donning ski masks, kerchiefs, and even the artisanal masks of the region. Practically, this serves as a means of concealing participants' identities and thus shields them from retribution. This masked concealment, however, is not an attempt "to become invisible, to pass unnoticed" (Paz 1982, 42). To the contrary, the insurgents' ski masks are a public proclamation of visibility, a statement that anybody in any place may be a Zapatista and that all participants are Marcos (see Marcos 1995, 83–86).

But equally important are the writings and speeches that emerge from behind Marcos's ski mask. These words are directly confrontational language acts regularly attached as (sometimes endless) postscripts to the pronouncements and press-releases of the CCRI. They are also circulated as independently released parables, biographies, and even children's stories. Invariably, they are discursive assaults upon the totalizing and exclusionary economic logic deployed to globalize neoliberalism. But most significantly, these words are couched in literary and poetic forms that are alternatively (and sometimes simultaneously) playful, heart-wrenching, obscure, magicorealist and hugely antiauthoritarian. They have earned Marcos specifically, and the Zapatistas in general, a tremendous readership.

The third element to have emerged from the uprising is its proliferation of tie-in merchandise. The most prolific of this merchandise is the *muñeca Zapatista* (Zapatista doll). There is a long history of backstrap loom weaving as a cottage industry among Mexico's Mayan women, and an equally long history of small human figurines assembled from the remnant textile scraps. First appearing in 1994, the muñeca Zapatista is much like these dolls in form and size, but with important modifications: the dolls are dressed in black homespun ski masks and ponchos with woven bandoleers. Some carry rifles made of blackened wood but, on others, the wood is left natural much like the dummy guns first carried into San Cristobál. In its most common version the doll is stitched with blue eyes like those of Marcos himself. But almost as common are the Comandante Ramona dolls, similarly topped by a ski mask but with long protruding pigtails braided with polychromed yarn. These dolls are dressed in *huipiles,* the elaborately woven blouses that signify localized Mayan identities (Ramona herself is a Tzotzil), and are invariably clung onto by baby Zapatista dolls with blue eyes. This latter is on one level a joking allusion to a Ramona/Marcos liaison. But on another, it is a celebration of the role of women in the uprising. Roughly one third of EZLN combatants are female. The size and position of the tiny Marcos on Ramona's back further points to the fact that, true to his rank title, Marcos is

Muñeca Zapatista from Chiapas.

a subordinate commander in the ranks of the EZLN. As a comandante and a member of the CCRI, Ramona is among those who issue orders to Marcos (and was also one of the principal draftspersons of the Women's Revolutionary Law; see Wolfwood 1997). But in addition to fighting, female Zapatistas also biologically reproduce the uprising's combatants. Thus, the tiny Marcos (or, in some cases, Marcoses) clinging to the Ramona doll announces that "all our children are Marcos." Further, such dolls are traditional elements of children's play in the region, a toy that is no less a tool for imaginatively trying out adult roles. Thus, these muñecas afford children the opportunity to play at the role of Zapatista. In so doing, both the dolls themselves and their makers play a part in reproducing the uprising through making the children Marcos. (The baby Marcoses have also performed double duty as hair clips, atop miniature horses, and loaded into the backs of rough-hewn wooden toy trucks.)

A full account of the Zapatista uprising's trajectory since 1994 would require many chapters, even many volumes. In some ways it has taken the form of a conventional war of attrition, punctuated by negotiations over cessation of hostilities and indigenous rights. For its part, the Mexican government has stayed a traditional course: deploy 25,000 soldiers to spatially quarantine and occasionally occupy Zapatista base communities while hired paramilitaries (the so-called "white guard") harass the restive population. Indeed, harassment is a polite euphemism in light of the December 22, 1997 massacre of forty-five peasants at Acteal (Villafuerte 2001, 17). The superficial efficacy of this strategy, reenforced by a general absence of armed response or expansionist territorial offensives by the EZLN, has led to aperiodic but frequent pronouncements of the uprising's imminent demise.

But the dolls tell another story. From 1995 onward, the muñecas Zapatistas began following established circuits of domestic Mexican travel, turning up across regions of southern and central Mexico most sympathetic to the uprising. And even more telling than this diffusion of the Mayan-made dolls out from Chiapas was their appearance in new forms clearly native to their new recipient regions. In Oaxaca, muñecas Zapatistas were crafted out of ceramic, and in other instances took the form of clay or papier maché skeletons (sometimes assembled in vignettes about a coffin labeled PRI, the acronym of the then-ruling party). In Michoacan, terra cotta figurines appeared that matched the Mayan dolls in size, armaments and, of course, ski-masks crowned with earthen pompoms. And at the swelling edges of the Federal District of Mexico City, muñecas Zapatistas were fabricated by squatters who were in many instances themselves recent migrants from the rural south. Kluged together from factory-made materials and salvaged industrial detritus, these dolls were commonly injection-molded action figures carefully rebuilt in the image of Marcos complete with miniatures of his bestarred dungaree cap, blue eyes, and signature pipe. (It is also vital to note, however, the extreme unevenness of this diffusion: for those inhabiting Mexico's free-trading northern frontier, the Zapatistas may as well be on some other globe entirely.)

During the late 1990s, this recasting of the muñecas Zapatistas into new materials commonplace to their multiplying locales of production replicated the extent to which the rebellion was itself being recast to fit new contexts. Throughout the period the Zapatistas reformulated and extended their battle to *not* seize power, and they did so by deemphasizing armed struggle in favor of a different sort of weapon: the word. The insurgency had

Muñeca Zapatista from Michoacan.

become "a war of ink, of written word, a war on the Internet" (Foreign Minister Jose Angel Gurría in Montes 1995, n.p.). Written, the Zapatista's words (and especially their formulation by Marcos) were disseminated through the Spanish language press, sometimes as often as two to three times per week, and broadly spread over the Internet. Spoken, these words served as centerpieces to nationally telemediated mass events like rallies, peace negotiations, and the coalition-building *encuentros* (encounters). These latter became a hallmark of Zapatista praxis, large-scale hybrids of the teach-in, the professional conference, the diplomatic summit and the late-1960s style "happening."

Muñeca Zapatista from Mexico City.

Originally conducted under the aegis and at the invitation of the Zapatistas, the encuentros have drawn from around the country organizations of the poor, the socially marginalized, the dissident, and the radicalized to hold dialogue on the non-representativeness of the federal state and its alleged conversion into an agent of NAFTA. The resultant national extension of the Zapatistas gave birth to numerous Civil Committees of Dialogue, base-community-style assemblies with open memberships. These committees are a mechanism for the widened practice of the aforesaid new political relationships, and consensually generate proposals for an associated polity. Such proposals in turn were the centerpiece of a September 1997 congress, attended by roughly 2,600 activists from every state in Mexico (except Nayarit), that gave birth to the nationwide Frente Zapatista de Liberación Nacional. Heavily couched in antivanguardist caveats, the FZLN constitutes a civilianization of the EZLN, "a space of convergence for various thoughts and intentions" functioning "[t]o organize the demands and proposals of common citizens such that they who lead, do so by obeying" (FZLN 1996, n.p.).

Thus, through the strategic deployment and mobilizing capacity of their words, the Zapatistas have periodically breached the military cordons surrounding their base communities. In the process they have galvanized popular pressure to ratchet down the state's military antiinsurgency operations in Chiapas. This has played no small part in preventing the Mexican state from definitively rolling its war machine over the rebels and their wooden guns, and so has preserved for the moment the Zapatista's alternative space for the exercise of decentered power. But more significant for the long term, the words of the Zapatistas have established a political vector articulating resistance movements, opposition groups and nongovernmental organizations (NGOs) nationwide. Thus, the Zapatistas have begun an experiment in exporting and scaling up their spaces for peace and new political relationships, an experiment in space making that is increasingly a collaboration with preexisting and expanding sectors of Mexican civil society.

Further, this is an experiment that, in its disseminatory travels, has become a festive pop-cultural event in its own right; nor is this accidental. The Zapatistas have periodically embodied their "spaces for peace" as a portable temporary autonomous zone (or TAZ; see Bey 1991) and, to much fanfare, taken it on the road. The most recent and dramatic instance, one that again challenged persistent rumors of the uprising's impending irrelevance (see, e.g., Ronfeldt et al. 1998), was in March of 2001. Preparatory to a congressional vote on legislation guaranteeing indigenous autonomy, a Zapatista caravan set out on a sixteen-day, 2,100-mile tour through twelve Mexican states. Their ultimate destination was Mexico City's central plaza and "political heart," the Zócalo. Officially christened the Caravan for Indian Dignity but quickly renamed the Zapatour by the Mexican press, this march to the capital consisted of fifteen busses and hundreds of additional vehicles carrying, among others, twenty-three Zapatista comandantes, Subcomandante Marcos, rank and file supporters, observers, journalists and police (AP 2001c). Throughout the tour the Zapatistas held rallies, conducted encuentros, and participated in the congresses of coalitional organizations like the National Indigenous Congress (Report from Nurío, 2001). The arrival in Mexico City, however, was particularly spectacular. It brought out from 100,000 (Romney and Smith 2001) to over 150,000 people (Robles 2001), including numerous rock bands, troupes of urbanized (and, increasingly, transurbanized) neo-Aztec *conchero* dancers, and more than a few giant puppets. Thus, a portable TAZ encamped as a traveling carnival of resistance in the public center of the country, directly between the national cathedral, the National Palace, and the excavated ruins of Tenochtitlan's highest temple. This tour came complete with merch tables selling black ski masks, CDs of rebel music, "Zappo" lighters (AP 2001c), and bunches of black balloons imprinted with a fleshtone strip of Marcos's eyes and nose bridge. And of course the ubiquitous muñecas, most prominently the Zapatista version in Mayan textile, but also a plastic doll of the architect of Mexican neoliberalization, ex-president Carlos Salinas de Gortari, now in de facto exile over alleged ties to official corruption and political homicide. This doll constitutes a particularly carnivalesque touch: it carries a large bag of loot in one hand and, when the head is pressed down upon, exposes an enormous erection out from under its black-and-white striped prisoner's smock.

But such merchandise wasn't the most exotic element to accompany the caravan. The Zapatour included legions of foreigners from the United States, Canada, and Europe, most notably some six hundred Italians. And some of these Italians were exotic indeed, dressed in white jumpsuits and padded rubber armor. These were the "white monkeys" (a.k.a. *monos blancos* or *tutte bianchi*), an auxiliary security force organized midway through the tour by the Zapatista comandantes in response to persistent death threats. Their presence points to the fact that the Zapatista uprising has traveled not only nationally, but globally as well. In the process, it has played an inarguable role in inspiring the global convergence of a distinctly Zapatista-esque, indirectly direct assault on plutocratically corporatist global formation. It has, in short, inspired a global movement for the deconcentration and reorientation of power, enacted via circuits of travel within the nonlocal networks of plutocratic globality itself.

Globalization against Globalization

I have had many encuentros of my own with the muñecas Zapatistas, but most have not occurred inside Mexico. Commonly, they have been in small shops scattered throughout the metropolitan centers of Europe and the U.S. Most of these shops have been cultural spaces, generally run by non-Mexican Zapatista sympathizers who travel intermittently to southern Mexico. Perhaps the most representative of these spaces is the cleverly (and tellingly) named Espresso Mi Cultura, a coffeehouse performance space at the eastern end of Hollywood. Here, the dolls sit among volumes of the Sup's writings, portraits of Cesar Chavez, and the Virgin of Guadalupe, refrigerator magnets bearing the visage of Che Guevara, and leaflets for the Aztec-revivalist Mexica movement. The pervasiveness of this outside support for the Zapatistas became particularly visceral for me in late 1998, when I entered Mexico hot on the trail of the muñeca Zapatista's commodity chain. Upon arrival, I discovered that none of my local colleagues could arrange me safe passage into Chiapas. Hundreds of visitors traveling on United States and European Union passports had just been ejected from the region, an attempt by the Mexican state to remove the "infestation of foreign activists who stir up and manipulate many indigenous groups contrary to constitutional order" (*Expreso Chiapas* 1998, 8). Given that this infestation consisted largely of human rights observers hunkered down in "civil peace camps" within Zapatista terrain, the claim of outside agitation would seem to have been targeted toward two ends: discursively delegitimizing the uprising as an alien intervention, and physically enabling antiinsurgency campaigns to proceed unobserved. Nonetheless, the fact of my being denied access was as revealing as anything I may have found in Chiapas itself. The Zapatistas had so successfully rallied support in the Americas and Europe that anyone traveling from those areas was now regarded as a potential sympathizer.

Chiapas is the poorest state in Mexico, but also one of the most stereotypically picturesque and archeologically significant. Thus, it receives a sizeable portion of its income from tourism. Given the EZLN's emphasis on discursive combat and its care in leaving noncombatants unharmed, the uprising has only served to enlarge Chiapas's appeal as a tourist destination. In this context the dolls are more than a toy and a popular expression of dissident sentiment. The prodigious volume of the dolls' production attests to the fact that the overwhelming majority are not likely to be consumed locally, whether as playthings or no (as is the case with woven Mayan dolls in general). They are also souvenirs and a source of tourist income. As such, they have taken canonical forms produced by the thousands, stacked like cordwood at open-air markets for sale to visitors, and diffused to the most travel-affluent corners of the globe. The implied disjunction between the dolls as popular expression and as commodity, however, is a false dichotomy both materially and symbolically. Chiapas's cities, villages, and Zapatista base communities trade extensively with one another, and even share members. As a result, the dolls function as a means by which wealth is transferred from tourists to the Zapatistas' supporters in both the towns and the countryside. Nor does this exchange necessarily entail a loss of meaning on either end. From the producer's end, as one Michoacaño ceramicist told me, "I make these to sell and get money, I am very poor. But it is because I am poor that I am proud to make Marcos, to show that I too am Zapatista" (Flusty 1999, January). And as we have seen on the receiving end, the dolls have a marked tendency to turn up in cultural spaces with strong leanings toward autonomism and, in the southwestern U.S. case, Chicanismo. The unwitting model for the dolls himself, Marcos, originally disparaged their mass cottage production and sale as disrespecting fallen rebels. But upon realizing that those buying the dolls supported the movement, and given that many of the dolls are produced by Zapatistas and even by members of the EZLN, he let the matter drop (Watson 2001).

The dolls, then, became one of a number of unconventional methods transporting the uprising into the larger world. Indeed, the Zapatistas have increasingly relied upon such unconventional linkage practices. This is implicit in Marcos's innovative use of print and broadcast media to disseminate the uprising's case. Of course, such media are not necessarily accessible. This is most notable in the United States, where the major television news outlets have consistently paid scant attention to the uprising (including the otherwise celebrated Zapatour, with U.S. journalists noteworthy for their absence from the caravan's international press contingent). It is debatable to what extent this is a product of the United States's long-standing status as the principle beneficiary of asymmetrical economic relations with its southern neighbor. Similarly, there is the fact that television news in the United States is now almost entirely subsumed by Olimem, parceled out among such constituent organs as AOL Time Warner, Viacom, Disney, and Rupert Murdoch's News Corporation/Fox Entertainment Group. But whatever its origins, the Zapatistas have largely overcome this obstacle, making extensive use of the Internet to disseminate their declarations, the CCRI's communiqués, and Marcos's postscripts and stories. This is perhaps the first revolution with its own Internet homepage, http://www.ezln.org (Gray 1997, 5–6), a precedent-setting instance of arguably effective "Netwar" (Ronfeldt et al. 1998). Zapatista autonomist practices have thus been translated into the globally diffuse space of the Internet, issuing calls for consensually derived spaces of peace and new politics into the "consensual hallucination" of cyberspace. Such translation has resonated with particular strength among relatively educated and disaffected youth throughout the postindustrial world, and has created a worldwide visibility that renders state assaults on Zapatista territory "politically inadvisable" (Ronfeldt et al., 1998, 86).

These electronically mediated calls have taken the form not just of communiqués and fables, but also of explicit invitations. Issued to foreign celebrities and intellectuals, NGOs and other potentially interested parties, the invitations have drawn thousands of tourists, observers, and sympathizers from the outside in to the otherwise isolated mountains of southern Mexico. In the process, many of these visitors became participants in the summer of 1996's First Intercontinental Encuentro for Humanity and Against Neoliberalism (as pointedly opposed to an inter*national* gathering). At this assembly, three thousand attendees from forty-three countries drafted the Second Declaration of Reality (a pun, given the assembly's location in the town of La Realidad). Using tropes that would make Manuel Castells glow, the Second Declaration set forth a framework for the creation of oppositional nonlocal fields: an "intercontinental network of resistance" and an "intercontinental network of alternative communication" (Zapatistas 1998, 52–53). This event lead to a Second Intercontinental Encuentro held in 1997 at five locations in Spain with some very cosmopolitanized Mayan locals in attendance, and an International Consulta and Jornada for the Excluded of the World in 1999. While these meetings have more often than not produced unenthusiastically unresolved resolutions, they have also brought together activists who would subsequently coordinate "the anti-capitalist mass demonstrations of London J18, Seattle N30 and those that followed in 2000 including A16 Washington and S26 Prague" (Flood 2001. 3). But these meetings constitute no less the hyperextension of the assemblies and consultas, the infusion of a Mayanized consultative decision making process into the ongoing global formation of resistance networks.

Thus, in their efforts to elide military containment within Chiapas and establish a global reach, the Zapatistas have played a role in refining new organizing methods for the performance of dissent, and in assembling organizers to carry those methods "intercontinentally." Through this dissemination the Zapatistas have become a rallying cry articulating linkages between numerous other causes previously understood as local and distinct, causes like freeing putative political prisoners, "Third World" debt forgiveness, and opposition to transgenic foods. Nor is this a happenstance occurrence, such linkages have been actively formulated and popularized by particular visitors to Chiapas. One clear example is the Los Angeles–based rock band Rage against the Machine. On CDs and cassette tapes and at sold-out concerts, this band's hybrid of hip-hop and heavy metal accompanied lyrics that, not unlike Marcos's own writings, deployed violent indignation, principled proclamations, pedagogic analysis, and poetic magicorealism. Their subject matter was consistently that of reclaiming power through direct practices in the here and now, specific actions directed toward freeing activists Mumia Abu Jamal and Leonard Peltier, confronting police brutality and systemic censorship, or supporting the Zapatistas to oppose the hemispheric enactment of neoliberal theory. Concrete methods and established activist networks towards these ends were provided on the band's website (www.ratm.com). Further, the themes carried through in the band's merchandising, as with T-shirts emblazoned with the hyperpatriotic slogan "We Support Our Troops" in stars-and-stripes spangled red, white and blue, subversively juxtaposed with a portrait of four EZLN insurgents.

Beyond this one band, the visage of Marcos, often accompanied by those of Zapata and Che, have traveled to CD and book covers, T-shirts, and posters across the planet. The pipe-studded ski mask has even turned up in primitivist illustrations for a readily available children's picture book (Marcos and Domínguez 1996), penned by the Sup himself (and from which, upon realizing the identity of the author, the U.S. National Endowment for the Arts withdrew previously committed funding). Thus, as the uprising has repeatedly moved in and out of a commodity form it has spread ever further afield. In the process its meaning has undergone varied degrees of slippage, but in so doing it has taken on new implications and mobilizing roles as it has been adapted for use in new contexts and a succession of ever more far-flung mass actions.

This is not to imply, however, that attempts have not been made to appropriate the uprising for less activist ends, most notably for the enhancement of sales to youth target markets. As early as 1995, the Veneto-based clothing company Benetton, famous for its deployment of socially controversial causes in advertising, offered Marcos a reportedly lucrative modeling contract (Watson 2001). In itself, this is nothing new. In 1914, Pancho Villa accepted $25,000 from the Mutual Films Company to allow its documentarians at his battles, and went so far as to fight during daylight hours and delay his assault on the city of Ojinaga out of consideration for Mutual's film crew (Bennett 2000). But unlike his predecessor, Marcos tacitly refused the offer by neglecting to answer it. He had, however, lampooned the offer a full year prior to its making. In a running series of "mercantilist postscripts" attached to a CCRI communiqué of February 16, 1994, Marcos inquires into the "going price, in dollars" for such commodities and services as his "dirty, smelly ski-mask," a "mug shot . . . from the waist down," the appearance of "a particular brand of bottled soda . . . on the dialogue table," and the grief of the uprising's dead (Marcos 1995, 142–43). Spurned, Benetton turned to the Middle East and ultimately produced a catalog featuring the portraits and biographies of Israelis and Palestinians in amicable (albeit sometimes ambivalent) everyday interactions, with all depicted parties conspicuously clad in the company's garments (UCB, 1998).

While Marcos may not have been available for licensing, the corollary upsurge in revolutionary chic was public domain, most notably in its earlier avatar as Che Guevara. In the more informal sectors of the U.S. Southwest's economy, this resulted in the sale of banners bearing Andy Warhol's iconic black-and-red graphic of (Alberto "Korda" Diaz Gutierrez's photograph of) Che Guevara from off the chain-link fences of vacant lots. On the opposite scalar end of the business spectrum, a similar portrait appeared on the face of the Swiss Societe de Microelectronique et d'Horlorgerie corporation's "Revolucion" model Swatch watches. Somewhere in between were the relatively costly Italian-made scarves printed, yet again, with the same image. The most extreme example, however, was another doll, the most perversely distaff form of the muñeca Zapatista to date. Roughly the same size as the

Mayan dolls, this one was factory produced in the People's Republic of China. It took the form of a Chihuahua clad in Che's signature black beret. The beret was adorned on front with a red flag which, upon closer inspection, proved to be the logo of Taco Bell, a subsidiary of the TNC Yum! Brands (nee Tricon Global Restaurants, newly spun-off from PepsiCo). When pressed on the belly, this plush Che-huahua heroically intoned "!Viva Gorditas!"

Introduced in 1999, this doll was part of a campaign conceived by advertising firm TBWA Chiat Day's Los Angeles office. The campaign played upon then wildly popular ads in which a talking Chihuahua proclaimed "Yo quiero Taco Bell." But it went further, fusing the dog with antiquated tropes of Latin American revolutionary machismo as a means of introducing gorditas tacos to the fast-food market. Taco Bell restaurants flew red flags emblazoned with the beret-clad animal. Car antennae sprouted red pennants, again adorned with the canine Che. And in television spots, on a balcony high above the throngs of a dusty colonial city, the Che-huahua appeared in heavy rotation at a bank of antiquated microphones. Upon the dog's echoing intonation of "¡Viva Gorditas!" adoring throngs chanted and sang in unison as giant red banners unfurled across the sides of buildings, each emblazoned with a massive arm holding a taco aloft. Throughout the campaign, the gorditas slogan was endlessly repeated: "The Revolutionary Taco."

White Monkeys, Black Blocs

This book began with a prognostication by Marcos' Miniature Comrade at arms, Durrito the Beetle, to the effect that the rebels are going to win. So, are they winning? Or has the revolution been commoditized? There is no definitive answer. There are, however, some inarguable facts. By mid-2000, the Che-huahua partisan of the revolutionary taco had been put to sleep. Sales had fallen, the talking Chihuahua had transitioned from popular to passé, and TBWA Chiat Day lost the Taco Bell account. Conversely, the same period that saw the demise of the revolutionary taco also witnessed the sudden appearance of mass actions at sites of globalist conclaves around the world. The prototype of these was the "Battle in Seattle." Occurring from November 29–December 2, 1999, Seattle was to be the place where the World Trade Organization would ceremonially ratify the Multilateral Agreement on Investment (or MAI). The MAI was not just another claim for the rights of capital, but an unprecedented claim to the absolute sovereignty of capital. This claim had been formulated in a strict absence of public dialogue by trade negotiators, heads of state, foreign ministers and representatives of numerous TNCs, and codified in a hefty confidential document.

Muñeca Zapatista from Taco Bell.

But in Seattle, this claim was made visible and its enactment terminated. At some point in the run-up to the WTO meeting, the text of the MAI had been leaked. In response, broad hyperextended coalitions of resistant NGOs coordinated over the Internet (Ronfeldt et al. 1998, 115) and ultimately turned out fifty thousand protesters to greet the WTO functionaries. But what was particularly notable about this protest was not just its size or electronic coordination, but the persistent diversity of its participants and practices. Shipped in from locales as disparate as Atlanta, Turin, Jakarta and Seoul, these included large labor unions, environmentalists, church organizations, fair-trade activists, human rights advocates, and assorted out-of-the-closet anarchists massed into Black Blocs for the occasion. Their tactics were no less diverse, ranging from multi-thousand person marches (and marches of dozens of persons costumed as endangered sea turtles), sit-ins on major thoroughfares, fifteen-foot tall puppet shows, drumming circles, the blockade of a WTO delegates' hotel by arm-in-arm bell-ringing Santas, and bricks tossed through the windows of Starbuck's coffeehouses. Meanwhile, heavily armored riot police took up positions in front of such vital public infrastructure as the city's NikeTown (see *Adbusters* 2001, 48–49), called upon to protect and serve the physical integrity of a retail concept (and one that, by Nike's own account, had become an imminently divestible revenue loser).

The Battle in Seattle thus announced the emergence of a new alternate globality that ridiculed the institutional contradictions, vulnerabilities and absurdities of its hegemonic other. It signified the coalescence of the much remarked "teamsters and turtles" coalition of workers and environmentalists around the issue of globalization. It demonstrated new practices of resistance centered upon the highly creative and generally playful intrusion of the body into commonplace spatial infrastructure (a practice some participants now refer to as "voting," a play on the perception that legitimized mechanisms of political participation through the ballot-box have become fiscally co-opted and practically ineffective). And it accomplished all this through the popular production of an environment most closely resembling a gigantic circus. Or, more to the point, a carnival.

In his definition of *carnival,* Mikhail Bakhtin (1984, chap. 3) characterizes it as the archetypal temporary autonomous zone, an event that makes space for the practice of the popular-festive form. Carnival marks the inevitable passage of time, the death of the old and the corollary renewal of the world, performatively literalized in a celebration the people give to themselves. At carnival time, shopworn truths and the mirthless authorities they reinforce are beaten down and mocked with blows that are painful but "gay, melodious and festive" (207). Thus, the high is abased and destroyed in the service of low bodily renewal. In the process, the "carnivalesque crowd" organizes itself in its own way, "outside of and contrary to all existing forms of the coercive socioeconomic and political organization" (255). In short, carnival is a collective and emplaced bodily practice that playfully dismembers the rigidly imposed body politic.

The Battle in Seattle, in its loosely collaborative horizontal organization, its spontaneity, its deployment of violently playful confrontation, and even in such material culture forms as its masks and puppets, signifies a resurgence of Bakhtinian festival. It brought plutocratic globality down from on high, humiliated its authority and subordinated it to the body. Thus the de facto supranational state, in its attempt to globally impose the logic of the export production zone, unintentionally generated a massive temporary autonomous zone that recovered the popular-festive form. And, as suggested by subsequent such carnivals of resistance (e.g., at meetings of the International Monetary Fund/World Bank in Washington, D.C., from April 16–17 and in Prague from September 26–28 of 2000), this TAZ arrayed against the EPZ has become more of a portable permanent autonomous zone (a PAZ, perhaps?). Thus, the gray, grim and self-seriously opaque global administration of creative destruction has come under sustained assault by the merrily destructive creation of a carnivalesque and anarchistic alternate globality.

This carnival bears strong isomorphisms with that of March 2001 in Mexico City's Zócalo. Further, it is suggestive that they emerge in conjunction with the Zapatista's intercontinental encuentros. Of course, there are some significant differences, most notably the fact that the anarchist bent of much mobilization against plutocratic globality is at odds with the Zapatistas' support of the nation-state and openness to capitalism. But despite these distinctions, it would seem that the Zapatistas have indeed "inspired and stimulated a wide variety of grassroots political efforts in many other countries" (Cleaver in Ronfeldt et al., 1998, p. 115). But the empirical demonstration of this 'Zapatista Effect' (Cleaver, 1998) is in the persons and practices of the protesters themselves. Attendees of the Ruckus Society's Democracy Action Camps are one instance of this. This camp is a traveling emplacement founded in 1995, devoted to training would-be resisters in "nonviolent direct actions" ranging from forming bodily blockades to rappelling down the sides of building while unfurling unauthorized banners. Consistently, Ruckus participants cite the Zapatistas as their inspiration, and many identify their own experiences as tourists in Chiapas as the trigger for their subsequent civilly disobedient practices upon their return home (see, e.g., Lewis 2000).

An even stronger case is made by those White Monkeys. They are a division of the Italian (although now global) Ya Basta! Association, founded in 1996 as an urban Italian Zapatista support group. Dozens of them were among the "foreign infestation" ejected from Chiapas in 1998. They have pioneered many of the new carnivalesque tactics of a "rebellion of the body" by interposing their own highly visible and well padded bodies (dressed in white, in day-glo hues, or in nothing at all, taped into foam rubber suits, strapped into nets full of brightly colored balloons, carrying garbage can lids) where authority wants them least. They tie these practices explicitly to Michel Foucault's ideas of "bio-power," arguing that only through the disorderly rebelliousness of bodies can the state's exercise of power through the ordering and silencing of bodies be countered. And they have personally transported these theories and practices to the mass protests in London, Prague, Québec, and Genoa. But ultimately the White Monkeys cite their experiences and firsthand observations of the Zapatistas' bodily resistance as their principle source, especially the combatants armed with dummy guns and the Zapatista women who've massed unarmed around Mexican soldiers to prevent them entering Mayan villages (see Ramirez-Cuevas 2000; Ya Basta! 2001). The White Monkeys, then, constitute a concretely identifiable link by which Zapatismo's theory and praxis has traveled so widely as to become the axis of articulation for a restive alternate globality. And the White Monkey's particular adaptation of the Zapatistas' practices has itself been exported as a replicable new paradigm of not-so-passive resistance, informing highly visible direct-action organizations like the United Kingdom's WOMBLES (White Overalls Movement Building Libertarian Effective Struggles) and Australia's WOMBATS (White Overall Mobile Buffer against Truncheon Strikes).

TAZ versus EPZ

The seriously playful practices of people like the White Monkeys, in conjunction with the blockading Santas, oversized green sea turtles and gigantic puppets, have mobilized the popular-festive imaginary in a more nuanced vision of festival than even Bakhtin's. This is, after all, not something "the people" as a unitary opposition have given to themselves. Instead, it is something diverse coalitions of people have jointly taken for themselves, a politically empowering recovery of a lost signified despite and to spite the supranationalizing state and its partnership with the TNC. Thus it is "a hybrid, syncretic movement based more on immediate results than on ideology," one with "black-clad militant anarchist[s] . . . on the frontlines" and more traditional activists taking their cues from "less-militant but equally revolutionary . . . anarchist direct-action coordinators" (Kuiper 2001b, n.p.). And in its hyperextension, this movement becomes a carnivalesque globality, a riotous postmodernism of resistance in the global landscape wherein multiple voices retain their differences while conjoining to leave globalism "bruisedblueandcontused" (Rabelais 1955, 483).

The old new order, however, is hardly decrepit—it is neither so close to death nor so easily knocked around as was feudalism in François Rabelais' time. And so it has responded to the new nonlocal mobilization of the popular-festive imaginary with a voracity that throws plutocratic globality's praetorian face into sharp relief. At its least vigorous, the official response has been denigrative characterizations of the globally networked dissidents as benighted "globalphobes" insufficiently schooled in macroeconomics. But more seriously, authorities have begun conflating carnivalesque globality with "terrorism" (e.g., L.A. Richard Mayor Riordan in Lewis 2000; Morales 2001, 11).

Could giant masked sea turtles, balloon-armored white monkeys and obstructive Santas possibly be terrorists? On the face of it, the claim is patently absurd. But upon closer inspection, the practices of carnivalesque globality's convergences do bear certain isomorphisms with terrorism. Both are tactics of subaltern geopolitics, unconventional attempts to wield influence despite disinclusion from decision- and place-making processes. Both choose their targets quasi-randomly from out of a clearly defined, symbolically significant population. Both are forms of political theater that rely upon careful staging and telemediated representation. And both have, upon occasion and with variable degrees of success, proven effective in bringing visibility to grievances, and far more powerful adversaries to the bargaining table (Zulaika and Douglass 1996). But central to the terrorist event is the pseudo-random enactment of sudden violence against undefended life and limb, a praxis of asymmetrical warfare as enacted against Manhattan and Washington, D.C., on September 11 of 2001. In this event, a very different alternate globality turned such technologies of memory and motion as online reservation services and jumbo jets into weapons of mass destruction. Conversely, this sort of praxis has been wholly absent from the mass-convergences against plutocratic globality, and is inconsistent with their theoretical and ethical underpinnings. Thus the deployment of terrorist characterizations against plutocratic globality's discontents by representatives of the supranational state is a cynically dangerous exaggeration, and a disingenuous one at that. After all, what could be more terrifying than the state's technopolitical enactments of distanciated push-button violence, irresistibly delivered en masse and from on high in the form of not-so-smart "smart bombs" and paradoxically inaccurate "surgical strikes" (Aksoy and Robins 1991; see also Herman 1982)?

In keeping with this predilection, the supranational state has been leaving the practitioners of carnivalesque globality gassedstunnedshotzappeddousedanddisappeared (to coin a Rabelaisianism). While bodies may well be the enactors of power, such enactments include the deployment of well-armored and organized bodies against others less cooperative and less well equipped. Thus, plutocratically globalist apparatuses have adopted a standard operating procedure of employing ever greater degrees of force against their discontents. This use of force in support of the EPZ was not absent in Seattle, where U.S. Army Delta Force commandos were brought on scene (Ehling 2002) and police at one point exhausted their prodigious supplies of oleoresin capsicum pepper spray. But such practices have escalated, extending to raids on demonstration-preparatory "convergence centers" and the detainment without cause of noted activists (all subsequently judged extrajudicial). Increasingly, these interdictions have been executed by extrajudicial enforcers as well. The most noteworthy case of this occurred at the January 2001 World Economic Forum in Davos, Switzerland, where the "Swiss financial establishment" created and armed the United Police Forces of Switzerland (Morales 2001, 11), a praetorian guard in contravention of rulings by the Swiss Supreme Court. In the process the development and distribution of "less lethal" materiel suited to the task of quelling civil dissent, technologies like chemical agents, bean-bag rounds and rubber bullets, has itself engendered a large and profitable oligopoly in its own right.

This escalation of the running battle between plutocratic globality and its subalterns has evolved a distinct spatial form, one visited upon host sites wherever globalist functionaries congregate. It is a form that will by now be distinctly familiar, an egregious caricature of my own descriptions of the interdicted metapolis and the new world bipolar disorder at large. Consider, by way of example, Québec. Québec hosted the Summit of the Americas, where final negotiations on the Free Trade Area of the Americas were to be conducted from April 20–22, 2001. Preparatory to this, the Nike distributors boarded up their windows and the McDonald's went so far as to take down its golden arches. Phalanxes of police were mobilized and the citidel atop the seventeenth-century walled citadel, the strategically selected meeting site, was cordoned off. Within this "security zone," thirty-four of the American hemisphere's heads of state hammered out an obtusely worded confidential document establishing a unitary mercantile order stretching from the Arctic Ocean to Tierra del Fuego. Surrounding them was 2.5 miles of concrete barricade topped with chain-link fence, the so-called Wall of Shame, reinforced (and, where the wall was subsequently breached, substituted) by six thousand police armored like Roman legionaries. Outside this perimeter seethed a mass of thirty thousand othered: environmentalists, trade unionists, native peoples, food purists, and anarchists of various stripes. In this context, color took on a particularly stark signification as protesters self-divided into three color-coded groups: green for nonviolent, yellow for passive resistant (and possible detainees), and a red front line of the directly confrontational (and imminently arrestable).

For three days, the story of these colors was one of marching en masse and attempting to breach the new palisade surrounding the old citadel. Despite this, the line between the TAZ and EPZ held, crossed only by tear-gas canisters and the spray of water canons. Here masks were again much in evidence among protesters, police, and journalists alike. But they were gas masks, indicating that as plutocratic globality gradually metamorphoses into a praetorian globality, the carnival is taking on a hard, dark edge. (This too was presaged at Seattle, where student-protest veterans from South Korea introduced fellow dissidents to a novel form of festive face painting: the application of toothpaste around the eyes to ward off the caustic effects of tear gas; see Garcia, 2000.) In the end the othered retreated to the "lower city" beneath the citadel and, pounding "unabated, for hour upon hour . . . on the actual structure of the city itself, on guardrails, signs, girders, bridge abutments," ensured that "no one in the city could hear anything at all" (Kuiper 2001a, 22–23).

For now, the trail ends here. Where it will ultimately lead is an open question. The omens, however, are hardly reassuring. At Genoa's G8 summit from July 20–22, 2001, the persistence of authoritative disregard and increasingly draconian interdictory practices (some imported from Los Angeles; see Ehrenreich 2001) pushed plutocratic globality's objectors from the serious play of festival into open street warfare. Official attempts to defend an intensely militarized 1.5-square-mile inner "red" and much larger outer "yellow" protest exclusion zone against as many as 150,000 protesters gave rise to bloodily indiscriminate mass police violence against activists and the press, the serious injury of five hundred participants (predominantly those on the dissident side), $45 million in damages, the shooting death of a twenty-three-year-old fire-extinguisher-wielding Black Bloc-er by a twenty-year old *carabiniere,* and two days of rioting by the most radical dissident factions provoked and abetted, according to some accounts, by law enforcement clad as Black Bloc-ed anarchists (Kuiper 2001c; *Economist* 2001b; BBC News 2001a, 2001b; see Nordland and Dickey 2001, for a more conscientiously disinformative report).

Meanwhile, back in Mexico, congressional passage of an eviscerated resolution on indigenous rights and culture has raised the specter of a return to armed conflict. Nor is it inconceivable that, in the Zócalo sometime over the next year or two, there may be priapic black-and-white striped dolls of Marcos. Carnival, after all, is the cyclical business of debasing last year's king by enthroning a parodic new one: sooner or later, that new one must in turn be dethroned and merrily beaten (perhaps by that Spanish scourge of Augusto Pinochet, Judge Baltasar Garzón; see Skeels 2002). Meanwhile, the International Monetary Fund summit in November of 2001 was hosted in well-out-of-the-way Doha, Qatar: a locale hardly noted for its tolerance of performative civil disobedience under normal circumstances and specially locked down for the occasion. During this summit, only five hundred approved representatives of NGOs were allowed into the country to attend (MacKinnon, 2001) raising the ominous possibility that in future the management of global formation will be commanded by means of stealth summits.

All this could be regarded a resounding victory for global plutocracy. Then again, this geographical peripheralization of the last IMF summit also underscores the potency of alternate globalities. The everyday practitioners of global formation can and do become cognizant of the global reach of their practices, and have taken to deploying them bodily so as to articulate new nonlocal fields that embody global resistances to real effect. These are effects so real that international summits now put putative world cities on the map in entirely perverse ways, as places where "globalization" is not only made but broken as well—simultaneous with the literal breaking of the city itself. As a result, prospective host cities now regard supranational state conclaves as costly, disruptive menaces best held somewhere else, *anywhere* else but *here*. It seems fair to say, then, that the peripheralized have taken a serious stab at peripheralizing the center, and for a time succeeded in concretely evicting its formal enactment to the ends of the earth.

Thus, resistance has given form to an alternate globality, one of playful contention and "leading by following," that has poached a plethora of social actors and turned them to new uses. It has been given shape by those who travel in oligopolistically conditioned spaces and times so as to deploy themselves against the neoliberalized management of global formation. While this has hardly attained the status of a revolution, it is at least an upwelling: a dislocalized continuation, hyperextension and augmentation of that uprising in the mountains of the Mexican southeast.

The first Mexican revolution, fought at the beginning of the twentieth century, was a localized struggle to wrest *tierra,* earth, from the *latifundistas.* It brought about the dismemberment of the latifundia and their redistribution among the peasants. The second, initiated at the beginning of the twenty first century, has become a worldwide effort to wrest the earth from the global latifundium and, in the process, has informed a vociferous refusal to stand idly by as the global is reduced to a single vision. Whether it will nonetheless end up enforced as a unitary order, however, remains to be seen.

Conclusion

> The rich became richer, the mighty yet mightier, and the poor poorer, as the gods have decreed. . . .
>
> —Mika Waltari, *The Egyptian*

Over the years I have conducted this research, I have found myself in ever more frequent encounters with globalities of increasingly monstrous aspect. Of these encounters, two have been particularly disturbing. The first was some three years ago, a run-in with the praetorian globality presently inheriting hegemony from its plutocratic progenitor. This encounter was not with a lurid headline describing police actions to ward off the disruption of some international economic summit or other, nor was it one of the true-crime stories about some blood-soaked new Transnational Criminal Organization that passes for reportage on the local television stations. It was an encounter with a snow globe, manufactured in the People's Republic of China and ensconced among statuettes and teddy bears on the shelf of a small souvenir shop. Normally, a snow globe would be among the things least liable to terrify me, and in many ways this snow globe was no different from any other. It consisted of a large glass bulb atop a cast resin base, fitted with a music box that played Bach's Minuet No. 3. When shaken, a smattering of polychromed mylar confetti floated about the dome's interior. What shook me was the figurines inside the globe itself: two SWAT (Special Weapons and Tactics) officers in tactical armor and combat helmets, crouched in combat-ready poses as they pointed their miniature Heckler and Koch MP5 machine guns at me through the glass. On closer examination, I saw the base of the snowglobe was festooned in high relief with tiny handcuffs, walkie-talkies, and an ammunition belt laden with bullets.

This curio, the most outré artifact in VanMark's "Blue Hats of Bravery" collectible figurine line, was displayed in conjunction with the advertising copy "Whenever we question the chaos found within our daily lives due to the unpredictable threat of Violence and Villainy, we always seem to turn to the courageous efforts of our Policemen, expecting immediate protection!" In finding this artifact troubling, I do not mean to imply that I find commemorative police merchandise inherently problematic. I am, however, less favorably disposed toward merchandise celebrating the growing militarization of civil law enforcement (Kraska and Kappeler 1997). And to valorize the most zealous, bellicose and excessively forceful civilian police units (Morales 1999) in a material form that is not only homey kitsch, but downright *cute*, strikes me as a dystopian surreality akin to a cuddly plush Intercontinental Balistic Missile that squeaks happily when hugged.

Nonetheless, there is clearly a demand for such objects, or else why go to the expense of designing, marketing, and distributing them at all? An entire line of them, for that matter, updated annually. A colleague's student suggested that this snow globe must be intended for "the moms and girlfriends of cops," and from merchants I've spoken with this does seem to be the primary market. But there is something else at work here, too. The double SWAT snow globe is starkly emblematic of the quaintification of the new world bipolar disorder. It throws into high relief ongoing attempts to render publicly acceptable and even laudatory increasing levels of surveillance and brute physical control, their suppression of dissent, and their recipients' social peripheralization at every geographical scale.

In the snow globe, then, are the commonplace practices of concerting, coordering, conserving and candy-coating privilege within the world city, across the metapolis, and throughout the world at large: privilege accreted and secured through the strategic deployment of othering, through the command and commodification of difference, and the simultaneous silencing, subordination, suppression, and exclusion of the different. In the snow globe is an authoritative global postmodernism of reaction, the imposition of its "pretty lie" (Relph 1987, 259) to disguise an ever more subtle and powerful rationality on the part of supranationalizing state apparatuses conjoined to the transnational corporations (TNCs). This rationality has engendered an intensely incivil society overseen by unaccountable semiformal supranational autocracies, densely interwoven with quasi-legitimized gangsterism and media-saturated disinformation. It has enabled a private retreat into cozy neotraditionalist preserves while the rest of the planet writhes.

The snow globe itself is a tiny thing, but the scope and scale of the authoritatively imposed pretty lie it signifies is beyond any previously imagined. According to the U.S. Space Command, "[t]he globalization of the world economy will . . . continue, with a widening between 'haves' and 'have-nots'" (USSC 1996, 6). The militarized "domination" of outer space by means of a Space Defense Initiative will keep those "have-nots" in line, while protecting "commercial national interests and investment" (USSC 1996, 3, 4; Grossman 2001, 27). Of course, such a militarization of outer space does not only keep the have-nots in line after the fact. It constitutes a belligerent and overarching new component in the machine that manufactures haves and have-nots in the first place. It is, in short, the triumphant ascendancy of a praetorian globality. And it is also a demonstration that no matter how outrageous my hypothesizing as I've pursued this work, the underlying realities have consistently exceeded my own darkest hypotheses.

By all appearances, then, the earth's surface in its entirety is fast on its way to becoming jittery space. But as we have seen, the higher the viewpoint, the lower the resolution. Overviews overlook, and what the satellites must necessarily overlook is global formation itself in its innumerable everyday practices. Or, in the words of the Subcomandante Insurgente Marcos, "The apparent infallibility of globalization clashes with the stubborn disobedience of reality" (1997, n.p.). While discussions of globalization occupy themselves with structural manifestations and efforts to derive predictive generalizations, the activities of poaching and bricolage are constantly remaking and redefining the globe by feeding accretions of fine-grain peculiarities up from the ground level. This dynamic of global formation can be a hopeful thing, a cause for celebration. Then again, it can be something else entirely.

My second, disturbing global encounter came in the wee hours of a September morning, visited upon me by telephone calls from colleagues around the world. One, from Tokyo, was a frantic inquiry into my physical well-being. Another, from an Israeli, was an insistence that per her own now-standard practice I immediately call any associates in Manhattan to verify *their* physical well-being. These were followed by another two calls, both from Helsinki, urging me with typically wry Finnish humor to turn on my television. "Your tallest buildings are disappearing," one of them bluntly stated. Through a haze of interrupted sleep, I reached for the remote control and flipped on CNN to discover that, sure enough, the skyline of Manhattan was in the midst of an abrupt transformation. Simultaneously, the Pentagon had suddenly become what one of my callers ruefully referred to as "the Quadragon" (Raento, 2001).

Displayed on my thirty-one-inch screen was a whole other postmodernity, vengeful and with a vengeance, and a violent mutation of postmodernism's methods. For the next few hours I was transfixed by a perverse strategy of detournement whereby jetliners turned into guided missiles, bombs made smart not through multibillion-dollar research and development programs but through their poaching by unauthorized pilots with aspirations to martyrdom. In the process, routine travelers became just so much expendable ballast. I saw a kluging together of distinct epochal tactics into a new hybrid: the hijackings-for-hostages common to the 1970s fused with the suicide truck bombings of the late 1980s, all at a heretofore unprecedented scale. I watched the targets dissolve, literally and figuratively, into a highly polyvalent discursive/material formation that became what it was depending upon how one looked. It was a monument of mythic proportions to American might. It was an architectonic machine engaged in the minutiae of global formation's fiduciary management. It was an abruptly defunct ZIP code, the unauthorized implosion of an oversized bureaucratic back office you had to brave if you needed your licenses renewed, and the unanchoring of a world city's southern skyline—Manhattan's own under-appreciated Solsol and Shahmama now reduced to a seething absence. And yet it remained irrevocably two 110-story glass and steel containers of thousands of biographies, a vast citidel of richly elaborated everyday life stories all coming to instantaneous, unexpected ends. In the discursive and subsequent material erasure of these life stories, I witnessed the blood-soaked collision of alternate globalities that are territorially interwoven but utterly incommensurable. And in the collapse of the towers and its aftermath I experienced Jean Baudrillard inverted, a recession of simulacra: I had watched cinematic representations of these fractured towers hurling their occupants into midair two years previous in the movie *Armageddon,* and a few months later depictions of a terrorist-beleaguered Manhattan under martial law in *The Siege.* It was, in short, a brief but thorough cooptation of Olimove's and Olimem's most vital components to orchestrate a postmodern shock-geopolitics of the spectacle.

The attack's postmodernity was inextricably bound up with how it highlighted the presencing of the global in everyday life. For me this presencing came direct from across the planet, where colleagues had awakened me telephonically while watching the disaster telemediated in progress (in the Finns' case, on a gigantic video display affixed to the wall of a popular downtown Helsinki shopping arcade). My subsequent experience of explosively vanishing jetliners and crumbling towers came from these same images, obsessively rebroadcast cross-country by satellites and ground stations. All these dislocalized skeins wove back together in my own bedroom, its walls flaring orange and yellow as the pixels on my television screen ordered themselves to articulate the disintegration of an edifice I myself had utilized for panoptic sight-seeing some scant months previous. In an instant, the compression of global time space had become a visceral implosion.

Yet in the same instant that global time space imploded, it also decompressed in extraordinarily uneven and counterintuitive ways. Manhattan's surviving phone line hubs and relay antennae were hopelessly overloaded, all civilian aviation was instantaneously grounded, the prodigious electronic flows of the international capital markets were frozen and the national economy itself began to founder. I had become used to seeing this sort of disruption elsewhere, imposed upon others as the product of surgical strikes and sanctions directed top-downward. Here, however, it was self-imposed, the reaction to strikes executed with an eerily similar precision but from the inside out. The effect was thus perversely isomorphic: like Iraq and Serbia in the 1990s, the U.S. became a space of no-fly zones and, in parts, fundamental infrastructural failure. Those who'd torn me out of bed were now thousands of insurmountable miles away instead of a day's flight. And while my friends in Manhattan were many miles closer they were also infinitely more distant.

Utterly unreachable for subsequent days, they had for all practical purposes disappeared from the planet entirely.

This paradoxically implosive decompression of global time-space has subsequently served to legitimize a counterpoised explosion. Suddenly, we are in the midst of a readily portable, ultimately indefinable and quite possibly prefabricated (Arney 2001) 'forever war' of a distinctly hybrid nature. It is an armed conflict that mixes together the job descriptions of soldiers, spies, and police to puncture the division between foreign and civil wars, authorizing the Pentagon to govern distant nation-states, infantry to patrol U.S. airports and border crossings, and intelligence agents to monitor my e-mails and credit card transactions. In this new kind of flexist warfare, campaigns are short-cycling, telematic, spatially discontiguous and readily retargeted toward new locations with quicksilver speed. And there are so many targets in the offing. Al Qaeda's militarized subaltern theocracy is a nonlocal field as diffuse as any other, comprised of hyperextended everyday practices that can be traced to implicate any number of unsuspecting peripheral nation-states, along with their burgeoning megacities and long-suffering populations. As a result, the everyday lives of these last are now experiencing a global presence far more disturbing than anything that had entered my own bedroom.

Of course, for many of these everyday lives such disturbance is nothing new. Generations of them have borne the weight of plutocratic globality and its praetorian shadow self. They have been repeatedly displaced, most commonly into the nearest accessible megacity, while their political elites were co-opted and their economies readjusted. It should come as no surprise, then, that these everyday lives are so often situated in an epochal hybrid of the Paleolithic and the postapocalyptic, and possessed of a voracious appetite for some form, *any* form of liberation. In some corners of the world, this sort of globalization has left mosques and *madrassas* to pick up the slack on the street, to provide material sustenance and readymade meaning to the immiserated. It has bolstered the most puritanically revanchist forms of Islam and grafted them to some very modern doctrines of nationalism (see Moussalli 1993). It has employed this hybrid to assemble hyperextended holy wars against that other globality of note, the socialist one (see Labeviere 2000) now languishing atop the ash-heap of history's end. And it has subsequently neglected those holy wars, leaving them to blow back upon their patron once they became obsolete.

These outcomes in turn have intersected to propagate al Qaeda's neomedieval thirdspace, a hieratic globality with a distinctly modern penchant for technologically dependent exterminating gestures. This paradoxically antimodern modernity constitutes a soft planet that articulates seething discontent with globalism's values as well as its violations; its secular pluralism and its surgical strikes; its cosmopolitanism and its creative destruction; its invisible hand and its hidden fist.

The events that pulled me out of bed, then, were the opening of a new front in a continuing war that has long pitted the imperious heights of the world class city against the most enraged in-beyond of its megalopolitan other. And to the extent that the world city and the megacity have converged, this war becomes one of the metapolis against itself. In the words of Pogo Possum, we have met the enemy and he is us (Kelly 1972). The inhuman logic that takes such quotidianly cost-effective ephemera as boarding passes, box cutters, cell phone calls, and office cubicles and angrily kluges them into the telegenic massacre of some three thousand everyday lives finds correspondence in the dehumanized rationality that enables applied discussions of collateral damage, soft targets and structural adjustments. The praetorian globality that spawns paramilitary music boxes and the hieratic globality that spawns passenger cruise missiles, then, are one another's shadows, forcible efforts to univocally reorder the world that are counterposed yet perversely complementary. And in the struggle to impose these incommensurable would-be new world orders, everyday life becomes ever more insecure, polarized and disordered.

In the United States, now referred to in federal circles as "the homeland" and even "the home front," the outcome of this disorder has been the domestic application and overseas projection of unprecedented levels of aggressive interdiction, legitimized no longer by an overblown fear of crime or vaguely perceived anxieties about diversity but as an apotropaic against pseudo-random irruptions of mass-annihilation (Levy 2001). From coast to coast, the United States has become very jittery space indeed. In the process, any terrain for an excavation of the whys and critiques of the hows has become foreclosed terrain, an untenable no-man's-land demarcated only days after the fact by Olimem's construction of an unitary and uncriticizable patriotic consensus. Even the most footloose, globally dispersed TNCs have since proudly rediscovered their status as patriots, and have been promptly rewarded for it with untold billions of dollars in state largesse (Greider 2001b).

Conversely, carnivalesque globality lies stunned beneath the rubble of the World Trade Center, an entombment strategically trumpeted by neoliberalism's staunchest partisans (see, e.g., Pinkerton 2001). In a traumatized time of prolonged flag-waving and vigorous flag-vending, there is no space for clownish malcontents no matter how numerous, how serious their clowning, and how vital their discontent may be to apprehending the current trauma. Indeed, such serious clowning may now be readily classified as "domestic terrorism" under the subsequently established (and spuriously titled) USA PATRIOT laws, and the even more intrusively draconian Homeland

Security Act. But in the final analysis this disappearance of critical inquiry and performative dissent is the greatest danger of all. Without them, we will only persist in constructing the global self-servingly, dysfunctionally, and by default.

Faced with this domination of daily life by the most brutal globalities, it can be a Herculean task to refrain from falling into deep despair. Fortunately, while such globalities do indeed condition us, we make globalities. We can, after all, imagine everyday life in the absence of globalization, but how could there be any such thing as globalization without everyday life? This entails opportunities to reenvision the global from the inside outwards, not as the outcome of conflict but as dialogical engagement and mutual affect. In so doing, we step into one another's shoes and discover that those things that may at first appear dissonant and even bizarre are in actuality comprehensible and creative ways to negotiate the dislocalized exigencies of everyday life, negotiations that through their performance produce the global. Unsettling juxtapositions of geographically disparate technologies, institutions, and life ways can become positively cozy when seen through the eyes of a Swedish-speaking Chilean kid who prefers knock-off Nike wear to the real thing, or an Angeleno who can begin to be Nigerian, too, without ever having to leave Los Angeles. Given the right perspective, strange disjunctures are neither strange nor disjunctive at all, and such perspectives are fast becoming one of the most common. To see the world through such adjustable lenses has come to define the hallmark of the postmodern worldview. But there are places where this way of seeing goes back quite some time, and in so doing it obliges us to look afresh not just at the spaces of the world, but at its times as well.

Alternative Postmodernities

Throughout this work I have pointed out the colonial bloodlines of such critical globally formative phenomena as the world city, interdiction, and the deterritorialized hybrids that elide it. This thing called postmodernism, too, shows all the symptoms of colonization. Consider, for instance, Ahmed Gurnah's (1997) description of his youth spent mixing Kiswahili *taarab* songs with those of Xavier Cugat, Richard Rogers and Oscar Hammerstein, and Elvis Presley, the writings of William Shakespeare with those of V. S. Naipaul, Raymond Chandler, and Che Guevara. A markedly post-modern strategy of cultural assemblage, it would seem. But occurring in the 1950s, a good two decades before postmodernism was allegedly birthed in the academies of Paris (and four decades before the emer-gence of such supposedly postmodern fusionary musical forms as 'world beat').

Similarly, Tridib Bannerjee describes cities like Calcutta and Shanghai as juxtapositions of seemingly incongruous fragments: mule-pulled wagons fashioned from the chassis of Volkswagen Beetles, livestock tied to the gates of luxury condominium complexes, and high-tech hospitals where old-school street vendors peddle expired antibiotics on the sidewalks adjacent (1993, 76). For his part, Bannerjee describes such places as a mixture of the traditional and the modern, yielding "technological discontinuities" (93) and a "paradoxical urbanism" (78). But to whom, precisely, are these things paradoxical discontinuities? I expect not to whoever remediated the VW Beetle's disutility and unhomeliness by hitching it to a mule! Certainly, it is a paradox if we buy into the developmentalist dichotomization of the traditional versus the modern. But absent such a priori categorizations, a mule-drawn VW becomes something very different: the entirely sensible embodiment of an "alternative modernity" (see Gaonkar 2001) in its own right. And the strong resemblance of such alternative modernities to those hybridic postmodern practices is impossible to miss.

In a conference paper presented in Los Angeles during late April of 1992, Anthony King clearly was nurturing similar suspicions, writing, "The (Eurocentrically) defined cultural conditions of postmodernity, irony, pastiche, the mixing of different histories, intertextuality, schizophrenia, cultural chasms, fragmentation, incoherence, disjunction of supposedly modern and pre-modern cultures were characteristics of early colonial societies, cultures and environments on the global periphery (in Calcutta, Hong Kong, Rio or Singapore) decades, if not centuries, before they appeared in Europe or the USA" (King 1992, 12–13; see also King 1997, 8). Driving home this lesson on postmodernism's buried colonial roots, the impromptu closing ceremonies of this conference consisted of the Los Angeles Riot. Or uprising, or civil disturbance, or *Sa-Ee-Gu* to the city's hard-hit Korean population (Abelmann and Lie 1995)–characterizations of the violence itself proved unprecedentedly polyvocal (see Baldassare 1994). Whatever the name, the event bore startling isomorphisms to the anticolonial uprisings in British India during 1857–1858, something of a Sepoy Rebellion on fast forward (Flusty 1993).

Locating postmodernism within colonial power relations is not without its own contradictions and discontinuities. To what extent might such disparate, presumedly hypermodernized and "European" (or perhaps Europeanized) places as Italy, Finland, and even the distant and hegemonic United States itself qualify as early instances of decolonization? Were these places then postmodernized prior to modernity, too? Indeed, seen in light of the retreat of the Roman Empire, might not the Dark Ages be read as a traumatic period of postcolonialism that left an *ur*-postmodern mark upon medieval Europe, from the British Isles to Iberia and eastward to Transylvania? In this line of inquiry resides the danger of an historical reductio ad absurdum, and neo-Spenglerian claims that what we now term postmodernism is nothing more than an autonomic trans-historical cultural reaction visible whenever a society finds itself in transitional decline.

But my intention here is not to throw in with those who assert that the postmodern is a return of the premodern, nor do I seek to deny the existence and relative uniqueness of the particular experiences and conditions we have taken to calling postmodern. Instead, I am trying to contextualize claims about their novelty and, in the process, I am necessarily delimiting the geographical realm in which such conditions and experiences do indeed occur after the modern. By way of example, the way of seeing we have labeled *postmodernism* clearly strikes many of us in the academies of Europe and the American north as still relatively novel. Beyond this turf, however, the attributes of postmodernism come off more like old news. The youth cultures of Zanzibar and the streetscapes of Calcutta reveal that other places have been polyglot and polarized for much of the past century, and longer. Or consider some other defining traits of postmodernism. The copresence of multiple interpretive truths? In Mexico City, where complex back-room politics have predominated for much of the past century, *chilangos* regard authoritative accounts of controversial events not as the truth, but as just one of so many "versions." Disillusionment with progress? Certainly, recent protests against the International Monetary Fund/World Bank's hyperextended enactments of developmentalism entail unprecedented global coordination and telemediation. But mass actions against the imposition of modernist technoeconomic rationality have been relatively commonplace across Africa and South Asia since at least the middle of the twentieth century, mobilizing hundreds of thousands of participants from the Maghreb to Karnataka and the Philippines (Walton and Seddon 1994). Further, these discontents and their practitioners have come to comprise vital preestablished axes along which current opposition to plutocratic globality is articulated and enacted.

For those outside the colonizers' hearths, conditions matching the description of *postmodern* have indeed obtained for quite some time. And in no small part they have emerged in tandem with, and in response to, the jarring importation of modernity itself. In these places, radical breaks and the personal microfractures through which they manifest have yielded a long-running and ongoing permanent cultural revolution. And the resultant conditions of everyday life aren't "postmodern," nor are they necessarily heard as a mind-numbing cacophony of incommensurably differing voices. Instead, these conditions constitute the baseline of daily life, just the unremarkable way things are and have been for quite some time.

So the conditions of postmodernity *are,* but it is principally among the latecomers to these conditions that they are necessarily post-the-modern. Further, it is indeed telling that the belated appearance of these conditions in the urban centers of Europe and the U.S. coincides with imperial malaise, new waves of immigration from the former colonies to the ex-metropole, and increases in "periphery-to-core" cultural transfers. We may think we invented it. We may dress it up, after a very modernist fashion, as an endogenous next step in some linear evolutionary progress that elevates us ever further above the benightedness of both premodernity and its modern successor. In this fashion, we make of it a "totalizing local" (Shiva 1993, 18) like the modern itself: a partial and contingent time- and place-bound way of seeing broadly disseminated as though it were a universal truth and historically inevitable higher good. But strip away our core assumptions about ourselves as the core, and our postmodernity looks an awful lot like a case of the imperial eagles coming home to roost. Multiple alternative worldviews suddenly assert their presence right smack in the heart of the colonizer's home turf—now *there's* some of that radical uncertainty so dear to postmodern theorizing.

So we must look beyond the assumptions, periodizing and otherwise, loaded into the term *postmodernism* and realize that not only is it not the "West's" alone—it wasn't the West's to begin with. Other parts of the world were compelled to cobble it together, albeit as just one of a number of possible responses, while the great powers were preoccupied with the production and exportation of high modern truths. But postmodernism as post-the-modern-ism, or perhaps modern-*was*-m, is an appropriate technology for our own wuzmoderne place and time—a tool for abiding within multiple divergent visions of what the world is, and an apotropaic against proclaiming the singular correctness of any one of these visions. (Given this, it is ironic, yet somehow unsurprising, that international aid agencies continue to export modernist technocratic development "solutions" as though they were yet more obsolete consumer product readily pawned off overseas.) It is an opportunity to dismount from our high warhorse, hitch it to our VW Beetle, and set off to collaborate in the processes of global formation instead of continuing to presume mastery over them; an invitation to go "forward in all directions" (3 Mutaphas 3 1989) and attain a state of 'heterogenous well-being' (Haraway 1997, 95). But how, in practice, do we go about this task?

Forward in All Directions!

Fortunately, this question is not so intractable as it may seem, as we are all already more or less going about it. Whether a *sarariman* posted to Los Angeles, a Guatemalteca housekeeper for a Beverly Hills mansion, an Angeleno academician conducting fieldwork gods-know-where, a laborer contracted from Thailand to harvest cloudberries in a Swedish forest or blood oranges on a plantation in Israel, our everyday lives are hyperextended and hybrid. Our lives are hyperextended in that axes of identity, in conjunction with technological mediation of the most and least celebrated sorts, keep us in step with our "own kind" across ever widening distances, and so form nonlocal collectives. But very few of our lives are predicated upon just one axis of identity. Most every one of us is a hybrid of "kinds," so we invest nonlocal collectives with the potential to overlap polythetically. And our lives are increasingly bound together in urban spaces, ensuring the inescapable and even intrusive presence of others. In the process cities become agglomerations of interoperating dislocalities, nonlocal collectives not only overlap but interpenetrate, and intercultural flows make our selves and our kinds hybrids of ever more diverse and disparate influences. In this way we are all "challenged by the immediacy and intensity of global cultural confrontations" (Morley and Robins 1995, 122) in an "ironic and imperfect world that is as dependent on chance, localized encounters, as on other forms of experience" (Gottdiener 1995, 243).

Chance, localized encounters, the imperfections of the world: these are the ingredients of everyday life. The people and artifacts I have narrated throughout this book, then—their interrelations and commonplace experiences and everyday practices—are not examples of some higher order phenomenon. Rather, they *are* the phenomenon. Just as world cities holographically constellate the metapolis, so do these people and practices constellate the world city and, through it, the global. In the process, they embody a festival of efficacious global reinvention, as often as not unselfconsciously and without even trying. Hence, our common project—the creation of the discursive/material formation that is the global.

We have seen the strategic imposition of othering in the streets of the world city and across the metapolis. But we have also seen the globalizing reassertions of those so othered and, in their reassertion, the potential to reforge both the world city and the world. This has engendered fluidly demarcated global fields where we all wrestle with the very definition of what constitutes legality and criminality, public and private, alien and citizen, foreign and domestic. And through this struggle emerges dislocalized localisms, strengthened expressions of minority claims, contingent popular coalitions of common interests, and a demotion of authoritarian polity from the status of fundamental truth to that of just another "version." As such, it is through the cooperative de-coca-colonization of our own consciousness that brutalizing globalities can be refused.

What remains to be done, then, is to do as we have been doing, but to do it with intention and with feeling. Some everyday practices of global formation clearly spread tears in our webs of social conventions. And some are specifically designed to do so. They take advantage of new circumstances to purposefully open unique spaces where we can turn around words and thoughts "in order to discover what they were actually hiding" and what's on the other side (Bakhtin 1984, 272). As plutocratic globality's carnivalesque other has made so apparent, such efforts are bodily practices that rehearse the radical break by breaking things, discursive and material things, radically. While I am personally more encouraged by the discursive breakages than by the material ones, neither is less significant than the other. Both practices are part of an ongoing movement to recarnivalize consciousness and recover the lost signified of "festival time," a time when we may sweep away still-very-much-alive official hierarchic limits and proceed to the "radical change and renewal of all that exists" (Bakhtin 1984, 273). Whether this is a revived medieval notion, a utopian modernist notion, a postcolonial or a postmodern one is immaterial. What matters is that it *is*.

Of course, the drive for radical change and renewal is no unitary project. Multitudes of voices speaking plethoras of tongues now demand and expect to be heard, respected and reckoned with. Barring recourse to systematic violence, these voices are unlikely to recede back into inaudibility. But at the same time, many of these voices are conversing and collaborating, and more often than not with a newfound sensitivity to one another's standpoints. Here it is the dialogue that's the thing, and that dialogue works best when it is tacitly underpinned by no small amount of xenophilia.

By xenophilia I do not mean the romanticization of some other and the consumption of othered cultural forms, although this at least can constitute a first step. I am thinking of xenophilia as a driving thirst to openly engage, and be engaged by, that which is unfamiliar, a mentality that regards difference as much more than just something that happens and needs to be grudgingly dealt with. Xenophilia prepares the psyche for deep relations with those who are different, and at the same time acts as both a remedy to and an inoculation against coca-colonization. So while all our perspectives are necessarily partial and our knowledges situated, and they can never be completely integrated, cultivating xenophilia goes a long way to help us occupy, appreciate, and respect each other's situated perspectives. Through xenophilic engagement we develop the capacity to experience divergent realities, and so interact dialogically with others to negotiate across differential positions (Bakhtin 1988) with amiability and mutual affect.

The real and continuing practice of such dialogical negotiations has placed the contingent assemblage of social categories, predicated upon common experiences in shared space, at center stage as a means of organizing and resisting. And in this ongoing process it should come as no surprise that anarchic play in general and anarchists in particular have taken up prominent roles. Undertaking collaborative resistance projects based upon a mutual consensus to do so finds precedent in anarchist thought reaching back more than a century, and Emma Goldman was very clear that if it didn't permit dancing, it wasn't worth being a part of (Goldman 1924, chap. 9).

Such practices in turn can tear down ways of seeing that, often subtly and even invisibly, inform practices whereby power strives to silence and disappear many, and order the world as a whole, for the benefit of a few. A society without power relations may be an impossible ideal. But we can excavate, and indeed are excavating, the power relations that do operate in the formation of globalities. We can choose to deploy these relations consciously and conscientiously, to reforge the global in the practice of our everyday lives. And in doing so, we can finally make plain "the problem of the world which globalization pretends to construct: the pieces don't fit . . .", and proceed "to make a new world, a world where many worlds fit, where all worlds fit" (Marcos 1997). Whether or not we *will* do so is entirely up to us.

Bibliography

AAPA (American Association of Port Authorities). 1998. *World Port Ranking.* Available online at http://www.aapa-ports.org/pdf/rankworld.pdf.

Abelmann, N. and J. Lie. 1995. *Blue Dreams: Korean Americans and the Los Angeles Riots.* Cambridge, Mass.: Harvard University Press.

Abu-Lughod, J. 1989. *Before European Hegemony: The World System A.D. 1250–1350.* New York: Oxford University Press.

ACI (Airports Council International). 2000. *The World's Busiest Airport: Top 30 ACI Airports.* Available online at http://www.airports.org/traffic/busiest.html.

Adbusters 36. 2001. "//Posessions//are//9/10//of//the//Law." 48–49.

Agnew, J., D. A. Livingstone, and A. Rogers. (eds.) 1996. *Human Geography: An Essential Anthology.* Oxford: Blackwell.

Aguilar Camín, H. and L. Meyer. (L. A. Fierro, trans.) 1993. *In the Shadow of the Mexican Revolution: Mexican History, 1910–1989.* Austin: University of Texas Press.

Ajami, F. 1993. "The Summoning." *Foreign Affairs,* September/October. 2–9.

Aksoy, A. and K. Robins. 1991. "Exterminating Angels: Morality, Violence and Technology in the Gulf War." *Science as Culture* 2–3, no. 12. 322–36.

Allen, J. P., and E. Turner. 1997. *The Ethnic Quilt: Population Diversity in Southern California.* Northridge: California State University, Northridge, Center for Geographical Studies.

Althusser, L. 1997. "Ideology and Ideological State Apparatuses (Notes Towards an Investigation)." In S. Zizek (ed.), *Mapping Ideology.* London: Verso. 100–140.

Anderson, B. 1983. *Imagined Communities.* London: Verso.

Anton, D. J. 1995. *Diversity, Globalization and the Ways of Nature.* Ottawa: International Development Research Centre.

AP (Associated Press). 2001a. "World Outcry Over Fate of Afghan Buddha Statues," March 4. "Afghan Taliban Say Part of Statues Blown Up," March 5. "UN Members Urge Taliban to Stop Destroying Statues," March 6. "Taliban Rules Out Compromise on Buddha Statues," March 6. "Taliban Shows Off Buddha Rubble," March 27.

———. 2001b. "U.S. Economic Downturn Hits Indonesia's Shoe Industry," April 6.

———. 2001c. "White Monkeys, Earth-Color Men: Zapatistas Play on Color, Race," March 12.

Appadurai, A. (ed.) 1986. *The Social Life of Things: Commodities in Cultural Perspective.* NY: Cambridge University Press.

———. 1990. "Disjuncture and Difference in the Global Cultural Economy." *Public Culture,* 2, no. 2. 1–24.

———. 1996. *Modernity at Large: Cultural Dimensions of Globalization.* Minneapolis: University of Minnesota Press.

Arendt, H. 1963. *Eichmann in Jerusalem: A Report on the Banality of Evil.* New York: Viking Press.

Arney, G. 2001. "U.S. 'Planned Attack on Taleban'." *BBCi News.* September 18. Available on-line at http://news.bbc.co.uk/hi/english/world/south_asia/newsid_1550000/1550366.stm.

Arruda, M. 1996. "The New World Order: Crises in Ethics and Rationality." Presentation to the Fifteenth National Conference of the Brazilian Bar Association (BBA), Foz do Iguagu, September 4–8, 1994. *Otherwise,* March/April.

Auerbach, S. (ed.) 1994. *Encyclopedia of Multiculturalism.* New York: Marshall Cavendish.

Bailey, A. J., R. A. Wright, A. Mountz, and I. M. Miyares. "(Re)producing Salvadoran Transnational Geographies." *Annals of the Association of American Geographers* 92, no. 1. 125–44.

Bakhtin, M. 1984. (H. Iswolsky, trans.) *Rabelais and His World.* Bloomington: Indiana University Press.

———. (M. Holquist, ed.) 1988. *The Dialogic Imagination: Four Essays.* Austin: University of Texas Press.

Baldassare, M. (ed.) 1994. *The Los Angeles Riots.* Boulder, Colo.: Westview Press.

Ballinger, J. 1992. "The New Free-Trade Heel: Nike's Profits Jump on the Back of Asian Workers." *Harper's*, August, 46–47.

Banerjee, T. 1993. "Transitional Urbanism Reconsidered: Post-Colonial Development of Calcutta and Shanghai." In G. Guldin and A. Southall (eds.) *Urban Anthropology in China*. Leiden: E. J. Brill. 76–100.

Banham, R. 1973. *Los Angeles: The Architecture of Four Ecologies*. London: Penguin.

Barber, B. 1996. *Jihad vs. McWorld: How Globalism and Tribalism are Reshaping the World*. New York: Ballantine Books.

Barnet, R. J. and B. Cavanagh. 1994. *Global Dreams: Imperial Corporations in the New World Order*. New York: Simon and Schuster.

Barns, I. 1991. "Post Fordist People? Cultural Meaning of New Technoeconomic Systems." *Futures*, November, 895–914.

Baudrillard, J. (S. F. Glaser, trans.) 1994. *Simulacra and Simulation*. Ann Arbor: University of Michigan Press.

Bauman, Z. 1992. *Intimations of Postmodernity*. London: Routledge.

———. 1998. *Globalization: The Human Consequences*. Cambridge: Polity Press.

BBC News, 2001a. "Eyewitness: Street Violence in Genoa." July 20.

———. 2001b. "Genoa Gets Million-Dollar Aid Package." July 23.

Beaverstock, J. V.; R. G. Smith, and P. J. Taylor. 2000. "World-City Network: A New Metageography?" *Annals of the Association of American Geographers* 90, no. 1. 123–34.

Bennett, C. "The Life of General Villa." *The Progressive Silent Film List*. Available online at http://www.silentera.com/PSFL/data/L/LifeofGeneralVilla1914.html.

Benzinberg Stein, A. B., and J. C. Moxley. 1992. "In Defense of the Nonnative: The Case of the Eucalyptus." *Landscape Journal* 11. 35–50.

Berry, B. J. L. 1990. "Urbanization." In Turner B. L., II, W. C. Clark, R. W. Kates, J. F. Richards, J. T. Mathews, and W. B. Meyer. (eds.) 1990. *The Earth as Transformed by Human Action: Global and Regional Changes in the Biosphere over the Past Three Hundred Years*. Cambridge: Cambridge University Press. 103–20.

Bey, H. 1991. *TAZ: The Temporary Autonomous Zone, Ontological Anarchy, Poetic Terrorism*. Brooklyn: Autonomedia. Also available online at http://www.t0.or.at/hakimbey/taz/taz.htm.

Bhabha, H. 1994. *The Location of Culture*. London: Routledge.

Bhaskar, R. 1998. "Societies." In Archer, M., R. Bhaskar, A. Collier, T. Lawson, and A. Norrie. (eds.) *Critical Realism: Essential Readings*. London: Routledge. 206–57.

Bird, J., B. Curtis, T. Putnam, G. Robertson, and L. Tickner. (eds.) 1993. *Mapping the Futures: Local Cultures, Global Change*. London: Routledge.

Blakely, E. J. and M. G. Snyder. 1997. *Fortress America: Gated Communities in the United States*. Washington, D.C.: Brookings Institution Press/Cambridge, Mass.: Lincoln Institute of Land Policy.

Blaut, J. M. 1993. *The Colonizer's Model of the World: Geographical Diffusionism and Eurocentric History*. New York: Guilford Press.

Bourdieu, P. 1977. *Practical Reason: On the Theory of Action*. Stanford, Calif.: Stanford University Press.

Boyd, T. 1996. "A Small Introduction to the 'G' Funk Era: Gangsta Rap and Black Masculinity in Contemporary Los Angeles." In M. Dear, H. E. Schockman, and G. Hise (eds.) *Rethinking Los Angeles*. Thousand Oaks, Calif.: Sage. 127–46.

———. 1997. *Am I Black Enough for You?* Indianapolis: University of Indiana Press.

Braudel, F. 1984. *Civilization and Capitalism: Fifteenth–Eighteenth Century*. (Vol. 3, *The Perspective of the World*.) New York: Harper and Row.

Bullard, R. D., J. E. Grigsby, and C. Lee. 1994. *Residential Apartheid*. Los Angeles: UCLA Center for Afro-American Studies.

Burkeman, O. and J. Borger. 2001. "The Ex-Presidents' Club." *Guardian*, October 31, n. p.

Caballero, R. J. and M. L. Hammour. 2000. "Creative Destruction and Development: Institutions, Crises and Restructuring." Cambridge, Mass.: National Bureau of Economic Research.

Caldeira, T. P. R. 1996. "Fortified Enclaves: The New Urban Segregation." *Public Culture* 8, no. 2. 303.

Calvino, I. 1974. *Invisible Cities*. Orlando: Harcourt.

Carpenter, E. 1972. *Oh What a Blow That Phantom Gave Me*. New York: Holt, Rinehart and Winston.

Castells, M. and P. Hall. 1994. *Technopoles of the World: The Making of the Twenty-first Century Industrial Complexes*. New York: Routledge.

Cavalli-Sforza, L. and M. Feldman. 1981. *Cultural Transmission and Evolution.* Princeton, N.J.: Princeton University Press.

Cavalli-Sforza, L., P. Menozzi, and A. Piazza. 1994. *The History and Geography of Human Genes.* Princeton, N.J.: Princeton University Press.

Certeau, M. de. (S. Rendall, trans.) 1984. *The Practice of Everyday Life.* Berkeley and Los Angeles: University of California Press.

Chaliland, G. and J. Rageau. 1997. *The Penguin Atlas of Diasporas.* New York: Penguin.

Chase, J., M. Crawford, and J. Kaliski. 1999. *Everyday Urbanism.* New York: Monacelli Press.

Chomsky, N. 1991. *Deterring Democracy.* New York: Hill and Wang.

Chossudovsky, M. 1996. "The Business of Crime and the Crimes of Business." *Covert Action Quarterly* 58. 24–30.

Christaller, W. (C. W. Baskin, trans.) 1966. *Central Places in Southern Germany.* Englewood Cliffs, N.J.: Prentice-Hall.

Christopher. A. J. 1994. *The Atlas of Apartheid.* London: Routledge.

Churchman, W. 1971. *The Design of Inquiring Systems: Basic Concepts of Systems and Organizations.* New York: Basic Books.

CCACOSTF (Citywide Citizen's Advisory Committee Open Space Task Force). 1990. *Open Space Downtown: A Citizen Task Force Case Study Report on Citicorp Plaza.* Los Angeles: Community Redevelopment Agency of the City of Los Angeles. 7

Cleaver, H. 1998. "The Zapatista Effect: The Internet and the Rise of an Alternative Political Fabric." *Journal of International Affairs* 51, no. 2. 621–40.

Clifford, J. 1992. "Traveling Cultures." In L. Grossberg, C. Nelson, and P. A. Treichler (eds.) *Cultural Studies.* New York: Routledge. 96–116.

Clifford, M. 1992. "Spring in Their Step." *Far Eastern Economic Review,* November, 56–57.

CLR (Campaign for Labor Rights). 1997. "Labor Alerts: Update on the Nike Campaign." March 23.

Coase, R. H. 1937. "The Nature of the Firm." *Economica* 4. 386–405.

Cocks, J. 1992. "Rap Around the Globe." *Time,* October 19, 70–71.

Cole, C. 1995. "Celebrity Feminism: Nike Style Post-Fordism, Transcendence, and Consumer Power." *Sociology of Sport Journal* 12, no. 4. 347–369.

CounterPunch. 1999. "Nike Chronicles: 20 Cents an Hour? It's the Market." October 15–30.

CRA/LA (The Community Redevelopment Agency of the City of Los Angeles). 1988. *Bunker Hill Redevelopment Project: Biennial Report, 1986–1988.* Los Angeles: CRA.

Crawford, M. 1988. *The Ecology of Fantasy.* Los Angeles: Los Angeles Forum for Architecture and Urban Design.

Curran, J., A. Smith, and P. Wingate. (eds.) 1987. *Impacts and Influences: Essays on Media Power in the Twentieth Century.* London: Methuen.

Curtiss, A. 1994. "At CityWalk, the Real City Intrudes on the 'Fake One.' *Los Angeles Times,* 13, August, B-1.

Cushman, J. H. 1998. "Nike Pledges to End Child Labor and Apply U.S. Rules Abroad." *New York Times, Business Day,* p. 1, 5.

Davis, M. 1990. *City of Quartz: Excavating the Future of Los Angeles.* Verso: London.

———. 1992a. "Fortress Los Angeles: The Militarization of Urban Space." In M. Sorkin. (ed.) *Variations on a Theme Park.* New York: Noonday Press. 154–80.

———. 1992b. "Chinatown Revisited? The Internationalization of Downtown Los Angeles." In D. Reid. (ed.) *Sex, Death and God in L.A.* New York: Pantheon Books.

Dear, M. J. 1988. "The Postmodern Challenge: Reconstructing Human Geography" *Transactions, Institute of British Geographers* 13. 262–74.

———. 2000. *The Postmodern Urban Condition.* Oxford: Blackwell.

Dear, M. J., and S. Flusty. (eds.) 2001. *Spaces of Postmodernity.* Oxford: Blackwell.

Dear, M. J. and J. R. Wolch. (eds.) 1989. *The Power of Geography: How Territory Shapes Social Life.* Boston: Unwin Hyman.

Debord, G. 1958. "Theory of the Derive." *Internationale Situationniste* 2.

———. 1994 (D. Nicholson-Smith trans.) 1994. *The Society of the Spectacle.* New York: Zone Books.

Deleuze, G. and F. Guattari. (R. Hurley, M. Seem and H. R. Lane, trans.) 1983. *Anti-Oedipus: Capitalism and Schizophrenia.* Minneapolis: University of Minneasota Press.

———. (B. Massumi, trans.) 1987. *A Thousand Plateaus: Capitalism and Schizophrenia.* Minneapolis: University of Minnesota Press.

Dennett, D. 1991. *Consciousness Explained.* Boston: Little, Brown.

Derrida, J. 1976. (G. C. Spivak, trans.) *Of Grammatology*. Baltimore: Johns Hopkins University Press.

———. 1978. (A. Bass, trans.) *Writing and Difference*. Chicago: University of Chicago Press.

Dicken, P., J. Peck, and A. Tickell. 1997. "Unpacking the Global." In R. Lee and J. Wills (eds.) *Geographies of Economies*. London: Arnold.

Dunning, J. H. 1993. *The Globalization of Business: The Challenge of the 1990s*. London: Routledge.

Ebbesmeyer, C. C., and W. J. Ingraham. 1992. "Shoe Spill in the North Pacific." *Eos, Transactions, American Geophysical Union* 75, no. 34. 361–68.

Eco, U. 1976. *A Theory of Semiotics*. Bloomington: Indiana University Press.

The Economist. 1994. "The Discreet Charm of the Multicultural Multinational." July 30, pp. 57–58.

———. 2001a. "Of Rich and Poor." April 26, p. 80.

———. 2001b. "Picking Up the Pieces: After the Genoa Summit." July 26, pp. 49–50.

Ehling, M. 2002. *Urban Warrior*. ETS Pictures.

Ehrenreich, B. 2001. "Baton Twirling: L.A.'s Finest Train Italian Police on Crowd Suppression." *Los Angeles Weekly*, August 17–23, p. 18.

Eisner, M., and J. Lang. 1991. "It's a Small World After All/The Higher the Satellite, the Lower the Culture." *New Perspectives Quarterly* 8, no. 4. 40–45.

ELF (Earth Liberation Front). 2001. "Earth Liberation Front Claims Responsibility For Attempted Arson At Nike Outlet Store In Albertville, MN." 4 April. Available online at http://www.earthliberationfront.com/news/2001/010404m1.html.

Elteren, M. van. 1994. *Imagining America: Dutch Youth and Its Sense of Place*. Tilburg: Tilburg University Press.

Entrikin, J. N. 1991. *The Betweenness of Place: Towards a Geography of Modernity*. London: Macmillan.

Expreso Chiapas. 1998. February 19, p. 8.

Feinmann, J. P. 1998. "Guevara y Marcos." *Página 12*, August 22, pp. 000.

Feyerabend, P. 1978. *Against Method: Outline of an Anarchistic Theory of Knowledge*. London: Verso.

Fiske, J. 1992 "Cultural Studies and the Culture of Everyday Life." In L. Grossberg, C. Nelson, and P. A. Treichler (eds.) *Cultural Studies*. NY: Routledge.

Flood, F. 2001. "What Is It That Is Different about the Zapatistas?" *Chiapas Revealed*, February, pp. 1–12.

Flusty, S. 1993. "One Year On: The Moaning of the Hurricane." *L.A. Architect*, April, p. 11.

———. 1996–2001. Field notes. Unpublished.

Fogelson, R. 1993. *The Fragmented Metropolis*. Berkeley and Los Angeles: University of California Press.

Foley, M. 1995. "Privatizing the Countryside: The Mexican Peasant Movement and Neoliberal Reform." *Latin American Perspectives* 84, Vol. 22 No. 1. 59–76.

Forte-Escamilla, K. 1994. *The Storyteller with Nike Airs, and Other Barrio Stories*. San Francisco: Aunt Lute Books.

Foucault, M. (A. Sheridan, ed. and trans.) 1979. *Discipline and Punish: The Birth of the Prison*. New York: Random House.

———. (L. Sawyer, trans.) 1982a. "The Subject and Power." *Critical Inquiry* 8, no. 4. 777–95.

———. (C. Gordon, L. Marshall, J. Mepham and K. Soper, trans. ed.) 1982b. *Power/Knowledge: Selected Interviews and Other Writings*. New York: Pantheon.

Frantz, K. 2001. "Gated Communities in Metro-Phoenix (Arizona): Neuer Trend in der US-Amerikanischen Stadtlandschaft." *Geographische Rundschau* 1. 12–18.

Friedman, A. 2003. "Build It and They Will Pay: a Primer on Guggenomics." *The Baffler* 1 no. 15. 51–56.

Friedman, J. 1994a. *Cultural Identity and Global Process*. London: Sage.

———. (ed.) 1994b. *Consumption and Identity*. Chur: Harwood Academic Publishers.

Friedman, M. 1992. *Economic Freedom, Human Freedom, Political Freedom*. Hayward, Calif.: Calforina State University, Hayward; Smith Center for Private Enterprise Studies.

Friedman, T. L. 1994. "When Money Talks." *New York Times*. July 24, E-3.

———. 1999. *The Lexus and the Olive Tree: Understanding Globalization*. New York: Farrar, Straus and Giroux.

Fukuyama, F. 1992. *The End of History and the Last Man*. London: Hamish Hamilton.

Fulton, W. 1992 "California Pulls Out the Stops." *Planning*, October, pp. XXX.

Fusco, C. 1995. *English Is Broken Here: Notes on Cultural Fusion in the Americas*. New York: New Press.

FZLN (Frente Zapatista de Liberación Nacional), 1996. *Zapatista Front of National Liberation.* October 22. Available online at http://www.ezln.org/archivo/fzln/fzln.html.

Gaonkar, D. P. 2001. "On Alternative Modernities." In D. P. Gaonkar (ed.) *Alternative Modernities.* Durham, N.C.: Duke University Press. 1–23.

Garcia, A. 2000. "The March: The WTO-Battle in Seattle." *Changelinks,* January, pp. 1, 7.

García Canclini, N. 1995. (C. L. Chiappari and S. L. López, trans.) *Hybrid Cultures: Strategies for Entering and Leaving Modernity.* Minneapolis: University of Minnesota Press. 1995.

Garreau, J. 1992. *Edge City: Life on the New Frontier.* New York: Anchor Books.

Gaslin, G. 2001. "Elf Discovery." *Los Angeles New Times,* April 19–25, pp. 10, 12.

Geddes, P. 1997. *Cities in Evolution: An Introduction to the Town Planning Movement and to the Study of Civics.* London: Routledge/Thoemmes.

Geertz, C. 1973. *The Interpretation of Cultures: Selected Essays.* New York: Basic Books.

Gereffi, G. 1989. "Development Strategies and the Global Factory." *Annals of the American Academy of Political and Social Scientists* 505. 92–104.

Giddens, A. 1991. Modernity and Self-Identity: Self and Society in the Late Modern Age. Cambridge: Polity Press.

———. 2000. *Runaway World: How Globalization is Reshaping Our Lives.* London: Routledge.

Gilbert, A. and Gugler, J. 1990. *Cities, Poverty and Development: Urbanization in the Third World.* New York: Oxford University Press.

Gillis, M., D. H. Perkins, M. Roemer, and D. R. Snodgrass. (eds.) 1996. *Economics of Development, Fourth Edition.* New York: W. W. Norton and Company.

Glassner, B. 2000. *The Culture of Fear: Why Americans Are Afraid of the Wrong Things.* New York: Basic Books.

Glasze, G. 2001. "Enclaves of Well-Being: Gated Housing Estates in Lebanon as Private Small-Scale Solutions for Nationwide Problems." Paper presented March 1 in the session "Gated Communities II" at the 2001 meeting of the American Association of Geographers.

Gleick, J. 1987. *Chaos: Making a New Science.* New York: Viking.

Global Exchange. 1996. *Report on Nike.* San Francisco: Global Exchange.

Golden, T. 2001. "Revolution Rocks: Thoughts of Mexico's First Postmodern Guerrilla Commander." *New York Times Review of Books,* April 8, pp. XXX.

Goldman, E. 1924. *My Further Dissillusionment in Russia.* Garden City, N.Y.: Doubleday, Page and Company.

Gómez-Peña, G., E. Chagoya, and F. Rice. 2000. *Codex Espangliensis: From Columbus to the Border Patrol.* San Francisco: City Lights Books.

Gordon, A. 1997. *Ghostly Matters: Haunting and the Sociological Imagination.* Minneapolis: University of Minnesota Press. 1997.

Gorostiaga, X. 1984. *The Role of the International Financial Centres in Underdeveloped Countries.* London: Croom Helm/New York: St. Martin's Press.

Gottdiener, M. 1995. *Postmodern Semiotics: Material Culture and the Forms of Postmodern Life.* Oxford: Blackwell Publishers.

Graham, S. and S. Marvin. 1996. *Telecommunications and the City: Electronic Spaces, Urban Places.* London: Routledge.

Gramsci, A. (Q. Hoare, and G. N. Smith, eds. and trans.) 1971. *Selections form the Prision Notebook.* London: Lawrence and Wishart.

Grannovetter, M. 1985. "Economic Action and Social Structure: The Problem of Embeddedness." *American Journal of Sociology* 91. 481–510.

Grant, R. and J. Nijman. 2002. "Globalization and the Corporate Geography of Cities in the Less-Developed World." *Annals of the Association of American Geographers* 92, no. 2. 320–40.

Gray, C. H. 1997. *Postmodern War: The New Politics of Conflict.* New York: Guildford Press.

Greider, W. 2001a. "The Right and US Trade Law: Invalidating the twentieth Century." *Nation,* October 15. Available online at http://www.thenation.com/doc.mhtml?i=20011015&s=greider.

———. 2001b. "Pro Patria, Pro Mundo." *Nation.* November 12. Available online at http://www.thenation.com/doc.mhtml?i= 20011112&s=greider.

Grigsby, E. 1995. Private conversation with the author.

Grossberg, L. 1993. "Cultural Studies and/in New Worlds." *Critical Studies in Mass Communications* 10, no. 1. 1–22.

Grossman, K. 2001. "Space Corps: The Dangerous Business of Making the Heavens a War Zone." *Covert Action Quarterly* 70. 26–33.

Gurnah, A. 1997. "Elvis in Zanzibar." In A. Scott (ed.) *The Limits of Globalization: Cases and Arguments.* London, New York: Routledge. 116–42.
HABITAT (United Nations Centre for Human Settlements). Various years. *Global Report on Human Settlements.* London: Earthscan Publications.
Hall, P. 1984. *The World Cities.* New York: St. Martin's Press.
Hannerz, U. 1992. *Cultural Complexity: Studies in the Social Organization of Meaning.* New York: Columbia University Press.
Hannigan, J. 1998. *Fantasy City: Pleasure and Profit in the Postmodern Metropolis.* London, New York: Routledge.
Haraway, D. 1991. *Simians, Cyborgs and Women: The Reinvention of Nature.* New York: Routledge.
———. 1997. *Modest_Witness@Second_Millenium.FemaleMan©_Meets_OncoMouse^{TM}.* New York: Routledge.
Hardt, M. and A. Negri. 2000. *Empire.* Cambridge: Harvard University Press.
Harvey, D. 1989. *The Condition of Postmodernity: An Inquiry into the Origins of Cultural Change.* Oxford: Blackwell.
Helm, J. 2000. "Saving Advertising." *Émigre* 53. pp. 4–20.
Herman, E. S. 1982. *The Real Terror Network: Terrorism in Fact and Propaganda.* Boston: South End Press.
Hetherington, K. 1997. *The Badlands of Modernity: Heterotopia and Social Ordering.* London; New York: Routledge.
Holston, J. and Appadurai, A. 1996. "Cities and Citizenship." *Public Culture.* 8, no. 2. 187–204.
Hoskins, J. 1998. *Biographical Objects: How Things Tell the Stories of People's Lives.* New York, London: Routledge.
Hotz, R. L. 1998. "Of Gadgets and Gizmos." *Los Angeles Times Review of Books,* December 6, pp. 3–4.
Huntington, S. P. 1993. "The Clash of Civilizations?" *Foreign Affairs,* Summer, pp. 22–49.
———. 1996. *The Clash of Civilizations and the Remaking of World Order.* New York: Simon and Schuster.
Hymers, S. H. 1976. *The International Operations of National Firms: A Study of Direct Investment.* Cambridge: MIT Press.
Jackson, J. B. 1984. *Discovering the Vernacular Landscape.* New Haven, Conn.: Yale University Press.
Jackson, P. and J. Penrose. (eds.) 1993. *Constructions of Race, Place and Nation.* London: UCL Press.
Jansen, M. B. 2000. *The Making of Modern Japan.* Cambridge, Mass.: Belknap Press of Harvard University Press.
Jenkins, H. 1992. *Textual Poachers: Television Fans and Participatory Culture.* London: Routledge.
Jones, B. 2000. "Mexicans in U.S. Return Home to Vote in Presidential Race." *Associated Press,* April 24.
Joseph-Witham, H. R. 1996. *Star Trek Fans and Costume Art.* Jackson: University Press of Mississippi.
Jules-Rosette, B. 1990. "Simulations of Postmodernity: Images of Technology in African Tourist and Popular Art." *The Society for Visual Anthropology Review* 6, no. 1. 29–37.
Kaplan, R. 1994. "The Coming Anarchy." *Atlantic Monthly,* February, pp. 44–76.
———. 1996. *The Ends of the Earth: A Journey to the Frontiers of Anarchy.* New York: Random House.
Kelly, W. 1972. *Pogo: We Have Met the Enemy, and He Is Us.* New York: Simon and Schuster.
Kieschnick, M. 1998. "Response to Maria Eitel." Personal correspondence. Working Assets Long Distance, June 24.
King, A. 1990. *Global Cities: Post-Imperialism and the Internationalization of London.* London: Routledge.
———. 1991 *Urbanism, Colonialism and the World-Economy: Cultural and Spatial Foundations of the World Urban System.* London: Routledge.
———. 1992. "The Times and Spaces of Modernity." Paper presented at the conference "A New Urban and Regional Heirarchy: Impacts of Modernization, Restructuring, and the End of Bipolarity," International Sociological Association, Research Committee 21.
———. (ed.) 1996. *Re-Presenting the City: Ethnicity, Capital and Culture in the twenty first-Century Metropolis.* New York: New York University Press.
———. (ed.) 1997. *Culture, Globalization, and the World System: Contemporary Conditions for the Representation of Identity.* Minneapolis: University of Minnesota Press.
Kingery, W. D. (ed.) 1998. *Learning from Things: Method and Theory of Material Culture Studies.* Washington, D.C.: Smithsonian Institution Press.

Knox, P. and Taylor, P.J. (eds.) 1995. *World Cities in a World City System.* Cambridge: Cambridge University Press.

Koptiuch, K. 1991. "Third-Worlding at Home." *Social Text* 28. 87–99.

Kopytoff, I. 1986. "The Cultural Biography of Things: Commoditization as Process." In A. Appadurai (ed.) *The Social Life of Things: Commodities in Cutural Perspective.* NY: Cambridge University Press, pp. 64–91.

Korten, D. C. 1996. *When Corporations Rule the World.* West Hartford, Conn.: Berrett-Koehler/Kumarian Press.

Korzeniewicz, M. 1994. "Commodity Chains and Marketing Strategies: Nike and the Global Athletic Footwear Industry." In G. Gereffi and M. Korzeniewicz (eds.) *Commodity Chains and Global Capitalism.* Westport, Conn.: Greenwood. 247–65.

Kotkin, J. 1993. *Tribes: How Race, Religion and Identity Determine Success in the New Global Economy.* New York: Random House.

Kraska, P. B., and V. E. Kappeler. 1997. "Militarizing American Police: The Rise and Normalization of Paramilitary Police Units." *Social Problems* 44, no. 1. 1–18.

Kretzmann, S. and Rolfes, A. 1998. *Shell Shocked.* Berkeley: Project Underground.

Krinski, H. 2000. Private conversation with the author.

Krugman, P. R., and A. J. Venables. 1995. *Globalization and the Inequality of Nations.* Cambridge, Mass.: National Bureau of Economic Research.

Krugman, P. R. 1996. *Pop Internationalism.* Cambridge, Mass.: MIT Press.

———. 1999. "Enemies of the WTO." *Slate Magazine,* November 23. Available online at http://slate.msn.com/Dismal/99-11-23/Dismal.asp.

Kuiper, D. 2001a. "Notes From the Front: The Wall Defines Two Americas in Quebec." *Los Angeles Weekly,* May 4–10, pp. 22–23.

———. 2001b. "Hybrid Movement: No Break for Anarchists in Long Beach." *Los Angeles Weekly.* May 11–17, pp. XXX.

———. 2001c. "Out of Control: The Attack on Protesters and the Press in Genoa." *Los Angeles Weekly,* July 27–2, August p. 19.

Labeviere, R. 2000. *Dollars for Terror: The United States and Islam.* New York: Algora.

de Laet, M. and A. Mol. 2000. "The Zimbabwe Bush Pump: Mechanics of a Fluid Technology." *Social Studies of Science* 30. 225–63.

Lalloo, K. 1998. "Citizenship and Place: Spatial Definitions of, and Agency in, South Africa." *Africa Today* 45, 3/4. pp. 439–459.

Lash, S. and J. Urry. 1987. *The End of Organized Capitalism.* Madison: University of Wisconsin Press.

Lasn, K. 2001. "The Smell of Swoosh." *Adbusters* 36. 58.

Latour, B. 1995. "A Door Must Be Either Open or Shut: A Little Philosophy of Techniques." In A., Feenberg and A. Hannay (eds.) *Technology and the Politics of Knowledge.* Bloomington: Indiana University Press.

———. 1997. "On Actor-Network Theory: A Few Clarifications." *Soziale Welt.* Available online at http//www.keele.ac.uk/depts/stt/stt/ant/latour.html.

———. (as Johnson, J.). 1998. "Mixing Humans and Nonhumans Together: The Sociology of a Door Closer." *Social Problems* 35, no. 3. 293–310.

Law, J. and Hetherington, K. 2000. "Materialities, Spacialities, Globalities (draft)." Lancaster University: Department of Sociology. Available online at http://www.comp.lancs.ac.uk/sociology/soc029jl.html.

Levy, S. 2001. "A High-Tech Home Front." *Newsweek,* October 8, pp. 43–45.

Lewis, J. 2000. "Terms of Resistance: Training at the Ruckus Society's Democracy Action Camp." *Los Angeles Weekly,* August 11–17, pp. XXX.

Ley, D. and C. Mills. 1993. "Can There Be a Postmodernism of Resistance in the Urban Landscape?" In P. L. Knox (ed.) *The Restless Urban Landscape.* Engelwood Cliffs, N.J.: Prentice Hall. 256–78.

Libra, C. 1995. "Interview with Marcos." *La Jornada.* August 25. Available online at http://flag.blackened.net/revolt/mexico/ezln/inter_marcos_consult_aug95.html.

Lipsitz, G. 1994. *Dangerous Crossroads: Popular Music, Postmodernism and the Poetics of Place.* London: Verso.

Los Angeles Times T.V. Times. 1993. "The Fugitives among Us. They're Walking Time Bombs. Murderers. Rapists. Robbers. They're on the run, on the streets, free to strike at will." Advertisement for Channel 4 KNBC News, November 28 December 4, front cover appendage.

Lyotard, J. (G., Bennington, and B., Massumi, trans.) 1984. *The Postmodern Condition: A Report on Knowledge.* Manchester: Manchester University Press.

McGuire, B and D. Scrymgeour, 1998. "Santeria and Curanderismo in Los Angeles." In P. Clarke (ed.) *New Trends and Developments in African Religion.* Wesport, Conn.: Greenwood, 211–22.

McKenzie, E. 1994. *Privatopia: Homeowner Associations and the Rise of Residential Private Government.* New Haven, Conn.: Yale University Press.

McMichael, P. 1996. "Globalization: Myths and Realities." *Rural Sociology* 61, no. 1. 25–55.

———. 2000. *Development and Social Change: A Global Perspective, 2d ed.* California: Pine Forge Press.

McWilliams, C. 1973. *Southern California: An Island on the Land.* Santa Barbara: Peregrine Smith.

MacKinnon, M. 2001. "WTO Finds a Haven: Qatar." *The Globe and Mail,* February 9, pp. XXX.

Malik, J. 2003. Personal correspondence with the author.

Marantz Henig, R. 2000. *The Monk in the Garden: The Lost and Found Genius of Gregor Mendel, the Father of Genetics.* New York: Houghton Mifflin.

Marcos, Subcomandante. 1995. *Shadows of Tender Fury: the Letters and Communiqués of Subcomandante Marcos and the Zapatista Army of National Liberation.* New York: Monthly Review Press.

———. 1997. "The Seven Loose Pieces of the Global Jigsaw Puzzle." *Le Monde Diplomatique,* July. English translation available online at http://flag.blackened.net/revolt/mexico/ezln/1997/jigsaw.html

———. 1999. "Teachers Are a Mirror and a Window." Presentation delivered to the Closing Session of the "Democratic Teachers and Zapatista Dream" Encuentro. August 1. Avaliable online at http://flag.blackened.net/revolt/mexico/ezln/1999/marcos_teachers_close_aug.html.

Marcos, S. and Domínguez, D. (Bar Din, A., trans.) 1996. *The Story of Colors/La Historia de los Colores.* Guadalajara: Ediciones Colectivo Callejero/Cinco Puntos Press.

Marshall, B. 1991. *The Real World.* London, Marshall Editions/Houghton Mifflin.

Martin, A. 1997. "Traveling Beyond Local Cultures." In J. Eade (ed.) *Living the Global City: Globalization as a Local Process.* London: Routledge.

Marx, K. 1978. "Capital, Volume One." In R. C. Tucker (ed.) *The Marx-Engels Reader.* New York: W. W. Norton.

Massey, D. 1993. "Power-Geometry and a Progressive Sense of Place." In J. Bird, B. Curtis, T. Putnam, G. Robertson, and L. Tickner (eds.) *Mapping the Futures: Local Cultures, Global Change.* London: Routledge.

Mattelart, A. 1983. *Transnationals and the Third World: the Struggle for Culture.* South Hadley, Mass.: Bergin and Garvey.

———. 1994. *Mapping World Communication: War, Progress, Culture.* Minneapolis: University of Minnesota Press.

Mayer, M. 2001. Personal correspondence with the author.

Memmi, A. 1991. *The Colonizer and the Colonized.* Boston: Beacon Press.

Mercer, K. 1994. *Welcome to the Jungle: New Positions in Black Cultural Studies.* London: Routledge.

Metcalfe, J. S. 1998. *Evolutionary Economics and Creative Destruction.* London: Routledge.

Metropolitan Structures. N.d. *California Plaza.* Promotional brochure.

Meyer, K. and P. Deuel, 1993. "The Unknown Nepal," *Kathmandu Post,* May 5, pp. 5–7.

———. 1994. "We Have Met the Future of Nepal," *The Kathmandu Post,* March 20, pp. 2.

Miller, D. 1987. *Material Culture and Mass Consumption.* Oxford: Basil Blackwell.

Millett, M. 1999. "Japan Pushes for a Less 'Euro' UNESCO." *The Age,* November 11, pp. XXX.

Monterey Country Club Association, Inc. January 18, 1992. *Association Rules.* Palm Desert, California. Brochure.

Montes, R. 1995. "Chiapas is a War of Ink and Internet." *Reforma,* April 26, pp. XXX.

Morales, F. 1999. "The Militarization of the Police." *Covert Action Quarterly* 67. 45–50.

———. 2001. "Welcome to the Free World: Gas Me—Stun Me—Shoot Me—Zap Me—Douse Me—Drug Me—Shut Me Up." *Covert Action Quarterly* 70. 6–13.

Morley, D. 1991. "Where the Global Meets the Local: Notes From the Sitting Room." *Screen* 32, no. 1. 1–15.

Morley, D. and K. Robins. 1992. "Techno-Orientalism: Futures, Foreigners and Phobias." *New Formations* 16. 136–56.

———. 1995. *Spaces of Identity.* London: Routledge.

Mountaingate at Brentwood. Undated. Promotional brochure.

Moussalli, A. 1993. *Radical Islamic Fundamentalism: The Ideological and Political Discourse of Sayyid Qutb.* Syracuse, N.Y.: Syracuse University Press.

NACEC (North American Commission for Environmental Cooperation). 2001. *Summary of Environmental Law.* Chapter 15. Available online at http://www.cec.org/pubs_info_resources /law_treat_agree/summary_enviro_law/publication/mx15.cfm?varlan=english.

Nederveen Pieterse, J. 1995. "Globalization as Hybridization." In M. Featherstone, S. Lash, and R. Robertson (eds.) *Global Modernities.* London: Sage Publications.

Nast, H. J., with L. Pulido. 2000. "Resisting Corporate Multiculturalism: Mapping Faculty Initiatives and Institutional-Student Harassment in the Classroom." *The Professional Geographer* 52, no. 4. 722–36.

Naumkin, V. 1993. *State, Religion and Society in Central Asia: a Post-Soviet Critique.* Reading, UK: Ithaca Press.

New York Times. 1999. "Gap Between Rich and Poor Found Substantially Higher." September 5, p. 16.

Nicholas, N. and A. Strader ("trans."); M. Shoulson, (ed.) 1996. *Hamlet, Prince of Denmark: The Restored Klingon Version.* Flourtown, Penn.: Klingon Language Institute.

Nike Incorporated. 1998. *Annual Report.* Beaverton, Ore.: Nike, Inc.

nikebiz.com. 2001. "Responsibility-Labor." April 12. Available online at. http://www.nikebiz. com/labor/.

nike.con. 2001. "Jamming the Jammers." Available online at http://nikesweatshop.net/.

Nordland, R., and C. Dickey. 2001. "First Blood." *Newsweek,* July 30, pp. 20–23.

NPR (Nuclear Posture Review). 2001. Submitted to the U.S. Congress, December 31.

Nugent, D. 1995. "Northern Intellectuals and the EZLN." *Monthly Review* 47. 24–138.

OTA (Office of Technology Assessment, U.S. Congress). 1993. *Multinationals and the National Interest: Playing by Different Rules.* Washington, D.C.: United States Government Printing Office.

Okrand, M. 1992. *The Klingon Dictionary.* New York: Pocket Books.

Ong, P., E., Bonacich, and L. Cheng (eds.) 1994. *The New Asian Immigration in Los Angeles and Global Restructuring.* Philadelphia: Temple University Press.

Oppenheimer, A. 1996. "Guerrillas in the Mist: What Do Mexico's Rebels Want?" *New Republic* 214, no. 25. 22.

Orwell, G. 1949. *1984.* New York: Harcourt, Brace.

Palm Springs Life. 1993. *Real Estate Advertisement.* July, rear inside cover.

Paske-Smith, M. 1930. *Western Barbarians in Japan and Formosa in Tokugawa Days, 1603–1868.* Kobe: J. L. Thompson.

Paz, O. 1982. (L. Kemp, Y. Milos, and R. Phillips Belash, trans.) *The Labyrinth of Solitude.* New York: Grove/Atlantic.

———. 1994. "The Media Spectacle Comes to Mexico." *New Perspectives Quarterly* 11, no. 12. 59–61.

Peet, R. 1996. "A Sign Taken for History: Daniel Shay's Memorial in Petersham, Massachusetts." *Annals of the Association of American Geographers* 86, no. 1. 21–43.

Peirce, N. R. 1993. *Citistates: How Urban America Can Prosper in a Competitive World.* Washington, D.C.: Seven Locks Press.

Perrin, N. 1979. *Giving Up the Gun: Japan's Reversion to the Sword, 1543–1879.* Boston: D. R. Godine.

Peterson, I. 1988. *The Mathematical Tourist: Snapshots of Modern Mathematics.* New York: W. H. Freeman.

Pfaffenberger, Bryan. 1992. "Technological Dramas." *Science, Technology, and Human Values* 17. 282–312.

Philippi, D. L. (trans.) 1977. *Kojiki.* New York: Columbia University Press.

Pinkerton, J. P. 2001. "Not Ready for Primetime: Peaceniks." *Los Angeles Times,* October 2, B-15.

Pitelis, C. N. and R. Sugden (eds.) 1991. *The Nature of The Transnational Firm.* London: Routledge.

Portes, A. 1996. Global Villagers: the Rise of Transnational Communities. *American Prospect* 25. 74–77.

Powell, I. 1995. *Ndebele: A People and Their Art.* New York: Cross River Press.

The Prudential Property Company. 1991. *Explore.* Poet's Walk promotional brochure.

Pulido, L. 1996. "Multiracial Organizing Among Environmental Justice Activists in Los Angeles." In M. Dear, H.E. Schockman, and G. Hise (eds.) *Rethinking Los Angeles.* Thousand Oaks, Calif.: Sage. 171–89.

———. 1998. "Development of the 'People of Color' Identity in the Environmental Justice Movement of the Southwestern U.S." *Socialist Review* 96, no. 4. 145–80.

Purcell, M. 2001. "Neighborhood Activism among Homeowners as a Politics of Space." *Professional Geographer* 53, no. 2. 178–94.

Raban, J. 1974 *Soft City*. New York: E. P. Dutton.

Rabelais, F. (J. M. Cohen, trans.) 1955. *Gargantua and Pantagruel*. Baltimore: Penguin.

Raento, P. 2001. Private conversation with the author.

Raento, P. and S. Flusty, Forthcoming. "Imagineered Worlds: The Design of Las Vegas Resort-Casinos."

Ramírez Cuevas, J. (irlandesa, trans.) 2000. "The Body as a Weapon for Civil Disobedience (and Other New Forms of Political Activism)." *La Jornada*, October 15. Available online at http://www.geocities.com/CollegePark/Classroom/8982/bodyweapon.html.

Rashid, S. (ed.) 1997. *The Clash of Civilizations?: Asian Responses*. Karachi, New York: Oxford University Press.

Relph, E. C. 1987. *The Modern Urban Landscape*. Baltimore: Johns Hopkins University Press.

Renegade. 1995. Issue 4 (Newsletter of the German Klingon organization 'Khemorex Klinzhai'). Available online at http://www.khemorex-klinzhai.de/renegades/.

Report from Nurío, Michoacán. 2001. Available online at http://mexico.indymedia.org/local/webcast/uploads/zapatistassgmqyd.txt.

Riggins, S. H. (ed.) 1994. *The Socialness of Things: Essays on the Socio-Semiotics of Objects*. Berlin: Mouton de Gruyter.

Robertson, R. 1992. *Globalization: Social Theory and Global Culture*. London: Sage.

———. 1997. "Social Theory, Cultural Relativity, and the Problem of Globality." In A. D. King (ed.) *Culture, Globalization and the World System: Contemporary Conditions for the Representation of Identity*. Minneapolis: University of Minnesota Press.

Robles, F. 2001. "Zapatistas Desbordan el Zócalo." *La Opinión,* March 12, pp. 1, 12.

Roett, R. 1995. "Mexico-Political Update, Chase Manhattan S Emerging Markets Group Memo." January 13, Memo.

Romney, L. and J. F. Smith. 2001. "At End of Trek, Marcos Declares Indians' 'Hour.'" *Los Angeles Times,* March 12, pp. 1, 4.

Ronfeldt, D. F.; J. Arquilla, G. E. Fuller, and M. Fuller 1998. *The Zapatista 'Social Netwar' in Mexico*. Santa Monica: Rand Corporation.

Rose, G. 1993. *Feminism and Geography: The Limits of Geographical Knowledge*. Minneapolis: University of Minnesota Press.

Rothberg, D. M. 1995. "Chase Bank Denies Urging Elimination of Mexican Rebels." *Associated Press,* February 15.

Routledge, P. 1996. "Critical Geopolitics and Terrains of Resistance." *Political Geography* 15. 509–31.

Rushdie, S. 1991. *Imaginary Homelands*. London: Granta.

Santos, C. 2001. "An Ethnic Mosaic Explodes." *Los Angeles Times,* March 18, M-2.

Sassen, S. 1991. *The Global City: New York, London, Tokyo*. Princeton, N.J.: Princeton University Press.

———. 1996. "Whose City Is It? Globalization and the Formation of New Claims." *Public Culture.* 8, no. 2. 205–223.

———. 1999. "Whose City Is It? Globalization and the Formation of New Claims." In R. A. Beauregard, and S. Body-Gendrot (eds.) *The Urban Moment: Cosmopolitan Essays on the Late-twenteith-Century City*. Thousand Oaks, Calif.: Sage. 99–118.

Schiller, H. I. 1989. *Culture, Inc.: The Corporate Takeover of Public Expression*. New York: Oxford University Press.

Schlereth, T. J. 1990. *Cultural History and Material Culture: Everyday Life, Landscapes, Museums*. Ann Arbor: UMI Research Press.

Schlosser, E. 1998. "The Prison-Industrial Complex." *Atlantic Monthly,* December, pp. 51–77.

Schoenberger, E. 1997. *The Cultural Crisis of the Firm*. Cambridge, Mass.: Blackwell.

Schwarz, A. 1991. "Pressures of Work" and "Running a Business." *Far Eastern Economic Review,* June 20, pp. 14, 16.

Scott, A. J. 1988a. *New Industrial Spaces: Flexible Production Organization and Regional Development in North America and Western Europe*. London: Pion.

———. 1988b. *Metropolis: From the Division of Labor to Urban Form*. Berkeley and Los Angeles: University of California Press.

———. 1993. *Technopolis: High-Technology Industry and Regional Development in Southern California.* Berkeley, and Los Angeles: University of California Press.

Sennett, R. 1990. *The Conscious and the Eye: The Design and Social Life of Cities.* New York: Alfred A. Knopf.

Seuss, Dr. (T. Giesel) 1960. *One Fish, Two Fish, Red Fish, Blue Fish.* New York: Random House.

Shiva, V. 1993. *Monocultures of the Mind: Perspectives on Biodiversity and Biotechnology.* Penang: Zed Books and Third World Network.

Short, J. R. and Y-H. Kim. 1999. *Globalization and the City.* Harlow: Addison Wesley Longman Ltd.

Sibley, D. 1995. *Geographies of Exclusion: Society and Difference in the West.* New York: Routledge.

Siderov, D. 2000. "National Monumentalization and the Politics of Scale: the Resurrections of the Cathedral of Christ the Savior in Moscow." *Annals of the Association of American Geographers* 90, no. 1. 548–72.

Silverstein, K. and A. Cockburn. 1 1995. "Major U.S. Bank Urges Zapatista Wipe-Out: 'A litmus test for Mexico's stability.'" *CounterPunch* 2, no. 3.

Skorstad, E. 1991. "Mass Production, Flexible Specialization and Just-In-Time." *Futures,* 23 no. 12 December, pp. 1075–1084.

Skeels, E. 2002. "The Return of Coyote Marcos." *Eat ths State* 7, no. 8.

Smith, D. A. and Borocz, J. 1995. *A New World Order? Global Transformations in the Late Twentieth Century.* Westport, Conn.: Greenwood.

Smith, D. E. 1987. *The Everyday World as Problematic.* Boston: Northeastern University Press.

Smith, M. P. 1999. "Transnationalism and the City." In R. A. Beauregard and S. Body-Genrot (eds.) *The Urban Moment: Cosmopolitan Essays on the Late-twenteith-Century City.* Thousand Oaks, Calif.: Sage. 119–40.

———. 2001. *Transnational Urbanism: Locating Globalization.* Oxford: Blackwell Publishers.

Smith, M. P., and L. E. Guarnizo (eds.) 1998. *Transnationalism from Below.* New Brunswick, NJ: Transaction.

Smith, N. 1992. "New City, New Frontier: The Lower East Side as Wild, Wild West." In M. Sorkin (ed.) *Variations on a Theme Park.* New York: Hill and Wang. 61–93.

Soja, E. 1989. *Postmodern Geographies: The Reassertion of Space in Critical Social Theory.* London: New York: Verso.

———. 1996a. "Los Angeles 1965–1992: The Six Geographies of Urban Restructuring." In A. J. Scott and E. Soja (eds.) *The City: Los Angeles and Urban Theory at the End of the Twentieth Century.* Berkeley and Los Angeles: University of California Press.

———. 1996b. *Thirdspace.* Oxford: Blackwell.

Soja, E. and B. Hooper. 1993. "The Difference That Space Makes: Some Notes on the Geographical Margins of the New Cultural Politics." in M. Keith, and S. Pile (eds.) *Place and the Politics of Identity.* London and New York: Routledge. 183–205.

Sollors, W. (ed.) 1989. *The Invention of Ethnicity.* Oxford: Oxford University Press.

Sorkin, M. (ed.) 1992. *Variations on a Theme Park: The New American City and the End of Public Space.* New York: Hill and Wang. 1992.

Spivak, G. C. 1987. *In Other Worlds: Essays in Cultural Politics.* New York: Methuen.

Storper, M. and R. Walker, 1989. *The Capitalist Imperative.* Cambridge: Blackwell.

Strasser, J. B. and L. Becklund, 1991. *Swoosh: The Unauthorized Story of Nike and the Men Who Played There.* New York: Harcourt Brace Jovanovich.

Sudjic, D. 1992. *The Hundred-Mile City.* Orlando: Harcourt Brace.

Summit at Warner Center. N.d. *Life as an Art Form.* Promotional brochure.

Suttles, G. 1972. *The Social Construction of Communities.* Chicago: University of Chicago Press.

Swyngedouw, E. 1997. "Neither Global nor Local: 'Glocalization' and the Politics of Scale." In K. Cox (ed.) *Spaces of Globalization: Reasserting the Power of the Local.* London: Guilford. 137–66.

Tao, J. and W. Ho. 1997. "Chinese Entrepreneurship: Culture and Economic Actors." In A. Scott (ed.) *The Limits of Globalization: Cases and Arguments.* London: Routledge. pp. 143–177.

Taylor, C. (A. Gutmann, ed.) 1994. *Multiculturalism: Examining the Politics of Recognition.* Princeton: Princeton, N. J.: Princeton University Press.

Telander, R. 1990. "Your Sneakers or Your Life." *Sports Illustrated,* May 14, pp. 36–38, 43–44, 46, 49.

Thuan, T. X. 2001. *Chaos and Harmony: Perspectives on Scientific Revolutions of the Twentieth Century.* New York: Oxford University Press.

Theroux, P. 1994. *Translating L.A.: A Tour of the Rainbow City.* New York: W. W. Norton.

3 Mustaphas, 3. 1989. *Heart of Uncle.* London: Ace Records.

The Times of India. 2001. "CIA Worked in Tandem with Pak to Create Taliban." March 7, pp. XXX.

Towers, G. February 2000. "Applying the Political Geography of Scale: Grassroots Strategies and Environmental Justice. *Political Geography* 52, no. 1. 23–36.

Truell, P. 1992. *False Profits: The Inside Story of BCCI, the World's Most Corrupt Financial Empire.* Boston: Houghton Mifflin.

Tuan, Y. 1996. *Cosmos and Hearth.* Minneapolis: University of Minnesota Press.

UCB (United Colors of Benetton). 1998. *Enemies.* Published by *Newsweek.*

UNESCO (United Nations Educational, Scientific and Cultural Organization) 2001. "Director-General Condemns Taliban's Crime against Culture." New York: UNESCO.

USSC (United States Space Command). 1996. *Vision for 2020.* Colorado: Peterson Air Force Base.

Universal City Studios, Inc. 1997. *Commander CityWalk: Welcome to CityWalk.* Brochure.

Vande Berg, L. R. 1996. "Liminality: Worf as Metonymic Signifier of Racial, Cultural, and National Differences." In T. Harrison (ed). *Enterprise Zones: Critical Positions on Star Trek.* Boulder, Colo.: Westview Press. 51–68.

Verité. 2001. *Comprehensive Factory Evaluation Report Prepared Verité on Kukdong International Mexico, S.A. de C.V., Atlixco, Puebla, Mexico.*

Vickery, M. 1984. *Cambodia: 1975–1982.* Boston: South End Press.

Villafuerte, A. A. 2001. "The Zapatistas in the Fox Era." *Voices of Mexico* 55. 15–18.

Vogel, S. 1991. *Africa Explores: Twenteith Century African Art.* New York: Center for African Art; Munich: Prestel.

Wade, R. 2001. "Robert Wade on Inequality." *Economist.* April 28, pp. 79–82.

Wainwright, J., S. Prudham, and J. Glassman. 2000. "The Battles in Seattle: Microgeographies of Resistance and the Challenge of Building Alternative Futures." *Environment and Planning D: Society and Space* 18, no. 1. 5–13.

Walker, S. 1980. *Popular Justice.* New York, Oxford: Oxford University Press.

Wallace, A. 1992. "Like it's so L.A.! Not really." *Los Angeles Times,* February 29, pp. 19.

Wallerstein, I. 1984. *The Politics of the World-Economy.* Cambridge: Cambridge University Press.

———. 1990. "Societal Development, or Development of the World System?" *Globalization, Knowledge and Society.* London: Sage.

———. 1997. "The National and the Universal: can there be such a thing as World Culture?" In A. King (ed.), *Culture, Globalization and The World-System Contemporary Conditions for the Representation of Identity.* Minneapolis: University or Minnesota Press, pp. 91–105.

Waltari, M. 1972. (N. Walford, trans.) *The Egyptian.* Helsinki: Werner Söderström Osakeyhtiö.

Walton, J. and D. Seddon. 1994. *Free Markets and Food Riots: The Politics of Global Adjustment.* London: Blackwell.

Watson, J. 2001. "Subcomandante Marcos Not Only Inspires and Leads, He Sells." *Associated Press,* March 1.

Watts, M. 1997. "Mapping Meaning, Denoting Differences, Imagining Identity: Dialectical Images and Postmodern Geographies." in T. Barnes and D. Gregory (eds.) *Reading Human Geography.* London: Arnold. 489–502.

Weiner, E. S. and J. Simpson (eds.) 1991. The Oxford English Dictionary, Second Edition Oxford, New York: Oxford University Press.

Weisband, E. 1989. (ed.) *Poverty Amidst Plenty: World Political Economy and Distributive Justice.* Boulder: Westview Press.

Welchman, J. C. (ed.) 1996. *Rethinking Borders.* London: Macmillan Press.

Werbner, P. and T. Modood. (eds.) 1997. *Debating Cultural Hybridity.* London: Zed Books.

White, K. 1995. "Sweet Portable Lifestyle." *Baffler* 7. 15–19.

White, M. 1991. "Improving the Welfare of Women Factory Workers: Lessons from Indonesia." *International Labor Review* 129, no. 1. 121–33.

Wilkerson, I. 1990. "Challenging Nike, Rights Group Takes a Risky Stand." *New York Times,* August 25, p. 10.

Wichita Eagle. 1998. "Four Children Taken into Protective Custody on Report of Father's Speaking Klingon," December 2, pp. XXX.

Wichita Eagle. 1999. "When Love Isn't Enough," July 11, pp. XXX.

Wolch, J. 1990. *The Shadow State: Government and Voluntary Sector in Transition.* New York: Foundation Center.

Wolch, J. 1996. "From Global to Local: The Rise of Homelessness in Los Angeles during the 1980s." In A. J. Scott and E. Soja (eds.) *The City: Los Angeles and Urban Theory at the End of the Twentieth Century.* Berkeley and Los Angeles: University of California Press.

Wolch, J. and M. Dear. 1993. *Malign Neglect: Homelessness in an American City.* San Francisco: Jossey-Bass.

Wolfwood, T. 1997. "Who is Ramona?" *Third World Resurgence* 84. pp. XXX.

Ya Basta! 2001. "New York City Ya Basta! Collective Calls for All Bodies to Resist the FTAA." February 13. Available online at http://www.infoshop.org/news6/padded_yabasta.html.

Yapa, L. 1996. "What Causes Poverty? A Postmodern View." *Annals of the Association of American Geographers* 86, no. 4. 707–27.

Yellin Company. N.d. *Bradbury 1893.* Promotional brochure.

Yeung, Y., and X. Li. 2000. "Transnational Corporations and Local Embeddedness: Company Case Studies from Shanghai, China." *Professional Geographer* 52, no. 4. 624–35.

Yonemura, A. 1990. *Yokohama: Prints from Nineteenth-Century Japan.* Washington, D.C.: Arthur M. Sackler Gallery/Smithsonian Institution Press.

Zapatistas. 1998. *Zapatista Encuentro: Documents from the 1996 Encounter for Humanity and Against Neoliberalism.* New York: Seven Stories Press.

Zulaika, J. and W. A. Douglass. 1996. *Terror and Taboo: The Follies, Fables and Faces of Terrorism.* London: Routedge.

Index